The MAILBOX®
The Idea Magazine For Teachers®
KINDERGARTEN

1998–1999
YEARBOOK

Jan Trautman, Editor

The Education Center, Inc.
Greensboro, North Carolina

The Mailbox® 1998–1999 Yearbook

Editor In Chief: Margaret Michel
Magazine Director: Karen P. Shelton
Editorial Administrative Director: Stephen Levy
Senior Editor: Jan Trautman
Editorial Traffic Manager: Lisa K. Pitts
Contributing Editors: Michele M. Dare, Ada Goren, Kim T. Griswell, Lori Kent, Angie Kutzer, Allison E. Ward
Copy Editors: Karen Brewer Grossman, Karen L. Huffman, Tracy Johnson, Scott Lyons, Debbie Shoffner, Gina Sutphin
Staff Artists: Cathy Spangler Bruce, Pam Crane, Nick Greenwood, Clevell Harris, Susan Hodnett, Sheila Krill, Rob Mayworth, Kimberly Richard, Rebecca Saunders, Barry Slate, Donna K. Teal, Jennifer L. Tipton
Contributing Artist: Lucia Kemp Henry
Cover Artist: Lois Axeman
Editorial Assistants: Terrie Head, Laura Slaughter, Wendy Svartz, Karen White
Educational Consultant: Nancy Johnson
Librarian: Elizabeth A. Findley

ISBN 1-56234-294-0
ISSN 1088-5528

The Education Center, Inc.
P.O. Box 9753
Greensboro, NC 27429-0753

Look for *The Mailbox*® 1999–2000 Kindergarten Yearbook in the summer of 2000. The Education Center, Inc., is the publisher of *The Mailbox*®, *Teacher's Helper*®, *The Mailbox*® BOOKBAG®, *Learning*®, and *The Mailbox*® *Teacher* magazines, as well as other fine products. Look for these wherever quality teacher materials are sold, or call 1-800-714-7991.

Contents

Bulletin Boards

Bulletin Boards ....

Chicka Chicka Boom Boom Look Who's Here In Our Room!

Let's all gather at the coconut tree! To make this literature-related display, cut out tree leaves and a tree trunk from bulletin-board paper. Fringe-cut the leaves; then mount the whole tree on a wall. To make a coconut, give a child a brown construction-paper circle along with a slightly smaller white one. Instruct the child to write his name in the center of the white circle, then glue that white circle on the brown one. Next have the child spread a coat of glue on the white circle, but **not** over his name. Then have him sprinkle flaked coconut over the glue. When the glue dries, have him shake off the excess coconut. Follow the same procedure and sprinkle crumbled shredded wheat cereal on the brown part of the coconut. Arrange all these finished projects around the titled coconut tree. See you there!

Krista Miller & Michelle Rinehard
Lincoln Elementary, Findlay, OH

This eclectic color collage is truly a group project. Begin by titling the board with white letters on a black background. Then staple on the color-word circles. When introducing a new color, encourage children to search their homes for appropriately colored items to add to the display. (Depending on your space, you might suggest that each item be no larger than an envelope, for example.) What a creative-classroom collage of color!

Tracy Voller, Pinewood Elementary, Monticello, MN

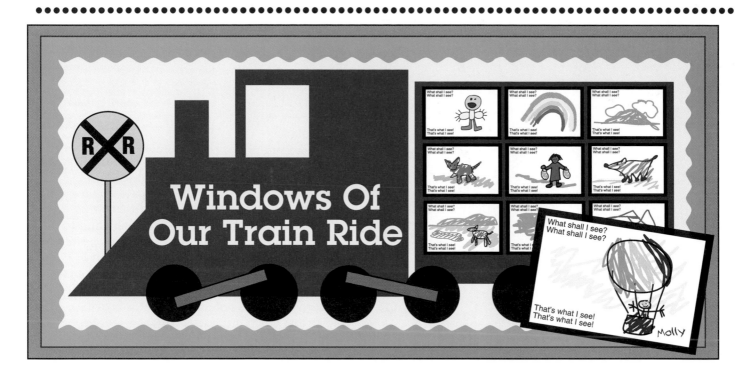

Creative writing is the beauty of this scenic train ride. In advance, mount a train engine and wheels on a board. Program a sheet of paper as shown; then duplicate a class supply. After sharing *The Train Ride* by June Crebbin, have each child illustrate an imaginary train-ride scene. Mount each scene on a sheet of slightly larger black paper; then staple each picture to the board to resemble a scene out of the train window.

Shandra Hathaway—Gr. K, Haverhill Elementary, Fort Wayne, IN

You'll have a place to show off bushels of learning with this year-round wall display. To begin, use a permanent black marker to draw a large basket on brown bulletin-board paper. Then cut it out. Mount the basket on a wall along with the title shown. From month to month, give each child an opportunity to make a different contribution to this display. In September, for example, you might fill the basket with child-painted apples; October, pumpkins; November, leaves; December, gifts; January, snowpeople; February, hearts; March, kites; April, butterflies; May, flowers; and June, suns.

Diane Bonica—Gr. K
Deer Creek Elementary
Tigard, OR

Bulletin Boards ....

When your students contribute to this display, entire families can take pride in its important message. Using the doll pattern on page 12, make photocopies on multicultural colors of construction paper. Ask each child to choose a doll cutout, then work with his family members to decorate his doll to represent his heritage. Provide adult assistance at school for those who need it. Then enlarge the Earth pattern (page 12) onto blue bulletin-board paper and cut it out. Have children sponge-paint the continents. Display the Earth, dolls, and title as shown. Encourage children to talk about their dolls and their heritages.

Mimi Duffy—Gr. K
Memorial School
Paramus, NJ

Let It Snow!

To make this wintry scene, encourage a flurry of activity several days in advance. During center times, have students stamp or stencil background paper with snowflake designs, make white paper chains, and trace and cut out green hand outlines. When the background is in place, staple the hand cutouts to the board to form a tree. Curl the fingertips of the cutouts by wrapping them around a pencil. Staple cotton batting to the board for accumulated snow. As the finishing touch, staple the paper chains to the board to form a snowman's body; then attach stick arms and a real scarf, hat, and mittens. Brrrrr! It's cold in here!

Christine Hammerschmidt—Gr. K Special Education, Hillcrest School, Morristown, NJ

How do you say "I love you" without saying a word? With sign language, of course! Teach your youngsters the hand sign for "I love you." Then decorate your classroom for Valentine's Day with this "hand-some" display. First have a student place her hand on an overhead projector. Trace the enlarged image onto bulletin-board paper; then cut it out. Fold the middle and ring fingers down and glue them to the palm. Attach the hand cutout to a wall with the title "I Love You!" Encourage each child to illustrate something or someone she loves; then display these pictures around the cutout. Love is in the air!

Pat Murray—Gr. K
St. Rita Of Cascia School
Aurora, IL

Whether for Groundhog Day or Presidents' Day, shadows and silhouettes are a must for February. At the beginning of the month, display your youngsters' silhouettes with a groundhog's shadow "hidden" somewhere in the collection. Then on Presidents' Day, record each student's dictation to "If I were the president..." on his silhouette.

Barbara Meyers—Gr. K, Fort Worth Country Day School, Fort Worth, TX

Bulletin Boards ....

"Bee" A Reader!

Even reluctant readers will be motivated to contribute to this honey of a display! In advance, duplicate a supply of honeycomb shapes on yellow construction paper. Also keep a large box of Honeycomb® cereal on hand. To make a large bee, cut out the simple shapes of the bee (see the illustration) from tagboard. Cover the abdomen and head with black construction paper. Cover the middle section with yellow fake fur or felt. Also cut out and glue on stripes from the same yellow fabric. Cover each eye circle with green foil paper; then add a smaller black construction-paper circle to each center. Attach curled pipe cleaners to resemble antennae. Finally, cover the wing shapes with waxed paper; then glue all of the parts together. Post the bee along with a title and some colorful tissue-paper flowers. When each child has read (or listened to) a book, give him a section of honeycomb. Have him write the title of his book and add an illustration. Each time a child adds a section to the honeycomb, invite him to scoop out a handful of cereal for a job well done!

adapted from an idea by Betty Kobes, West Hancock Elementary School

Cover a board with a lightly patterned pastel fabric. Use an opaque projector to enlarge the bunny pattern (on page 13). Using a black marker, trace the pattern onto white poster board. Color in the pink parts as shown. Mount the bunny on the board; then add the title and fringe-cut, construction-paper grass. After studying various types of decorated eggs, have each child design and paint a very large egg to add to the display.

Teresa Hatton—Gr. K, Hutchison Beach Elementary, Panama City Beach, FL

Sneaking Into Spring

This adaptable board provides each child with her own display space. Cut out a large construction-paper circle for each child, plus one extra. Decorate the extra circle to resemble a caterpillar's head. For each child, duplicate a pair of construction-paper sneakers (page 14). Have each child color and cut out her sneakers, then glue construction-paper legs and sneakers to her personalized caterpillar body part. Mount the body parts behind the caterpillar head, going as far around your room as necessary. Use each body part to display that student's choice of work. (Adapt the title to coincide with your studies—for example, "Sneaking Into Summer…Books…Manners…Science…etc.")

Pamela Buettner—Gr. K, Belleville, IL

KINDERGARTEN FLOWERS

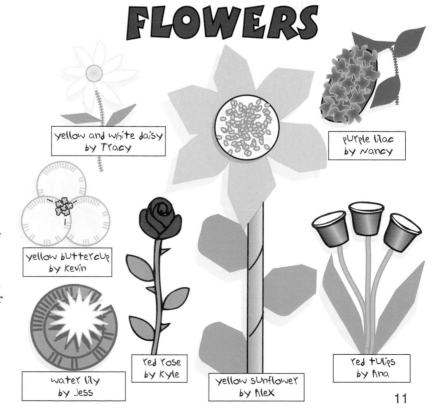

Combine science, art, and language arts to create this eye-catching display. As you study flowers, encourage each child to choose one particular flower that he likes. Provide books such as *The FLOWER Alphabet Book* by Jerry Pallotta and *Flowers* by David Burnie. Then ask each child to use the books to study his chosen flower. Next invite him to use a variety of art supplies to create an artistic expression of that flower. Encourage each child to write a label for his flower and sign his name. As each child finishes his flower project, display it near the title. A beautiful array of kindergarten flowers!

Karen Cook—Gr. K (Resource Teacher), McDonough Primary School, McDonough, GA

11

Earth Pattern

Use with the bulletin board on page 8.

Doll Pattern

Use with the bulletin board on page 8.

Sneaker Pattern

Use with "Sneaking Into Spring" on page 11.

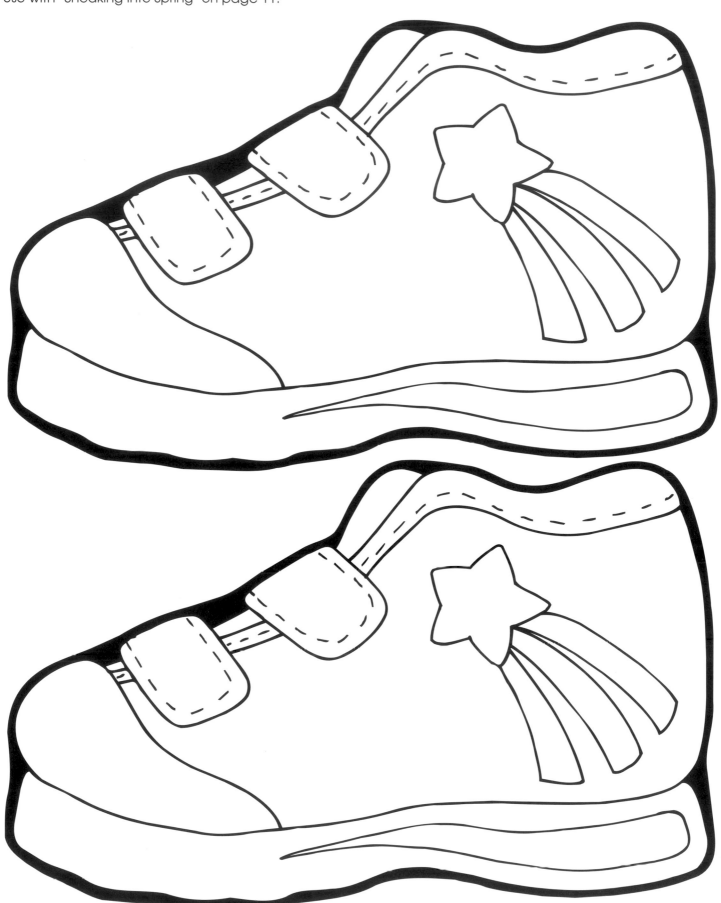

Arts & Crafts

Arts & Crafts
For Little Hands

Sunny sunflowers bring the golden glow of summer's sunshine into your classroom. Use this crop of sunflower ideas to brighten your learning environment and to reinforce fine-motor skills, creativity, and design.

Height And Hands

Height and hands are the major components of these child-size sunflowers.

Materials needed:
1 margarine-tub lid (for tracing)
1 sheet of art paper per child
yellow tempera paint mixed with dishwashing liquid
   (or washable yellow paint)
brown tempera paint
paintbrushes

sunflower seeds
green bulletin-board paper
green construction paper
1 tape measure or yardstick
glue
scissors

To begin, help a child trace the lid on a sheet of art paper. Then instruct her to paint one of her hands with the yellow paint. Have her make yellow handprints around the edge of the traced circle. After she rinses her hands, instruct the child to paint the inside of the circle brown. When the paint dries, invite the child to glue sunflower seeds to the center. When the glue is dry, have the child cut out her flower. Next measure the child from toe to shoulder. Cut out a bulletin board-paper stem of that height. Have the child cut out two large construction-paper leaves, then glue the stem and leaves to the flower. Mount all of these child-size flowers on a classroom wall.

Judy Kelley—Gr. K, Lilja School, Natick, MA

Sunflower Mosaics

This sunny sunflower project provides fabulous fine-motor practice and offers lots of opportunities for children to plan designs. To prepare, stock your art area with sturdy art paper, yellow and green construction paper, glue, and dried beans. Encourage each child to tear the yellow and green construction paper, then arrange and glue the pieces on the art paper to make a sunflower picture. Then have him glue the dried beans to the center. (This is one time when a *lot* of glue will be necessary.) Encourage each child to take his sunflower mosaic home to share with his family.

Laura Crymes—Gr. K
Canongate Elementary
Sharpsburg, GA

Wild, Wild Sunflower Child

Smiling faces will beam from these giant blossoms. Have each child don one as you read aloud *Wild Wild Sunflower Child Anna* by Nancy White Carlstrom or for a delightful touch at Open House. To make one, cut out the center of a paper plate. Have a child cut out lots of large yellow petals and two green leaves, then glue them to his plate. Then have him glue sunflower seeds around the opening, at the base of the petals. To make a headband, cut two 1 1/2" x 10" construction-paper strips. Staple one strip to each side of the plate. Fit the headband to the child; then staple it. Next staple the other strip to the top of the plate and to the headband for stability. If desired, cut a U-shaped space in the center for the chin.

If your class is recognizing National Hispanic Heritage Month (beginning September 15), these craft ideas have arrived just in time! Or you can use them for anytime arts-and-crafts fun.

Sombreros

The beautiful colors on these sombreros are fashioned entirely by your students. To make a sombrero, cut out a 16-inch circle from poster board. Center an upside-down paper bowl on the circle; then trace around it. Cut out a hole from the poster board approximately 1/2-inch smaller than the traced circle. Then glue the inverted bowl around the hole. When the glue dries, staple on a length of elastic for a chin strap. Then use brightly colored paints and markers to decorate the hat. Olé!

Martie Eernisse—Gr. K
Cincinnati Christian School
Fairfield, OH

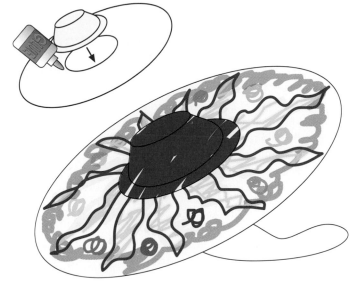

Maracas

Can you hear the rhythm of the beat? The magic of these maracas is contagious! On a sheet of tagboard, draw simple illustrations and write the directions as shown. (If desired, you can just enlarge and duplicate the illustration on this page.) Then stock a center with a supply of dried beans, plastic cups, masking tape, bottles of dimensional craft paint, and the directions. To make a maraca, have a child follow the directions. Encourage youngsters to shake their completed maracas to the beat of some traditional and some contemporary music from various Hispanic countries.

Maurie F. Ganther
Virginia Beach, VA

① paint

② dry

③ 10 beans

④ upside down

⑤ tape

⑥ shake

Arts & Crafts
For Little Hands

Fun Fall Scarecrows

Scare up some fun for fall with these seasonal art projects. Ask each student to bring in a brown paper grocery bag. Cut off the bottom of each bag; then flatten the bag. Fold in the corners; then staple them in place. Have each child gently stuff his scarecrow head with newspaper, then staple the bottom closed and turn the bag over. Invite each child to use art supplies—such as markers, construction paper, raffia, buttons, and fabric scraps—to create a scarecrow. Display these finished projects on a bulletin board or around your classroom. They're sure to scare up some classroom fall fun!

Michelle Hall—Gr. K, Biddeford Primary School, Biddeford, ME

Discard

Stuff here, then staple.

Sand-Art Scenes

Colored sand adds new dimension and texture to your youngsters' artwork. Collect six small margarine tubs with lids. Fill each tub about 3/4 full of sand. Add 8–10 drops of food coloring to each one to make a different color of sand. After securing the lids, shake the tubs until the sand is evenly colored. Then give each child a sheet of construction paper, a paintbrush, and a 4:1 mixture of glue and water. Instruct each child to use the glue to paint *one part* of a landscape, such as the trees, grass, or mountains. Then have him sprinkle a color of sand onto the glue and shake off the excess. Encourage the child to paint the next part of his scene, painting and sanding as before. Continue in this manner until the picture is finished. Back the sandy scenes with a complementary color for display.

Note: If you're studying Native Americans of the Plains, these sandy scenes make the perfect backgrounds for tepees. To make a tepee, wrap and staple half of a small paper plate as shown. Decorate the tepee with markers and pipe cleaners; then staple it on the scene.

Sandie Bolze—Gr. K, Verne W. Critz School, East Patchogue, NY

Halloween Carriers

There's no trick to getting youngsters to make these handy little carriers for classroom work, other papers, and Halloween treats. To make one carrier, paint the bottoms of two paper plates orange. When the paint dries, use black markers or construction-paper shapes to add "hall-o-wonderful" faces. Staple the plates together (with the pumpkin faces to the outside), leaving the top half unstapled. Cut a 6" x 2" strip of green construction paper to make a handle. Staple the handle to the inside top of each plate. During October, encourage each child to use her carrier to transport work from school to home. Every once in a while, toss in a few candy treats with children's work, and watch them light up like jack-o'-lanterns.

Native American Patterned Bags

Your "kinder-crafters" can learn to use patterns as creatively as Native American craftsmen when they make these shoulder bags. Ask parent volunteers to help cut out a class supply of felt shapes using pattern block templates. Give each child two sheets of felt and a two-foot length of cord. Instruct her to glue along three edges of one felt sheet, then press the two felt pieces together. Invite each child to choose felt shapes to form a pattern on her bag. Have her arrange the pattern, check her work, and then glue the shapes in place. After the glue dries, punch a hole in the upper right- and left-hand corners of the cloth. Thread the cord through each hole and tie a knot to secure it in place. Display these bags on a bulletin board during the month of November.

Janet S. Witmer—Preschool and Gr. K, Harrisburg, PA

Jack Frost Magic

This magical art project will turn any frosty frowns upside down! Make the Jack Frost solution by combining one cup of Epsom salt and one cup of water. Bring the mixture to a boil; then let it cool just slightly. Then instruct children to cut out leaves from construction paper. Invite youngsters to paint their leaves with the warm Jack Frost solution, then let the leaves dry overnight. The next day, encourage each child to use other art supplies to create a fall scene on a large sheet of paper. Have him add the finishing touches by gluing on his frosted leaves. Display the finished projects on a board titled "Jack Frost Magic!"

Judy Kelley—Gr. K, Lilja School, Natick, MA

Ceramics Studio

This creative center will make your little ones feel like they have their very own ceramics studio. Set up a center with plaster of paris, water, plastic cups, craft sticks (for mixing), and a variety of flexible molds, such as plaster-craft molds and candy molds. Also provide a variety of craft paints and paintbrushes. Then illustrate step-by-step directions according to the directions on your particular plaster of paris. Display these directions in the center. Supply each child with a small box or box lid for the pieces he is working on. (Also set aside space nearby for projects to dry.) With adult supervision, encourage each child to visit this ceramics studio during center time and create to his heart's content.

Bonnie McKenzie—Pre-K and Gr. K, Cheshire Country Day School Cheshire, CT

Arts & Crafts
For Little Hands

Put Your Name In Lights

Since little ones love seeing their names in print, they'll be thrilled to make—and show off!—these high-voltage necklaces. In advance, use the lightbulb patterns (page 23) to make a class supply of tagboard lightbulb tracers. (If desired, dreidel patterns are also provided.) Then cut a 30-inch length of yarn for each student and a large supply of black 1" x 2" construction-paper strips. To begin, provide each child with colorful construction-paper choices, a lightbulb (and/or dreidel) pattern, and the length of yarn. Instruct each child to trace the pattern one time for each letter in her name, then cut out all the patterns. For each bulb, have each child fold a black paper strip (a socket) over the yarn, insert the bulb, and glue it shut. (Follow the same procedure for the dreidel option using the black paper strip as the dreidel's handle.) Next have each child write one letter of her name (in order) on each light or dreidel. Then help each child tie the yarn ends together. During the holidays, encourage children to wear these nifty necklaces.

Wendy Svenstrup
St. Mary's Preschool
Lafayette, IN

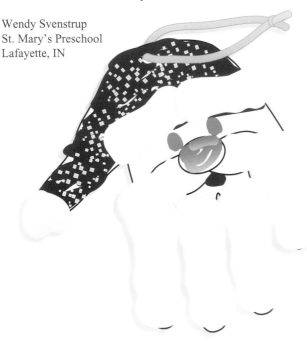

"Hand-some" Santa Hangers

Here's a "hand-some" holiday decoration that little hands will be eager to create. To make one, trace your hand onto white tagboard; then carefully cut it out. Turn the cutout upside down (as shown); then draw a line from the base of the thumb across the palm to distinguish the hat area. Draw a Santa face in the palm area; then color the hat. Next glue one cotton ball to the tip of the hat and a stretched-out cotton ball (or two) across the forehead area. For Santa's beard, glue several stretched-out cotton balls on the fingers. Embellish Santa's hat with glitter or holiday confetti, if desired. When each project is dry, punch a hole at the top and tie on a ribbon hanger. Ho, ho, ho!

Kelly Dobias—Gr. K, St. Columba School, Chicago, IL

Heart In Hand

This lovely holiday ornament is a lasting keepsake. To make one ornament, cut two identical mitten shapes from white felt. (Be sure the cutouts are large enough for a child's hand to fit inside them.) Next help a child paint his hand with green paint, then press it onto one mitten. When the handprint is dry, have the child cut out a small, red felt heart. Hot-glue the heart in the center of the handprint; then also glue the edges of the mittens together. Have the child use a paint pen to write his name and the year on the back of the mitten. When the paint is dry, punch a small hole in the top and attach a ribbon for hanging. These precious ornaments are perfect for very special holiday gift giving.

Kathy Martin—Gr. K, Nellie Reed Elementary, Vernon, MI

Lovely Angels

Grace your classroom with these delightful holiday angels. To make an angel, start with one red heart-shaped doily. Make an angel robe by gluing half a coffee filter horizontally across the center of the doily, covering the point of the heart. To make the head, trace a juice-can lid onto any color of skin-toned construction paper; then cut it out. Draw facial features on this cutout; then glue it near the top of the doily so that it slightly overlaps the robe. Hot-glue a garland halo to the very top of the angel's head. If desired, decorate the angel's robe by gluing on sparkly sequins. Then accordion-fold two tagboard arms. Glue the arms to the back of the doily; then wrap them around the front. Then tape a construction-paper songbook or a small holiday treat in the angel's hands. These heavenly holiday projects make a sweet classroom display.

Lori Hamernik—Gr. K, Prairie Farm Elementary, Prairie Farm, WI

Pasta-Perfect Wreaths

These unique wreaths provide plenty of pleasing holiday possibilities!

For each child you will need:

1 waxed-paper workmat
white glue
approximately 1 cup of cooked, drained, and cooled pasta pieces (such as *rotini*)
1 small (waxed) paper cup
green tempera paint
red pom-poms, sequins, or beads
glitter

To begin, stir together a mixture of one part paint to four parts glue. (For one cup of cooked pasta, you'll need approximately one tablespoon of paint to four tablespoons of glue.) Then gently stir the pasta into the glue mixture. (In order for the pasta to form a wreath, it must be *thickly* coated with glue.) Next place the cup upside down on the waxed paper. Arrange the colored pasta around it, being sure that the pasta pieces are all overlapping. While the glue is still wet, decorate the wreath with red decorations and glitter. When the wreath is partially dry, remove the cup and use a pencil or straw to make a hole near the top to attach a hanger. When the wreath is completely dry (three to five days), peel off the waxed paper. Display these wreaths just as they are, use them for tree ornaments, or convert them into picture frames by taping special photos to the backs.

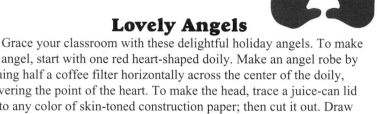

Sandra Ziegler, St. Mary's Catholic School, Strongsville, OH

Dominick

Artichoke Trees

Are you interested in a new tree-printing activity? Try using swirly artichokes! To make one printer, slice off the top of an artichoke, leaving the stem end intact. Place several folded, damp paper towels in a shallow tray and spread green tempera paint on them. Dip the artichoke in the paint. Center the first print near the top of a large sheet of construction paper. Then create a triangle tree shape by making two prints in the second row, three prints in the third row, and so on. Paint or color a brown trunk at the bottom of the tree if desired. When the paint is dry, use art supplies (such as sequins, pom-poms, beads, ribbon, and lace) to add festive touches to the tree. Then display a forest of these terrific trees!

Sandie Bolze—Gr. K, Verne W. Critz Primary School
East Patchogue, NY

Picturesque Poinsettias

Brighten your classroom and enhance fine-motor skills with these pretty poinsettias. First paint a large sheet of manila paper with red tempera paint. To create *bracts* (the red petal-like leaves), tear the dried paper into petal shapes. Arrange the bracts on the back of a small paper plate; then glue them in place. Next glue unpopped popcorn kernels in the center. Add torn green construction-paper leaves for a finishing touch.

To vary this activity, glue torn red tissue-paper pieces onto a white construction-paper background; then add green tissue-paper leaves. Decorate the center section by squeezing on dabs of neon yellow-colored glue. Display these holiday beauties in your classroom. It's beginning to look a lot like Christmas!

Julie Robinson—Gr. K
Club Boulevard Humanities Magnet
Durham, NC

Cristie Bagwell—Gr. K
Robert Lee Elementary
Robert Lee, TX

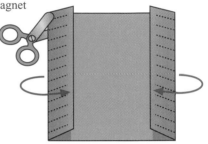

Kwanzaa Mats

Habari gani? (What's the news?) It's Kwanzaa time! If your class is studying Kwanzaa, celebrate these special days by making *mkekas* (traditional woven mats that represent a firm foundation and tradition). In advance, collect one brown grocery bag for every two children. To prepare, cut a supply of colorful, 1" x 18" construction-paper strips. Then cut out the large front and back panels of each bag. For each panel, fold in two inches on each short side. Cut the folded sections for weaving (as shown). To begin the activity, give one panel to each child. Instruct her to draw a picture of her firm foundation—her entire family. Then show each child how to weave the paper strips, in and out, on each side of the mat, and then trim and glue the ends of each strip to the mat. Laminate the finished mkekas; then use them as placemats or for other Kwanzaa-related activities. Happy Kwanzaa!

Penguin Pals

Pondering the perfect penguin project? Make these little guys with your class! Collect paper egg cartons; then cut apart two cups for each child. To make a penguin, glue two cups together as shown. (It might be helpful to press a dab of clay into the bottom cup for added stability.) Paint the resulting egg shape with black and white paints to resemble a penguin's body. Glue on triangle-shaped, construction-paper wings, flippers, and a beak. Then glue on wiggle eyes for a finishing touch.

Encourage children to take their finished penguins to the block center. Then have them build structures on which to perch these popular pals. If desired, cover the block structure with a smooth, white sheet; then invite youngsters to slide their penguins down the icy hill!

Suzanne Bell Ward—Gr. K,
Ancaster, Ontario, Canada

glue
together

Sweet Snowmen

It's fun to make these sweet, little snow creations—and they won't melt in your classroom! Begin with a blue construction-paper background. Use dabs of white glue and large marshmallows to build a snowman on the paper. Then poke in toothpicks to resemble arms. Add details with fine-tipped permanent markers and construction-paper scraps. Then complete the scene by gluing small marshmallows in the sky and on the ground. (Remember to have extra marshmallows on hand for snacking!) When the glue is dry, display the finished projects with a banner that reads "We're 'SNOW' Glad To Be Here!"

Martha Ann Davis—Gr. K
Springfield Elementary
Greenwood, SC

Patterns
Use with "Put Your Name In Lights" on page 20.

lightbulb

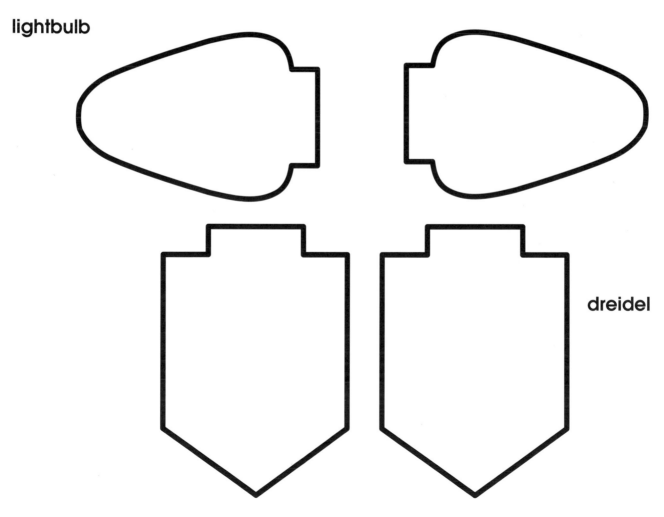

dreidel

Arts & Crafts
For Little Hands

Serve Up Some Hearts

Little ones will enjoy making these pretty placemats for your valentine party! To make a placemat, use crayon to draw and heavily color a variety of hearts on a 10" x 16" sheet of white construction paper. (Make sure each heart is covered with a thick coat of wax.) Then paint a thin, red tempera wash over the entire sheet. The crayon will resist the paint, leaving delicate hearts on the placemat. When the paint is dry, have each child choose a background color of 12" x 18" construction paper, and glue his mat onto it. Laminate the mats for durability if desired. Who's ready to party?

Valentine Collage

These tactile valentines are just right for little hands! In advance, use alcohol mixed with a few drops of food coloring to dye a large quantity of dry pasta shapes (such as rotini, macaroni, and wheel); then spread the pasta on newspaper to dry. To make one collage, spread a thick coat of glue on a small area of a tagboard heart. Arrange dyed pasta and dry white rice on the glue as desired. Continue working until the heart is covered in pleasing designs. When all the heart collages are thoroughly dry, encourage children to give their hearts to sweethearts or other loved ones. What a touching gift!

Log Cabin Creations

Culminate discussions of Abraham Lincoln's birthday and his rustic beginnings with these creative cabins! To prepare, cut a large supply of 1/2"-wide, brown construction-paper strips. To make a log cabin, arrange the strips on a sheet of paper, tearing them as different lengths are needed. Then glue on paper scraps to resemble windows, doors, and other details. To complete the picture, draw in background details with crayons. Abe would be proud of these endearingly rustic cabins!

Susan Logan
Hickory Tree Elementary School
St. Cloud, FL

Lovable Lambs

Youngsters won't mind the March bluster when they have these lovable lambs to remind them that spring is coming! Provide each child with a coffee filter, a large supply of cotton balls, and a sheet of black construction paper. Encourage the child to glue cotton balls onto the inside bottom of the coffee filter. Then have him cut a head, legs, and a tail from the black paper. Have him glue the parts in place, then draw on features with a white crayon. These fuzzy little lambs will help usher in spring weather!

Amy Ross—Gr. K
Community School Age Day Care
Downingtown, PA

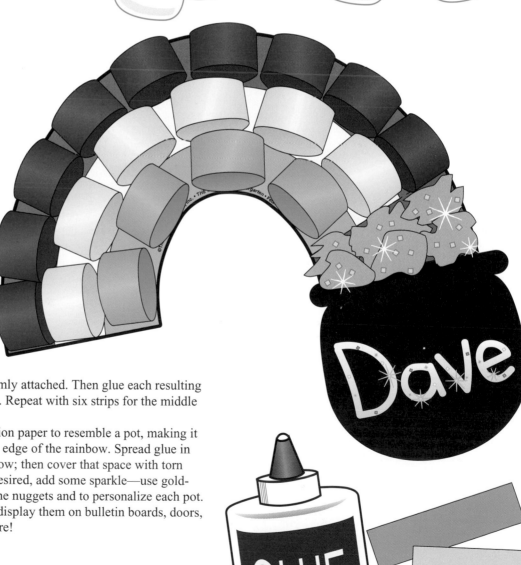

Lucky Rainbows

The luck o' the Irish will fill your classroom when your students make these three-dimensional rainbows. In advance, cut a large supply of colorful 1" x 5" paper strips. To make one rainbow, color a white construction-paper copy of the rainbow pattern (page 30) with three colors of your choice; then cut it out. For the top band of color on your rainbow, count out nine matching construction-paper strips. Curve each strip until the ends overlap; then glue them together. Hold the ends in place until they are firmly attached. Then glue each resulting ring to the corresponding rainbow band. Repeat with six strips for the middle row and four strips for the bottom row.

Trim a four-inch square of construction paper to resemble a pot, making it as large as possible. Glue this pot to the edge of the rainbow. Spread glue in the space between the pot and the rainbow; then cover that space with torn yellow construction-paper nuggets. If desired, add some sparkle—use gold-glitter fabric paint to dab gold dust on the nuggets and to personalize each pot. Let these rainbows dry overnight; then display them on bulletin boards, doors, or wherever your little leprechauns desire!

JoEllyn Larrison—Gr. K
Northside Elementary
Geneseo, IL

Arts & Crafts
For Little Hands

Bunny Surprise!

Youngsters will enjoy making—and especially giving—these unique springtime cards!

For each card you will need:

white and colored construction paper
crayons, colored pencils, or pastels
identically sized egg tracers
Easter grass (optional)

scissors
markers
a stapler
glue

To make one card:

1. Trace two egg shapes onto white construction paper; then cut them out. (See egg patterns on page 186, if desired.)
2. Decorate one of the eggs. Then, beginning at the narrower end, cut a slit partway down that egg.
3. Place the decorated egg on top of the plain egg and staple them together at the wider end. Fold back the top egg; then draw and color bunny features inside.
4. Glue the back of the plain egg to a folded piece of colored construction paper so that the decorated egg is showing and the staple is at the top.
5. Add details to the outside of the card and write a spring or Easter message on the inside.

Michele Hertz—Gr. K
Central Islip Early Childhood Center, Central Islip, NY

Beautiful Blooming Bonnets

These flowery spring bonnets will bring visions of bygone days when ladies wore fancy hats to Easter parades! A few days before children begin these projects, display a sample bonnet. Tell boys and girls that they can make these hats for themselves or to give away, or to display as springtime decorations. Then set up a flower-making factory as a center option. Encourage all students to chip in to make an abundance of flowers (see the directions below). When you have a large supply of flowers, you're ready to begin making these beautiful blooming bonnets!

Flower-Making Supplies:
a large supply of colorful tissue-paper pieces (approximately 5" x 6")
a stapler

To prepare one flower:

1. Align three tissue-paper pieces on top of each other.
2. Accordion-fold, as shown.
3. Fold the resulting strip in half; then staple it on the fold.

For each bonnet you will need:

a paper plate
a stapler
crayons

a craft knife (for adult use only)
5 feet of 2-inch-wide ribbon

To make one bonnet:

1. Color the back of a paper plate.
2. Use the craft knife to cut two slits in the paper plate as shown. Thread the ribbon through the slits to create a hat tie.
3. Staple the base of a flower onto the hat. Gently separate and fluff the tissue-paper layers. Repeat this step, adding flowers to the hat as desired.

adapted from an idea by Barbara Meyers—Gr. K
Fort Worth Country Day School, Fort Worth, TX

Hurry-Scurry Hummingbirds

Are you studying birds this spring? These child-made projects will help familiarize youngsters with one of the tiniest and fastest-flapping birds of all. In advance, display color illustrations of hummingbirds. To make one hummingbird, cut out a white construction-paper copy of the hummingbird body (page 31). Use a pencil to draw on eyes and a beak. Using a thin watercolor wash, lightly paint three paper cupcake liners and the body. When the liners are dry, fold two in half for wings; then fold the remaining liner into quarters for the tail. Assemble and glue the hummingbird on a sheet of construction paper. Create an aviary effect with a display of these birds around your classroom.

Johanna Clinton—Gr. K
Rosemont Elementary
Dallas, TX

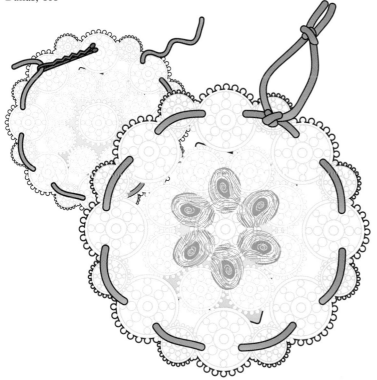

Mother's Day Sachet

Moms and special ladies everywhere deserve a treat on their special day, so make these sachets that smell as good as they look! To make one sachet, run a thin bead of glue all the way around the edge of a paper doily. Sandwich a folded fabric-softener dryer sheet between this doily and an identical one. Allow the glue to dry. Using a bobby pin as a child-safe needle, sew a length of narrow ribbon around the edges of the doilies to create a decorative effect. Tie a knot in the ribbon; then use the ribbon ends to make a loop for hanging. Add a personal touch by making a thumbprint flower on one side of the sachet. Encourage children to give their sweet-smelling sachets to the special ladies in their lives.

Judy Kuen—Gr. K
Lomira Elementary
Lomira, WI

Sweet Peas

Picture your sweet peas in these adorable frames that make excellent anytime gifts! To make one frame, glue four large craft sticks together to form a square. Paint the frame yellow; then set it aside to dry. Cut out green construction-paper copies of two pea pods (page 31). To make one pod, glue only the bottoms and sides of the patterns together, forming a boat shape. When the glue is dry, tuck three or four green 1/2-inch pom-poms inside the pod and glue them in place. Poke a short length of green pipe cleaner through one end of the pod; then twist the pipe cleaner to look like a vine. Use a permanent marker to write "I'm Your Sweet Pea!" on the dry frame. Glue the pea pod to the bottom of the frame. After each child has made a frame, help him glue a picture of himself into it. Finally, attach magnetic tape to the back of the frame. How sweet it is!

adapted from an idea by Patricia Draper—Gr. K
Millarville Community School
Millarville, Alberta, Canada

27

Arts & Crafts
For Little Hands

Island Silhouettes

Escape to the islands with these tropical sunset silhouettes. To make one, paint a piece of white construction paper with plain water. While the paper is wet, overlap strokes of multi-colored watercolor paints. Set the paper aside to dry. Then cut out island shapes from black construction paper. Glue these shapes to the dried, painted background. Display these island-inspired projects with the title "Island Getaway."

Gloria Burciaga
Peppermint Junction—County Station, Ventura, CA

My Very Own Goldfish

In this independent project, each child will go for the goldfish! To prepare, photocopy a class supply of the fishbowl pattern (page 32) on light blue construction paper. Place the patterns in the art center along with green scrap paper, a shaker of gold glitter and sand, white glue, scissors, and a bowl of fish-shaped crackers.

To create the scene, have each child cut out a fishbowl. Instruct her to spread glue along the bottom of the bowl and sprinkle on the glitter-and-sand mixture. Next, encourage her to glue on torn pieces of construction paper to resemble plant life. To add the feature attractions, have each child glue on several fish-shaped crackers. When the glue is dry, invite her to take these pretend pets home to enjoy.

Denise K. Clay, Kehoe France School, New Orleans, LA

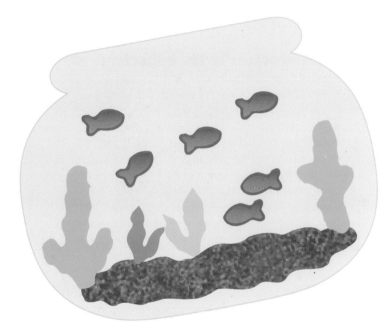

Stunning Starfish

Captivate your little beachcombers with these pretty starfish. In advance, mix up enough salt dough (see the recipe shown) for each child to have a lime-sized portion. To make a starfish, roll the dough into a long rope; then divide it into five equal pieces. Arrange the five pieces to resemble a starfish; then press the center together. Use a pencil to add texture to the surface of the starfish; then set it aside to dry for two to three days. (Turn the starfish over midway through the drying time.) Finally, paint the dry starfish with a light coat of coral-colored tempera paint. Then sprinkle kosher salt on top of the wet paint. Display these starfish along a long strip of child-made ocean. Say—did you see that stunning starfish?

Christine Guanipa—Gr. K
Covenant School
Arlington, MA

Salt Dough Recipe

2 parts salt
4 parts flour
1 part water

Mix the ingredients together with your hands; then knead it until it is smooth. (Add more water if necessary.)

Father's Day Wallets

Treat Dad (or a favorite male friend) to this cool wallet filled with Father's Day credit cards—*at zero percent interest!*

To make one wallet:

1. Use the side of a crayon to rub a textured pattern onto a 9" x 12" sheet of construction paper. (Tree bark, for example, creates a nice, rough leather look.)
2. Fold the paper in thirds (colored side out).
3. Unfold the paper; then glue one of the outer sections to the middle.
4. Refold the remaining flap; then fold the sides in, about one inch each. Glue the sides down, holding them firmly until they are dry.
5. Fold the wallet as shown.

To fill the wallet with several child-made credit cards, photocopy a supply of the credit-card patterns (page 31) on construction paper. To make one credit card, have a child write or dictate a special treat for Dad in the space provided. Then have him sign his name and color the card as desired. After a child slides his credit cards into his wallet, it's ready for a very special delivery! What a thoughtful gift for a loving dad or special male friend!

adapted from an idea by Nancy Hatch—Gr. K
South Bristol Elementary School
South Bristol, ME

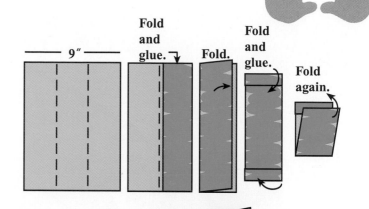

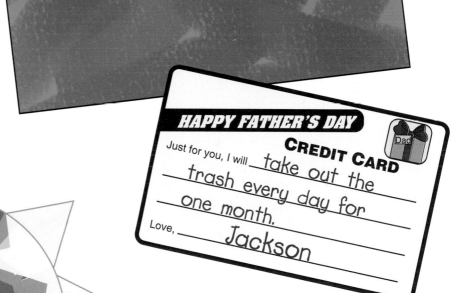

HAPPY FATHER'S DAY
CREDIT CARD
Just for you, I will take out the trash every day for one month.
Love, Jackson

Let The Sunshine In

For those days when the real thing isn't smilin' down on you, try this project that's guaranteed to bring bright sunshiny rays into your classroom. To prepare, cut or tear yellow, white, and orange tissue paper into small pieces. Then brush a solution of one part glue to one part water over a white paper plate. While the glue is still wet, arrange tissue-paper pieces on the plate, being sure to cover it completely. When all the tissue is in place, paint the entire surface again with the glue mixture, sealing any loose edges. Sprinkle clear glitter on the wet glue. Then cut out construction-paper triangles and glue them to the back of the plate to resemble sun rays. To make a hanger, poke a partially straightened paper clip through the top of the plate. Suspend these suns anywhere that needs a little cheer. See? It's gonna be a bright sunshiny day!

Rainbow Pattern
Use with "Lucky Rainbows" on page 25.

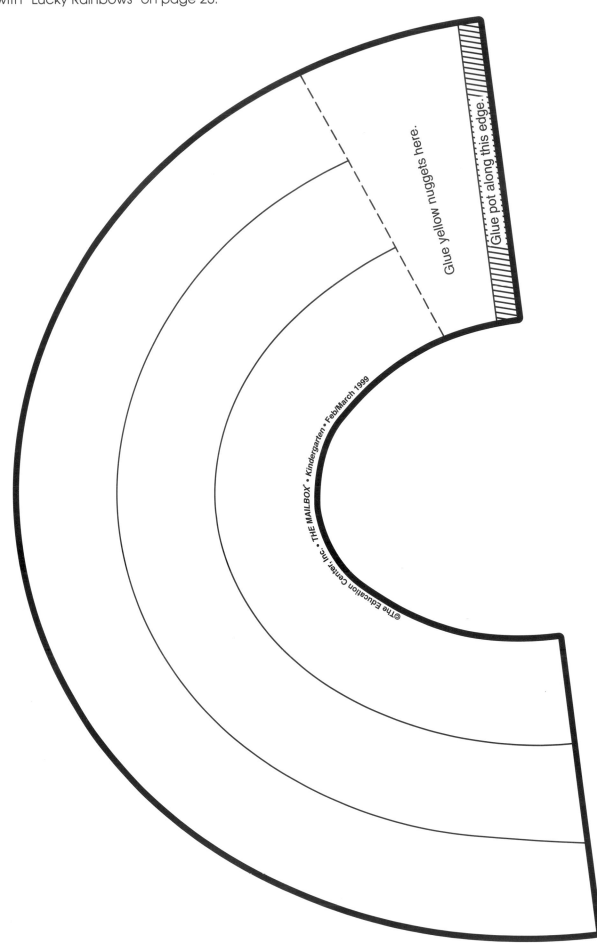

Glue yellow nuggets here.

Glue pot along this edge.

©The Education Center, Inc. • THE MAILBOX® • Kindergarten • Feb/March 1999

Hummingbird Body Patterns

Use with "Hurry-Scurry Hummingbirds" on page 27.

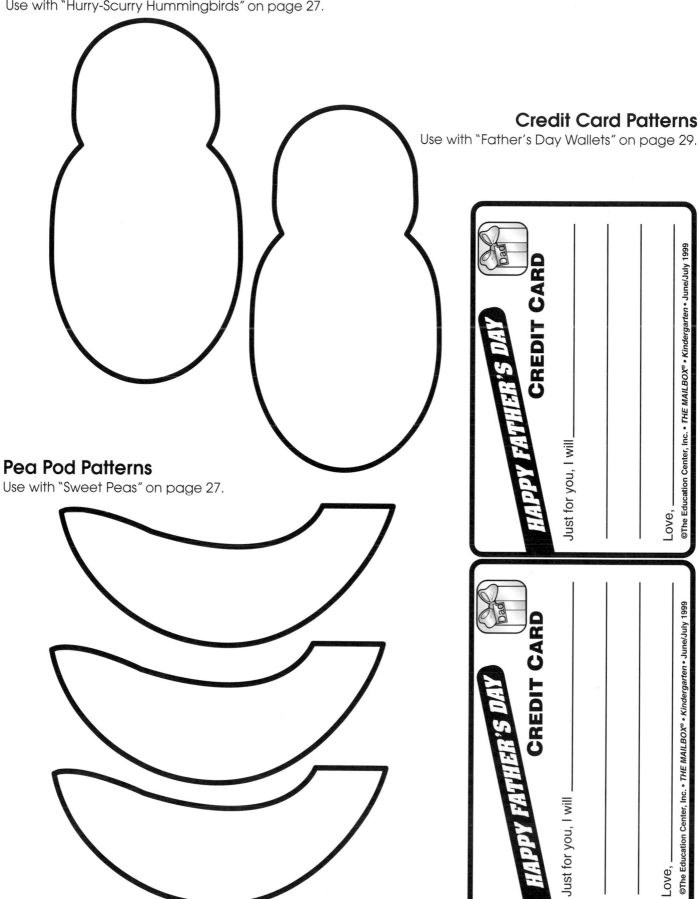

Credit Card Patterns

Use with "Father's Day Wallets" on page 29.

Pea Pod Patterns

Use with "Sweet Peas" on page 27.

HAPPY FATHER'S DAY

CREDIT CARD

Just for you, I will _____

Love, _____

©The Education Center, Inc. • THE MAILBOX® • Kindergarten • June/July 1999

HAPPY FATHER'S DAY

CREDIT CARD

Just for you, I will _____

Love, _____

©The Education Center, Inc. • THE MAILBOX® • Kindergarten • June/July 1999

Fishbowl Pattern

Use with "My Very Own Goldfish" on page 28.

LEARNING CENTERS

Learning Centers

Mr. Jones' Bones

Dem bones, dem bones make just the right teaching tools for this October learning center. To prepare the components, follow these steps:

1. Use an opaque projector to enlarge the skeleton pattern (page 41). Trace the skeleton on a large sheet of poster board—on any color except white.

2. Trace the enlarged pattern again on white poster board.

3. Cut apart the white poster-board bones along the bold outlines.

4. Laminate the whole colored sheet of poster board (with the intact skeleton drawing) and all the white pieces.

To prepare the center, use permanent markers or taped-on labels to program each section of the intact skeleton picture with a different skill. (Our illustration shows colors and color words. Other examples include dot sets and numerals, upper- and lowercase letters, sight words and pictures, simple addition facts and sums, etc.) Next program each bone with the corre- sponding skill. Lay the skeleton poster on a flat surface in the center, and store all of the bones in a bucket or string-tie envelope. When a child visits this center, his task is to give Mr. Jones all of his bones—but they will only fit with careful thinking! Will Mr. Jones get all his bones?

* To change the programming on Mr. Jones' Bones, simply wipe the bones and poster clean with a spritz of hairspray.

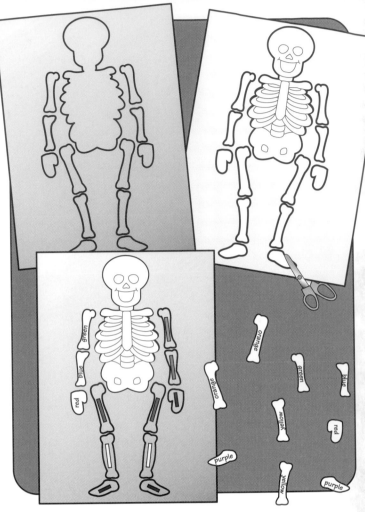

Trick Or Treat, We Repeat!

This center calls on patterning skills with a little seasonal art and creativity whisked in for good measure. Stock the center with seasonal sponge cutouts, paints, and long strips of painting paper. (If sponges are not available, duplicate a large supply of the patterns on page 41 and use them in a similar manner.) Invite each child to use these supplies to create a pattern on one or more strips of paper. When their patterns are dry, display them—one at a time—to your class. Encourage youngsters to identify each of the patterns. As each pattern is correctly named, write that pattern on the back of the strip(s). For further patterning practice, put the patterns in a center. Have a child look at a pattern, identify that pattern, and then turn the strip(s) over to check his answer. (When your center work is done, these patterns make nice bulletin-board borders!)

Laurie Birt—Gr. K, Belinder Elementary, Prairie Village, KS

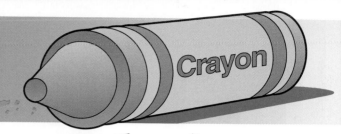

Spelling, Anyone?

Is anybody ready for spelling? Or perhaps some beginning-sound work? Or maybe your students need to stick with matching letters for a little while longer. This center has it all! In advance, collect simple pictures from magazines or decorative notepads. Mount each picture on a different sheet of paper. Laminate each page; then use a permanent marker to program each page according to your youngsters' abilities (see the illustrations for programming options). Then arrange these pictures in a center along with a supply of manipulative letters. When each child visits this center, encourage her to complete each page by placing the appropriate letter(s) in place. "Hey—that 'urkey' needs a *t!*"

Kathie Deann Thornton, In Home Day Care, Wake Forest, NC

"Gotta" Dance!

Here's the perfect creative outlet for those toe-tappin', finger-snappin', foot-stompin' kindergartners of yours. Designate an area with some open floor space to be your *dance studio.* Cover a low table (or another piece of furniture) with butcher paper to resemble a *barre.* Mount a mirror on a nearby wall, or attach a large sheet of silver wrapping paper or tinfoil to the wall. Set up a cassette or CD player in the area. Stock this center with a variety of dance costumes and props, such as tap shoes, ballet slippers, and cowboy boots. Each week, provide a different type of music, such as classical, country, or even show tunes. When children visit this center, prompt them to use the costumes and props of their choice and dance, dance, dance!

Bonnie McKenzie—Pre-K & Gr. K
Cheshire Country Day School, Cheshire, CT

Tell It Again, Sam!

Your little learners will enjoy telling stories again and again with these portable storytelling bags. In advance sew a simple bag from approximately one yard of felt. Then sew on two lengths of sturdy cord for handles. Each time you'd like to offer a different book in your storytelling center, make flannelboard pieces by tracing the story's characters onto sheets of Pellon®. Then color and cut out each character. After you introduce this book to your class, put the book and the flannelboard pieces in the bag. Then place the bag in a reading center that has a doorknob or hook (from which to hang the bag). Encourage children to visit this center in pairs or small groups so they can assume the roles of *storyteller* (who holds the book), *props person* (who manipulates the flannelboard figures), and *audience.* After each telling of the story, invite youngsters to switch roles and tell the story again. And be sure to keep an ear out: you might hear some pretty creative additions authored in the story as time goes on!

Cynthia G. Besosa—Gr. K, Tuloso-Midway Primary, Corpus Christi, TX

Learning Centers

The Spirit Of Giving Goes On

After the holidays, set up this center to reinforce recycling, creativity, and the spirit of giving. Before the holidays, ask children to save some wrapping paper from their holiday gifts. Pool the samples and put them in your art center along with large sheets of construction paper and glue. When a student visits this center, invite her to choose several samples of wrapping paper and to tear those samples into pieces. Next have her arrange and glue the pieces onto a construction-paper background. Display each finished project on a board titled "The Spirit Of Giving Goes On." Then ask, "If you could give any gift you choose to any person you choose, what would you give to whom?" Then have each child write or dictate her response on a strip of paper. Staple each child's response under her project. What a spirited display!

Daphne M. Orenshein, Yavneh Hebrew Academy, Los Angeles, CA

I'm going to buy my Mom a weighing thing because she said it's broken.
Haley

Christmas-Cookie Station

Combine one of the best parts of the holiday season—baking cookies!—with this fine-motor and matching activity. To prepare, use your favorite recipe to make a supply of red, green, and brown play dough. (If desired, provide a sensory surprise by adding a few drops of sweet-smelling extracts to the dough.) Then trace several different holiday cookie cutters on tagboard sheets. Color the shapes; then laminate the tagboard cookie sheets. Store the cookie cutters in a seasonal tin and put it in a center along with the play dough, the cookie sheets, a holiday cookie tray, spatulas, and rolling pins.

To use this center, have a child select a cookie sheet and create a play-dough cookie to match each shape on the sheet. Then invite him to pretend to bake the cookies. (If you have a play oven in your housekeeping center, that would be the perfect place!) Next have him use a spatula to remove the cookies and arrange them on the tray. As each new child visits the center, invite him to follow the same procedure and add his cookies to the tray. It's beginning to look (and smell) a lot like Christmas!

Adapted from an idea by Mary F. Philip—Gr. K
Relay Children's Center, Baltimore, MD

Sounds Like Letters!

Letter-sound association is a snap with this language-center idea. In advance, collect empty film canisters and lids. Program a lid with each letter you'd like to include. Then place small objects whose names begin with each of the letters in different canisters. (For example, use plastic ants for *A*, buttons or beans for *B*, a toy cow or car for *C,* etc.) Store the open canisters upright in a decorated shoebox. Store the programmed lids in a small basket. To use this center, invite a child to examine the contents of each canister, then snap on the correct lid. (If desired, make this center self-checking by attaching a labeled sticker to the bottom of each canister.) When all the letters are matched, have the child remove the lids and put them back in the basket for the next child who visits the center.

Rochie Kogan, Yeshiva Ohr Yisroel, Forest Hills, NY

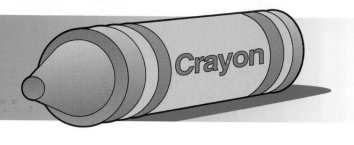

Musical Review

Got an ear for music? Your students will develop their abilities to hear musical patterns when they visit this center! Obtain a xylophone with colored bars (or use stickers to color-code the bars on a plain one). Draw simple color patterns on tagboard strips; then place them in a container. Stock a center with the xylophone, patterns, markers, and blank pattern strips. Invite students to choose patterns to play. When they have sampled several—and seem to get the hang of it—have your little maestros use the blank pattern strips and the markers to create their own masterpieces. Ah, music to their ears!

Kelly Williams—Gr. K, Jacksboro Elementary, Jacksboro, TX

Valentine Memory

Recycling is only one of the benefits of this seasonal center! You'll also find visual discrimination, reading, and turn-taking tucked in here and there. In advance, gather a collection of old valentines. Find all the matches among your collection; then glue each of those cards to a different construction-paper heart. Laminate all the heart cards. Then arrange all the cards facedown in the shape of a heart. Have children visit this center in pairs and instruct them to use the cards to play a memory game. (One child turns over two cards. If they match, she keeps the pair and continues play in the same manner. If the cards do not match, she returns them to their original positions and play continues with the next child. Children continue in this manner until all of the cards have been matched.) As they play, encourage children to read the familiar valentine vocabulary on each of their pairs. A perfect valentine match!

Sharon Schmidt—Gr. K, Theresa Learning Community, Theresa, WI

Wind-Catching Patterns

Not only are these pretty patterns fun to make and display, but they serve as terrific wind catchers too! Place a class supply of paint-stirring sticks, a colorful variety of 14-inch crepe-paper streamers (at least six per child), and glue in your art center. Invite each child who visits this center to make a wind catcher. First, have her apply a thin line of glue along a paint stick. Then have her glue on at least six streamers to create a pattern on the stick. When the glue is dry, hot-glue a length of yarn to the back of each paint stick to form a hanger. Suspend students' wind catchers near a window or on a tree branch, or have children carry them as wands during graceful movement activities. Enjoy those balmy breezes!

adapted from an idea by Terri Whitaker—Gr. K
Barrington Place School
Sugar Land, TX

Learning Centers

Children And The Chocolate Factory

Since the season for chocolate bunnies and such is upon us, set up a chocolate factory in your fine-motor or art center! In advance, mix up a batch or two of chocolate-scented play dough by adding a few tablespoons of baking cocoa to your favorite play-dough recipe. Also provide a class supply of individually wrapped chocolates. Then arrange the play dough and wrapped chocolates in a center along with rolling pins, plastic knives, spatulas, and pastel-colored workmats. *When children visit this center, remind them that this play dough is not edible.* Then encourage each child to create the ultimate chocolate creation. When he has finished working, invite him to enjoy a real chocolate treat. Mmm—this chocolatey center sure smells fun!

Lori Kent
Hood River, OR

Flower Phonics

Watch letter-sound associations come to full bloom in this language center. To make one flower, cut out a large construction-paper blossom, two leaves, and a stem. Program the blossom with a capital letter and the stem with the matching lowercase letter. Then glue a different picture beginning with the corresponding sound on each of the leaves. Make as many flowers as desired; then laminate all the pieces. Store the flower parts in a basket. Arrange the flowers and a supply of pushpins near a bulletin board. To use this center, a student matches the leaves and stems to the correct blossoms, then pins the matching parts to the bulletin board. There you have it—easy, attractive letter-sound practice!

Trish Draper—Gr. K
Millarville Community School
Millarville, Alberta, Canada

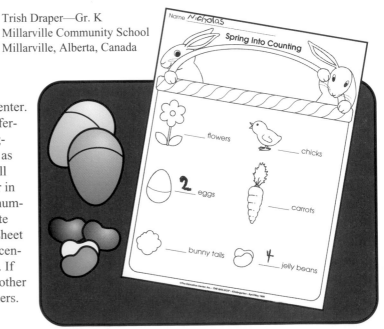

Spring Into Counting

Along with spring fever comes this higher-level counting center. To prepare, post a counting chart in your math center. Then, referring to the recording sheet on page 43, collect six sets of spring-related items for counting practice. You can use objects—such as toy chicks, plastic eggs, silk flowers, jelly beans, and cotton ball bunny tails—or pictures of these items. (Determine the number in each set based on your students' abilities. And remember, the number 0 can be practiced too!) Place each type of item in a separate basket in the center. Duplicate a class supply of the recording sheet on page 43; then place the copies near the baskets. To use this center, a child counts and records the number of each type of item. If desired, vary this idea during different seasons by substituting other seasonal items and corresponding recording sheets and containers.

Trish Draper—Gr. K

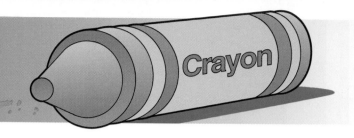

All The King's Men (And Women!)

Provide springtime visual-discrimination and problem-solving practice with this puzzle center. In advance, cut out large egg shapes from laminated wallpaper samples. Puzzle-cut each egg into an appropriate number of pieces for your students' abilities. Then store all the pieces in a basket. To introduce this center, read a version of "Humpty Dumpty." Then have each child who visits this center sort the egg pieces into like patterns, then put each egg together. Did all the king's men and women get Humpty together again?

Ann Rudolph—Gr. K
Rich Pond School
Bowling Green, KY

Seeds Of Spring

Sow the seeds of scientific discovery, then reap language and visual-discrimination benefits with this center! In advance, obtain pairs of spring seed packets made by different companies. Glue each packet and several seeds to individual index cards. Fill a plastic planter with the cards and hand-held magnifiers; then place the planter in a center. Invite each child who visits this center to spread out the cards, examine them with a magnifier, and then match each pair using seed or word clues.

Saraellen Johnston—Gr. K
Elm Road School
Mishawaka, IN

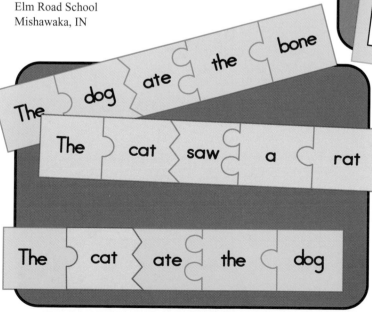

Silly Sentences

This center is sure to be a treat for your emergent readers! To prepare, write simple sentences on different colors of sentence strips. Then cut the words apart to form puzzles. (Using the same puzzle cut between each part of speech will allow students to mix up the words to build new sentences. See the illustration for clarity.) Be sure to throw in some silly sentence options to keep reading fun!

Karen Smith
Pensacola, FL

Learning Centers

My, You Look Important!

Use the official feel of clipboards to entice each child to do some thematic reading and writing. To prepare this center, write 10–15 vocabulary words from your current theme on sentence strips. (If desired, code these words with theme-related stickers to distinguish them from other classroom print.) Cut the words apart; then position them around your room. Finally, place a supply of paper and several clipboards in a center. When a child visits this center, invite her to go on a word search. Instruct her to clip a sheet of paper on a clipboard, then search the room for five to ten theme words. Have her write the words on her paper. When she is finished, instruct her to read her list of words to an adult. Then have her take the list home to read to her family.

Donna Peduto—Gr. K, Neshobe Elementary School, Brandon, VT

Hooked On Math

Fishing for fun math practice? Hook up to this idea! Begin by duplicating an equal number of the fish and worm patterns (page 44) on construction paper. Program each fish with a simple math problem and each worm with a corresponding answer. Cut out the fish and worms. If desired, program the back of each fish for self-checking; then laminate them. Next hot-glue a clothespin to the back of each fish. Store all these pieces in a plastic fishbowl; then place the fishbowl in a center along with a supply of counters. To use this center, a student chooses a fish, uses the counters to solve the problem, and then clips on the corresponding worm. It's the catch of the day!

Karen Smith—Grs. K–1, Pace, FL

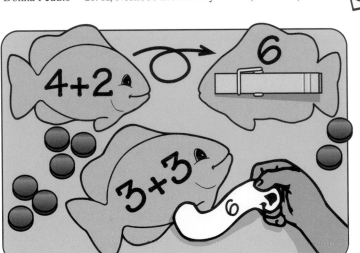

Colorful Pizza Pizzazz

This colorful pizza will satisfy your students' appetite for color-word reinforcement. To prepare, obtain a large cardboard circle and a clean pizza box. Decide how many colors you'd like to include; then use a marker to divide the cardboard circle into that many sections. For each slice in your pizza, cut out one colored construction-paper pizza slice and one white one. Cut off a crust shape from each colored slice; then glue that crust to a white pizza slice. Program each white slice with the color of the crust. Then glue these slices to the cardboard circle. Next, program each (crustless) colored slice with the corresponding color word. Place the pizza and the pieces in the box and store it in your center. To use this center, a child matches each colored slice of pizza to the crust and the color word. Isn't it time for a colorful slice of pizza?

Erin Roeske, Woodbury, MN

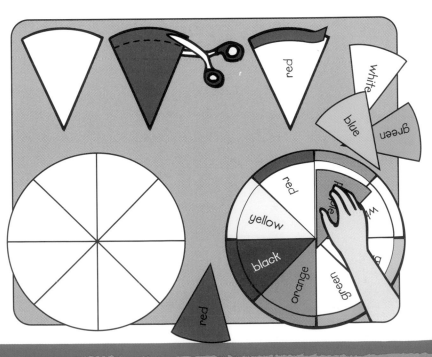

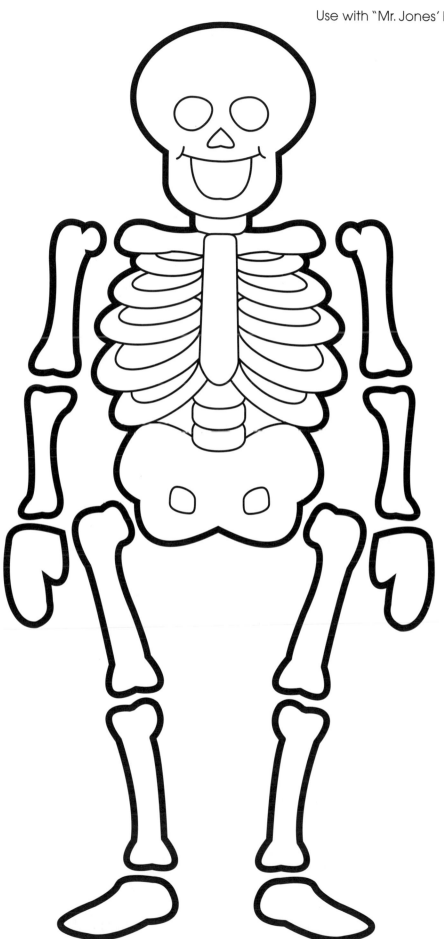

Seasonal Patterns

Use with "Trick Or Treat, We Repeat!" on page 34.

Name _____

Spring Into Counting

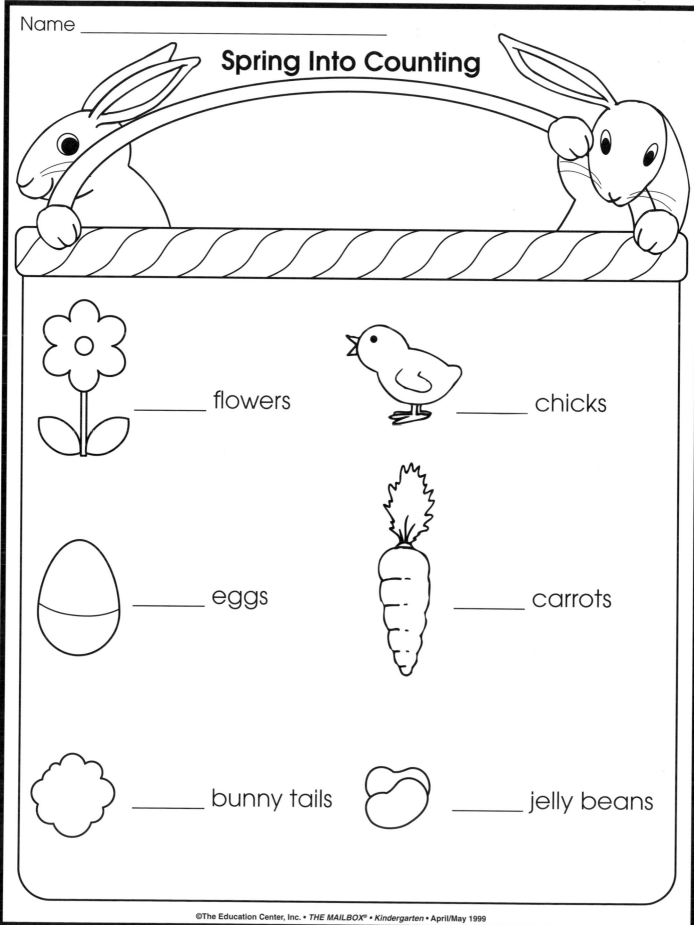

_____ flowers

_____ chicks

_____ eggs

_____ carrots

_____ bunny tails

_____ jelly beans

Fish And Worm Patterns

Use with "Hooked On Math" on page 40.

CHILDREN'S LITERATURE

FALL FRIENDS

Greet the autumn season with this crop of literature-related ideas featuring fall-weather friends and cool-curriculum fun. From fall festivities to friendly frights, your youngsters are sure to fall head over heels for these special characters.

introduction, reviews, and ideas by Anne Bustard and Mackie Rhodes

RATTLEBONE ROCK

By Sylvia Andrews
Illustrated by Jennifer Plecas
Published by HarperCollins
Publishers, Inc.; 1995

What a night to remember! What a night to recall! When the Rattlebone Rock stirred one and all!

This cumulative tale is sure to stir up one and all of your students! To begin, tap your foot to a steady beat while reading the rhythmic tale. Afterward assign each sound effect in the story to a different small group of children. Then read the book again. As each sound is introduced, have the appropriate group create that sound and perform a corresponding action or dance. As each new sound is added, invite the previous groups to repeat their sounds in turn. By the end of the book, your whole class will be doin' the Rattlebone Rock! Are you ready? Dim the lights and tap your feet. It's time to read along to the rattlebone beat!

SIX CREEPY SHEEP

By Judith Ross Enderle and Stephanie Gordon Tessler
Illustrated by John O'Brien
Published by Boyds Mills Press, Inc.; 1992

All dressed up and someplace to go! But one by one, five of the six creepy sheep are scared away by creepier costumed characters. Finally only one brave creepy sheep remains. Will it be trick or treat for that little sheep?

Once your youngsters have heard this story, the stage is set for a little subtraction action. In advance collect six old sheets and/or pillowcases to use as ghost costumes. Using the art in the book as a reference, add accessories, such as a necktie, a red cap, a green hat, and a pair of glasses. Choose six students to each don a ghost costume. As you read the story again, encourage these actors to pantomime the script. Six...five...four...three...two...one... now what? At the very end, invite your whole class to shout, "Happy Halloween!" Repeat the performance until each child has had a chance to star in the play.

Further extend this tongue-twisting tale with a bit of phonics fun. As you return to each page that describes a different group of trick-or-treaters, guide children to notice that several words on that page begin with the same sound. Then share a few sayings that contain initial-consonant alliteration, such as "Sally sells seashells by the seashore." Afterward invite each child to choose a letter and write/dictate and illustrate an original sentence using that letter as her guide. Have each child share her work with the class; then display it under the corresponding letter label.

A babe bug bited a brown bear.

Jon

THE VANISHING PUMPKIN

By Tony Johnston
Illustrated by Tomie dePaola
Published by G. P. Putnam's Sons, 1983

Who snitched the Halloween pumpkin? A 700-year-old woman and an 800-year-old man encounter some very zany characters while searching for their missing pumpkin. And at the end of their journey, a surprise awaits!

A cooperative pumpkin search is in order after reading this delightfully teasing tale. Assign one student the role of the old woman and another the old man. Send the assigned students out of the room while another child, the wizard, hides a small pumpkin. Then ask the old woman and old man to link their elbows and return to the room. Have them keep their elbows linked while they search for the missing pumpkin. Invite the other students to say either "vanish" or "appear" to help clue the searchers about their proximity to the pumpkin. After the couple finds the pumpkin, reassign the roles to three different students, and repeat the game. During the last round, have the wizard hide a box labeled with a pumpkin cutout—and containing a surprise pumpkin pie! When the couple finds this special pumpkin, invite the whole class to share in the findings. "Now what do you think of that?"

FIVE LITTLE PUMPKINS

By Iris Van Rynbach
Published by Boyds Mills Press, Inc.; 1995

Bold, colorful illustrations sing anew this fingerplay's tribute to Halloween. It's a countdown to fun!

This Halloween rhyme is just right for reinforcing shape and number concepts. After sharing this book, discuss and compare the different shapes and features of the five jack-o'-lanterns on the first two-page spread. Then have each child cut out a large, construction-paper pumpkin. Instruct her to create a jack-o'-lantern using an assortment of precut construction-paper shapes and a variety of craft items, such as buttons, sequins, and yarn. Then invite groups of five children to recite and perform the rhyme, using their student-made jack-o'-lanterns as manipulatives.

JEB SCARECROW'S PUMPKIN PATCH

By Jana Dillon
Published by Houghton Mifflin Company, 1992

When Jeb Scarecrow learns that the pesky crows want to party in his pumpkin patch, he devises an ingenious plan to keep them out. Watch out, crows!

After reading this story, challenge youngsters to devise their own scarecrow schemes with this activity. To begin, enlarge the scarecrow pattern on page 51. Use this enlarged pattern to make several tagboard tracers. Then have each child trace and cut out a tagboard scarecrow. Invite her to decorate her cutout as desired using a variety of craft items, such as fabric scraps, raffia, buttons, and yarn. Ask each child to dictate her plan to prevent a crow party from happening in her scarecrow's pumpkin patch. During group time, encourage each child to introduce her scarecrow and share her scarecrow scheme. Then display each child's work on a pumpkin-patch background labeled "Scarecrow Schemes" (you might want to decorate this bulletin board with the jack-o'-lanterns made in *Five Little Pumpkins*).

We use good manners.

We wait for our turn to talk.

We walk in a quiet line.

We raise our hands.

We help our friends.

We follow directions.

We keep our hands to ourselves.

We share with each other.

STELLALUNA

By Janell Cannon
Published by Harcourt Brace & Company, 1993

"Flump!" Stellaluna, a baby fruit bat, lands in a bird's nest and is soon adopted by the bird family. But some of a bat's ways are very different from those of a bird—and Stellaluna feels she must adapt. Will she ever fit in? This award-winning gem gently nourishes the essence of friendship and diversity.

After reading this story, discuss with students the different ways that Stellaluna had to adapt in order to live with the birds. Then ask students to name some ways they have adapted to their school environment. Write their responses on a large poster-board bat. Laminate the bat and cut it into puzzle pieces. Place these puzzle pieces in a center. Next guide children to discuss that when we adapt to different situations, we are helping each other to live peacefully together. Invite student pairs, in turn, to assemble the bat puzzle and then read the puzzle as reminders of how they have adapted to school.

BAT JAMBOREE

By Kathi Appelt
Illustrated by Melissa Sweet
Published by Morrow Junior Books, 1996

This "bat-talion" of performers shakes the house down with its incredible music, dancing, and stunts. And the grand finale is topped by none!

After sharing this entertaining extravaganza with your class, youngsters will be inspired to perform some counting acts of their own. Use a copy of the bat outline (page 52) as a pattern to create a felt bat beanbag. Write the numerals 1–55 on a chalkboard. Then invert a large hat to use as the beanbag target. Invite each child, in turn, to try to toss the beanbag into the hat. For each toss, circle the corresponding numeral to indicate a hit, or draw a slash through the numeral if the target was missed. After 55 tosses, have the class chorally count the hits and misses, then compare the totals. Repeat this game as student interest dictates.

THE BAT IN THE BOOT

By Annie Cannon
Published by Orchard Books, 1996

Based on a true story, a family tenderly cares for a tiny bat found in Dad's boot. Then—to everyone's dismay and also delight—Mother Bat returns to take her baby home.

With these special book reports, youngsters will be more than willing to retell this tender tale again and again. To make a boot, prepare a tagboard tracer using the pattern on page 52. Fold a large sheet of construction paper in half. Place the tracer on the fold, as shown. Cut out the boot outline through both thicknesses. Glue only the edges of the boot together, leaving the top open. Next cut out a construction-paper copy of the bat pattern (page 52). On this bat, illustrate and dictate a memorable moment from the book. Then fold the bat's wings over its body. Insert the folded bat into the open top of the boot. To use this, have a child remove the bat from his boot and share the story using his illustration as a reminder.

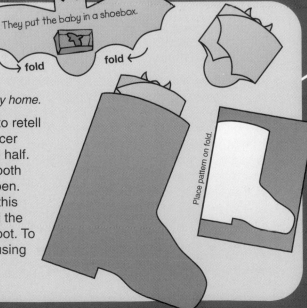

They put the baby in a shoebox.

fold

fold

Place pattern on fold.

MISS SPIDER'S TEA PARTY

By David Kirk
Published by Scholastic Inc., 1994

All the insects refuse Miss Spider's invitation to tea until an act of kindness convinces them that she means no harm. Playful, rhyming text sets the perfect table for this extraordinary counting book with exuberant illustrations.

Invite youngsters to have their own spidery teatime after reading this charming story. To make a placemat, cut two sheets of clear Con-Tact® covering for each child. Remove the backing from one sheet; then have the child arrange small pieces of torn or cut tissue paper onto the sticky side of this sheet. Then help her remove the backing from the second sheet and place this sheet over the tissue paper (sticky side down). Next invite each child to make her own spider treat (see the recipe and directions on pages 267–268). Then serve each child her spidery treat with tea (or juice) on her personal placemat.

THE ROLY-POLY SPIDER

By Jill Sardegna
Illustrated by Tedd Arnold
Published by Scholastic Inc.

What an insatiable appetite! When hunger strikes the roly-poly spider, she knows just what to do. Beware, bypassing bugs!

When this spider extends a dinner invitation to a passerby, she's not looking for company! After reading this tale, reinforce story recall by inviting each child to create a spiderweb for bug-catching. To prepare, duplicate a class supply of the bug strip on page 51. Give each child a bug strip, a sheet of waxed paper, and a large paper clip. Instruct him to bend one end of the paper clip out, then use that end to scratch a spiderweb on his sheet of waxed paper. Then have him cut apart the bug strip. Ask the child to tape each bug that the roly-poly spider caught to the back of the waxed-paper web so that it is visible in the web. Then glue the bug-filled web to a dark sheet of construction paper. Encourage each child to use a permanent marker to label each of the captured creatures. Then invite each student to make a construction-paper spider to use with his web in retelling the story.

MORE FALL FRIENDS

THE BIGGEST PUMPKIN EVER

By Steven Kroll
Illustrated by Jeni Bassett
Published by Holiday House, Inc.; 1984

Unaware of each other's activities, two mice tend the same plant as it grows into an enormous pumpkin. When they discover each other—and each other's goals for the pumpkin—the mice quickly reach a compromise that makes them both winners.

THE LITTLE OLD LADY WHO WAS NOT AFRAID OF ANYTHING

By Linda Williams
Illustrated by Megan Lloyd
Published by HarperCollins Children's Books, 1986

The spooks in this cumulative tale can't scare the brave little old lady. But with her help, they unite for a common cause.

SHEEP TRICK OR TREAT

By Nancy Shaw
Illustrated by Margot Apple
Published by Houghton Mifflin Company, 1997

After a night of trick-or-treating, the disguised sheep head home past a group of wolves in waiting. But who's afraid of whom?

A HALLOWEEN MASK FOR MONSTER

By Virginia Mueller
Illustrated by Lynn Munsinger
Published by Albert Whitman & Company, 1986

All of Monster's masks are much too scary. But a glance in the mirror convinces Monster that being himself is just right for a night of trick-or-treating. A charming Halloween treat!

BAT IN THE DINING ROOM

By Crescent Dragonwagon
Illustrated by S. D. Schindler
Published by Marshall Cavendish Corporation, 1997

Guests panic and flee when a lost bat swoops into a hotel dining room. But order is restored when a concerned and resourceful girl helps the bat make a safe exit.

Sheila Krill

scarecrow Use with *Jeb Scarecrow's Pumpkin Patch* on page 47.

bug strip Use with *The Roly-Poly Spider* on page 49.

Patterns

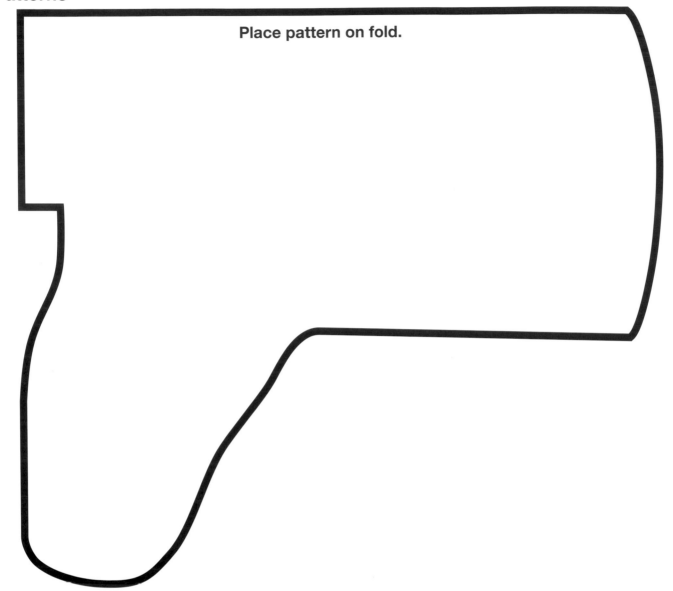

Place pattern on fold.

boot   Use with *The Bat In The Boot* on page 48.

bat   Use with *The Bat In The Boot* and *Bat Jamboree* on page 48.

Color Zoo

By Lois Ehlert
Published by HarperCollins Publishers, Inc.; 1989

Nine shapes are creatively combined to concoct a colorful zoo filled with some common and some not-so-common animals. A template of each shape adds a multisensory dimension to this Lois Ehlert masterpiece.

After touring the pages of this shape-filled zoo, have youngsters examine a number of toy or pictured zoo animals. As they study each one, help students identify parts of the animal that might represent different shapes—such as circle eyes, triangle ears, or a rectangle body. Then invite each child to create a zoo animal by arranging and gluing an assortment of construction-paper shapes on a sheet of paper. Have him cut a loose outline around his animal; then write his dictation about it on a paper strip. Display each child's cutout with his dictation on a bulletin board titled "Our Shape Zoo."

This is a lion from Africa.

Circle up your youngsters for some high-spirited learning fun with this five-star collection of shape literature and related ideas. As children pour their hearts into these activities, they will discover gems of knowledge more precious than diamonds. So be there or be square!

introduction, reviews, and ideas by Anne Bustard and Mackie Rhodes

The Shape Of Things

By Dayle Ann Dodds
Illustrated by Julie Lacome
Published by Candlewick Press, 1994

"A shape is just a shape, but look again and see…" With jaunty rhymes and vivid drawings, each simple shape is converted into much, much more.

Inspire shape discoveries in your classroom with these special shape viewers. Introduce each basic shape in the first reading; then revisit the book, this time pointing out the borders on each two-page spread. Explain that the artist created the borders with potato prints. Then have each child border a tagboard ring with tempera-paint potato prints corresponding to one of the shapes in the book. To use the resulting shape viewer, have the child peer through the center opening and search for a shape matching that on the viewer. Ask her to share her discoveries with a classmate. On a signal, have each child switch viewers with a child whose viewer represents a different shape; then send youngsters on another round of shape searching.

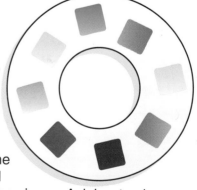

My First Look At Shapes

A Dorling Kindersley Book
Published by Random House, Inc.; 1990

What do a chocolate bar, an envelope, and a door have in common? They are all rectangles! With each turn of the page, youngsters will ogle the bountiful photographic delights found in this exploration of nine different shapes.

After sharing this shape-inspired picture book, engage youngsters in a game of shape dominoes. To prepare, collect a variety of magazines and color sale flyers. Cut out small pictures of items representing the shapes found in the book. Then glue a separate cutout onto each end of a seven-inch-long sentence strip to create a domino. Laminate all the dominoes for durability. To use the domino set, have a child match the ends of the dominoes according to the shape of the pictured items.

Shapes, Shapes, Shapes

By Tana Hoban
Published by Greenwillow Books, 1986

Shape up your view of people, places, and more through the camera lens of Tana Hoban. Her quick clicks prove the pervasive presence of shapes in our world.

After sharing this book, return to the page with the lunchbox on it. Review the shapes in the meal; then invite youngsters to create this special book. Obtain a hinged Styrofoam® tray for each child. Trim five sheets of paper to fit inside the tray. Label each page with a different day of the school week. Instruct the child to glue shape cutouts onto each page to represent different lunch items. Encourage the child to embellish his shapes with art supplies to resemble the foods represented. Then have him write or dictate a label for each food. Assemble the sequenced pages into a book as shown; then use a permanent marker to title the book "What's For Lunch?" Invite each child to share his book with the class.

Beach Ball

By Peter Sis
Published by Greenwillow Books, 1990

Follow Mary's windblown beach ball across the pages to discover the wide assortment of shapes found along the seashore. Then trace the ball's path again and again to emphasize the other concepts highlighted in this sunny sensation.

Zoom in on shapes as you page through this entertaining book with your class. Then invite students to toss around their shape knowledge with this game. To prepare, cut out a supply of laminated construction-paper shapes. Punch a hole in a shape and thread it on yarn to create a necklace for each child. Give each child a necklace; then have all your students stand in a circle. To play the game, have children toss a beach ball at random around the circle. Each time a child catches the ball, encourage her to name the shape worn by the ball thrower. To vary this game, direct students to toss the ball around the circle in a clockwise direction. Before each child passes the ball, have her name the shape she is wearing and the shape worn by the person on her left. For example, a child might say, "Square passing to Triangle."

The Patchwork Quilt

By Valerie Flournoy
Illustrated by Jerry Pinkney
Published by Dial Books For Young Readers, 1985

Pieced together with love, Tanya's patchwork quilt is full of squares representing special memories for each family member. A tender story radiating warmth and love.

Square is the catchword when youngsters piece together this dandy duo—a class quilt and a companion memory book. After reading the story, encourage each child to ask her parent to help her find an old fabric piece that holds special memories. Help each child cut several squares from her fabric. Have her glue one square onto a sheet of paper; then write her dictation about the memory that particular fabric holds for her. Have each child glue her remaining squares onto a length of bulletin-board paper, arranging them to make a class patchwork quilt. Stack the student pages between two construction-paper covers. Use the title "Sentimental Squares" for both the book and a display area for the quilt and book. Quilt admirers will enjoy matching squares from the quilt to those in the book to learn about students' special memories.

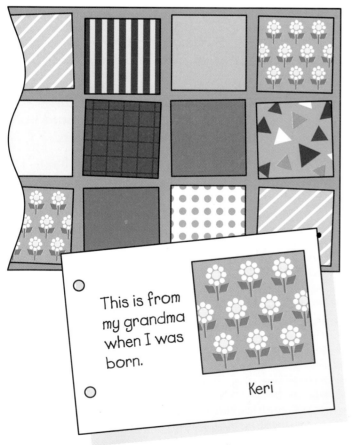

This is from my grandma when I was born.

Keri

Circles, Triangles, And Squares

By Tana Hoban
Published by Simon & Schuster Books
For Young Readers, 1974

Hoban's sharp black-and-white photos zoom in on the everyday occurrences of these common shapes. This visual geometric adventure inspires readers to take a closer look at the world of shapes.

After sharing this book with youngsters, encourage them to try their hands at origami—paper folding—to create a special creature. Give each child in a small group a five-inch square of construction paper or wrapping paper. Then demonstrate each step shown, having students follow your lead. Invite each child to add marker details to the resulting animal head. Afterward provide a variety of shapes for youngsters to fold and manipulate into imaginative creatures and whatnots.

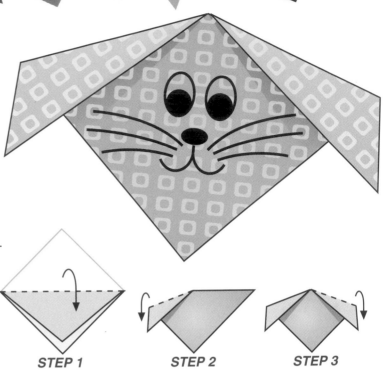

STEP 1   **STEP 2**   **STEP 3**

Shape Space

By Cathryn Falwell
Published by Clarion Books, 1992

Hop, rock, swing, and dance your imagination with this colorful, creative book. The shape-related movement and make-believe possibilities are endless!

Share this book with your class; then get youngsters into shape with this action-packed activity. Collect an assortment of foam-rubber blocks in a variety of shapes, colors, and sizes. (Or create a set of laminated construction-paper shapes.) Then invite each child, in turn, to perform an action with a described block. For instance, you might instruct the child to hop over a small yellow circle or to dance around a large blue triangle. Afterwards, place the blocks and this book—for inspiration—in a center. Challenge youngsters to manipulate the blocks into their very own dreamed-up, schemed-up creations.

Brown Rabbit's Shape Book

By Alan Baker
Published by Kingfisher, 1994

What shape will Brown Rabbit's mysterious package take? Discover the delightful surprises along with curious Rabbit in this fun-filled learning experience.

Wrap up some essential shape-identification skills with this idea. In advance collect an assortment of paper bags. After sharing the book, invite youngsters to create their own mysterious shape gifts. To begin, have each child choose a paper bag from your collection. Then encourage her to decorate her bag using shape stamps. Next have the child search the classroom for a shaped item, then secretly place it in her gift bag. Then, at group time, give a mysterious gift to each child. In turn, invite each student to open her gift, then to name the shape of the mystery item found inside. After all the items are revealed, challenge youngsters to sort themselves according to the shape gifts they received. Then encourage the groups to gather as many similarly shaped classroom items as they can. Afterward invite each group to share its shapely finds with the class. Then, if desired, use each group's collection to steer children right into a concrete graphing activity.

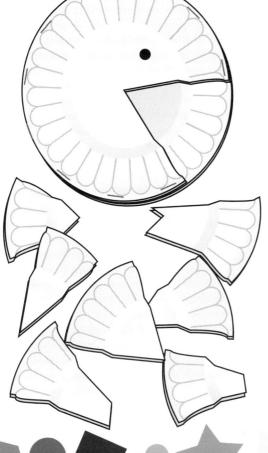

The Missing Piece

By Shel Silverstein
Published by HarperCollins Children's Books, 1976

Simple black-and-white drawings depict an incomplete and unhappy circular fellow in search of his missing piece. But when that perfect missing piece is finally found, our little guy begins to sing a different tune. A Silverstein classic!

"Hi-dee-ho, here I go, lookin' for my missin' piece." Youngsters will echo the circle's song in this critical-thinking activity. After the story, give each child three small, foam plates. To create a missing-piece circle, cut out a wedge from one of the plates. Invert that plate over another one; then staple the rims together to create a circle pocket. Use a permanent marker to draw an eye on the cut plate to resemble the circle in the story. Then cut the extra plate into an assortment of shapes, including a few wedges. Insert the shapes, along with the original missing piece, into the circle. Next have each child in a pair exchange circles. Encourage each student to look through all the shapes inside the circle and guess which one might be the missing piece. Have her explain how she arrived at her choice, then try it out and see. If it doesn't fit exactly, encourage her to rethink her choice and try again. "Hi-dee-ho, here I go!"

It Looked Like Spilt Milk

By Charles G. Shaw
Published by HarperCollins
Children's Books, 1947

Stir the imagination with these vivid contrasts of white shapes against royal blue backgrounds. It might look like spilt milk…or a rabbit…or a mitten, but surprise! It's just a cloud in the sky!

Inspire little ones for this reading by taking them outdoors for some puffy-cloud observing; then share the book. Afterward have each child use a glue stick to draw and fill in a shape on a sheet of dark blue construction paper. Sprinkle flour over the entire shape; then shake off the excess. Following the story's text pattern, use a white crayon to write the child's dictated description of his picture on his page. Then spray hairspray over the page to affix the flour. Assemble the pages into a class book titled after the original story. During group time, invite each child to read his page to the class.

Sometimes it looked like a dragon.

But it wasn't a dragon.

The Shape Of Me And Other Stuff

By Dr. Seuss
Published by Random House Books
For Young Readers, 1973

The imaginative, rhyming text of Dr. Seuss causes readers to marvel at the wonderful variety of shapes in which people and things are packaged. Detailed silhouettes perfectly complement the text.

Extend this book's celebration of the diversity of shapes and give your students a visual discrimination workout at the same time. To prepare, gather a collection of solid objects that your students could likely identify by their shapes. Then hang a white sheet in front of a table. Position a flashlight on the table so that the light shines toward the sheet. Turn off the lights; then turn on the flashlight. Place an object between the light and the sheet. Challenge youngsters to identify the object by the resulting shape on the sheet. Follow up this activity by having students trace objects on white paper, then color in the outlines. Encourage children to guess the identity of their classmates' pictures.

MORE SHAPE BOOKS

Three Pigs, One Wolf, And Seven Magic Shapes

By Grace Maccarone
Illustrated by David Neuhaus
Published by Scholastic Inc., 1997

This magical twist on the classic folktale uses tangram shapes to help the third little pig outwit the wolf. The tangram cutout makes a great center activity!

Ten Black Dots

By Donald Crews
Published by Greenwillow Books, 1986

Ten black dots. Ten black circles. Readers will be amazed at the limitless creations made with such simple shapes.

Ed Emberley's Picture Pie: A Circle Drawing Book

By Ed Emberley
Published by Little, Brown And Company; 1984

Take a circle, cut it into pie pieces, and then let your imagination soar! This colorful book will inspire readers to explore the numerous creations that can be made with circles and parts of circles.

The Greedy Triangle

By Marilyn Burns
Illustrated by Gordon Silveria
Published by Scholastic Inc., 1994

A triangle, unhappy with its dull life, repeatedly asks to be given "just one more side and one more angle" to make life more interesting. But when things begin to go downhill, the three-sided life takes on new appeal!

Spirals, Curves, Fanshapes & Lines

By Tana Hoban
Published by Greenwillow Books, 1992

Take a close look at this fascinating pictorial introduction to these special shapes. Hoban's camera magic casts a spell on readers once again!

Mouse Tales

Your little learners will become avid "mouse-keteers" when you introduce them to this collection of mouse tales. With each literary mouse morsel comes a curriculum-flavored activity that's just right for students to sink their paws into. So gather these books and let the furry-friend fun begin. Squeak! Squeak!

introduction, reviews, and ideas by Anne Bustard and Mackie Rhodes

Inside, Outside Christmas

By Robin Spowart
Published by Holiday House, Inc.; 1998

With gentle, bold-and-bright illustrations, mouse families are celebrating the holiday season—inside and outside. There's writing and lighting, mingling and jingling, waiting and skating. A sweet seasonal read to reinforce opposites, rhyming, and cozy Christmas cheer.

To prepare for this activity, title a board or section of a wall "Happy Holidays—Inside And Out!" Then share this new, wonderfully simple read-aloud with your class. After discussing the book, ask each child to think of what her family does during the holidays—inside and outside. Then give each child a large sheet of art paper. Ask her to draw a line to divide the paper in half. Have her draw an *inside* event on one half of the page and an *outside* event on the other half. Invite each child to share her page with the group. Then offer that child a pair of scissors to cut her paper in half. Help her post the *inside* picture on the left side of the board and the *outside* picture on the right side. Left or right, outside or in—it's Happy Holidays to you!

Do You Want To Be My Friend?

By Eric Carle
Published by HarperCollins Children's Books, 1971

A tiny, little mouse asks of one animal after another, "Do you want to be my friend?" But none of the other creatures are interested in befriending this furry little fellow. The predictable text and illustrations, along with the surprise ending, make this story a class favorite.

This book makes a natural springboard for a discussion on friendship. After sharing the story, invite each child to create two candy-cane mouse decorations—one for himself and one to give to someone else as a gesture of friendship. To make a mouse, use the patterns on page 65 to make tagboard tracers for the mouse body and ears. Using a fine-tip marker, trace each pattern onto felt. Cut out the felt patterns; then cut slits in the body as indicated on the pattern. Assemble the pieces as shown. Use a fine-tip permanent marker to draw on eyes; then hot-glue thread whiskers to the felt mouse. (Sturdy buttonhole thread works well.) Finally, slide a candy cane through the slits (as shown) to resemble a tail. Encourage each child to give one of his crafted mice to someone special as a gesture of friendship. Then suggest that he take the other one home to serve as a reminder of that special friendship.

First Snow

By Emily Arnold McCully
Published by HarperCollins Children's Books, 1988

This wordless winter wonderland features a timid little mouse who is reluctant to follow the lead of her eight brothers and sisters who are sledding down an enormous snow-covered hill. But when the little mouse finally summons up the courage to give it a try, the rest of the story is simply downhill…and downhill…and downhill!

Youngsters will give their thinking caps a good workout with this simulated sledding experiment. In advance, mask the dotted lines on an enlarged copy of the mouse-body pattern (page 65); then duplicate a tagboard mouse for each student. Also cut one six-foot length of thin nylon string for every two children. After sharing the book, have each child color and cut out her mouse. Also encourage youngsters to color and cut out construction-paper sleds, then glue them under their mice. Next help each child punch a hole at the top of her mouse. Then pair students and give each pair a length of string. (If the string ends ravel, wrap them with Scotch™ tape.) Have one child hold one end of the string on the floor. Instruct her partner to insert the other end of the string through the hole in one of the mice. Then encourage that partner to adjust the height and/or length of the string to make the mouse slide down to the floor—as if it's sledding down a hill! Encourage each pair to experiment with the position of the string to obtain the best results. Then have the partners switch roles and try it again with the second mouse. During a group time, discuss and compare each pair's discoveries. Swoosh!

If You Give A Mouse A Cookie

By Laura Joffe Numeroff
Illustrated by Felicia Bond
Published by Scholastic Inc., 1985

In this modern-day classic, a boy innocently gives a mouse a cookie. From that moment on, a chain of charming events results, eventually wrapping the story right back to where it began. A perfectly yummy read!

'Tis the season for giving, but this little boy's good-hearted gesture results in a domino effect. Before reading the story aloud, draw a circle on a flat surface. Then gather pictures or objects that represent the events in this story (such as a cookie, glass of milk, straw, napkin, mirror, pair of scissors, broom, sponge, box and pillow, book, crayon, pen, and roll of tape). After sharing the story, use the following activity to reinforce sequencing of the story's events, and also to introduce your children to the meaning of a *domino effect.*

Begin by giving each different picture (or object) and a domino to a different child. As you reread each event in the story, have the child with the corresponding picture stand his domino on the circle outline. When the story is finished, tap one domino to start the chain reaction. Compare the circular collapsing of the dominoes to the circular events of the story. Then prepare for the next domino effect—the fact that youngsters will want to do this activity over and over again. So much so, in fact, that they'll probably want you to set up a domino center for free exploration! But be careful—if you give a kid a domino…

Mouse Paint

By Ellen Stoll Walsh
Published by Harcourt Brace & Company, 1989

Three mice stir up some fun—and new colors—when they take a dip in what they think is mouse paint. This book, filled with lively hues, easily translates into a lesson in primary and secondary colors.

After sharing this colorful tale, invite your youngsters to make their own painted mice. To begin, have youngsters help you mix up a batch or two of mouse dough. (If desired, make enough dough to create three additional mice to use with *Mousekin's Family.*) Give each child a portion of the dough; then ask her to shape the dough into a mouse. While the dough is still moist, have the child poke in construction-paper ears and a pipe-cleaner tail. Set the mice aside to dry. On the second drying day (when the ears and tail are secure), have each child dip her mouse into red, yellow, or blue water-thinned tempera paint. When the mice dry thoroughly (up to two full days), challenge youngsters to use their mice to mix and mingle in the following activity.

First, group students and their mice by mouse color. Then call out a secondary color. Have the students in the appropriate color groups mix together to represent the two primary colors that make up that secondary color. Then signal students to return to their original groups. Continue in the same manner using all the secondary colors. Then send each child home with her mouse to tell family members her own colorful version of *Mouse Paint.*

Mouse Dough
(makes approximately 15 mice)

1 cup cornstarch
1 cup flour
up to 1 cup water

Pour cornstarch and flour into a bowl. Slowly mix in water until a stiff dough forms.

Squeak, squeak,
squeak,
squeak!

Mousekin's Family

By Edna Miller
Published by Simon & Schuster Trade, 1972

Mousekin had been away for a short mousetime and knew it was time to return to his young. But a case of mistaken identity prevents Mousekin from seeing the little family members that were scampering around him all along. Solid science and a sweet story are featured in this tale for little ones.

A game of "hide-and-squeak" is the perfect follow-up to this story. (To play, you will need three dough mice. See the recipe in *Mouse Paint.*) After reading and discussing the story, appoint a child to be Mousekin. Ask Mousekin to leave the room momentarily while three children each hide a dough mouse in your classroom. Then invite Mousekin to return to look for his young. Encourage the class to squeak clues to help Mousekin locate his babies—loud squeaks indicate he is close, while soft squeaks mean he is further away. When Mousekin finally finds all three babies, have him give an "enor-mouse" squeak of delight! Continue play, giving each child a turn to be Mousekin.

Cat And Mouse In The Rain
By Tomek Bogacki
Published by Farrar, Straus & Giroux, Inc.; 1997

It's raining. It's pouring. But the rain's no longer boring! A rainy day turns into a splashing adventure when Cat and Mouse learn the joys of puddle jumping—with a friend, of course!

After sharing this splish-splashy story, give youngsters a jump on counting practice with this puddle-jumping game. Ask each child to make his choice of a cat or a mouse headband. Then arrange several plastic hoops of different colors on the floor to represent water puddles. (If hoops are not available, tape shape outlines on the floor.) Then invite students to don their headbands. To play, call on a cat-and-mouse pair. Give the pair specific directions, such as "Jump four times in the red puddle, then two times in the blue puddle." Encourage the remaining cats and mice to count aloud with the jumpers and keep tabs on their progress. Continue in the same manner with new pairs, increasing the complexity of the directions as appropriate. Come on in—a rainy day is fun!

Lunch
By Denise Fleming
Published by Henry Holt And Company, Inc.; 1992

Mouse becomes a delightfully colorful mess during his lunchtime feeding frenzy. Acquaint your youngsters with a host of colorful, nutritious foods with this Fleming favorite. It's time for Lunch!

After sharing this story, invite students to create this colorful mouse book to reinforce colors and food identification. To prepare, mask the dotted lines on the mouse-body pattern on page 65. For each child, enlarge and duplicate the pattern on gray, white, orange, yellow, green, blue, purple, red, and pink construction paper. To make one book, have a child cut out one of each color of the mouse pattern. Then invite him to add construction-paper ears and marker details to the gray mouse. This will be the cover. Then have him illustrate each page with a simple line drawing of the corresponding food from the story. (Some students might even want to label and sequence their pages, so be sure to have the book available for student reference.) Next have the child stack all his illustrated pages behind the cover. Then help him punch a hole as shown. Finally, bind the pages together with a pipe-cleaner tail. Encourage each child to bring his book home to share with his family.

Seven Blind Mice
By Ed Young
Published by Philomel Books, 1992

Is it a pillar? A snake? A rope? No, it's an elephant! In this Caldecott Honor Book, Ed Young humorously retells an ancient fable using seven blind mice. The mouse moral? SEE for yourself!

Imaginations will be primed after reading and discussing this story. So challenge your youngsters to try their *hands* at *seeing* with this feely-bag activity. In advance, place common objects in a pillowcase or an opaque bag. (Suggestions include a box of gelatin mix, a pencil, an orange, a spool of thread, a cassette tape, a bottle of nail polish, etc.) After sharing the story, invite each child, in turn, to reach into the bag to grasp one object—but not to look at or remove it! Then ask her to describe the parts of the object according to what she feels. Encourage the class to guess the identity of the object. Then have the child show the object to the class. Now they know!

Mouse Tales, Too!

Cathedral Mouse

By Kay Chorao
Published by E. P. Dutton, 1988

More than anything else, Mouse wants a real home that is safe. Scurrying around and about a vast, mysterious cathedral, Mouse finds a place that's not exactly a home—but seems to do just fine. But just when Mouse finally begins to feel comfortable in his new spot, something else is moving in!

Four Brave Sailors

By Mirra Ginsburg
Illustrated by Nancy Tafuri
Published by Greenwillow Books, 1987

Ahoy, mates! Join four brave mouse sailors on their dreamy sailing adventures. There's nothing to fear—except, of course, "you-know-who"!

Lilly's Purple Plastic Purse

By Kevin Henkes
Published by Greenwillow Books, 1996

Now here's a mouse of the '90s! And she has a brand-new purple, plastic purse. AND she's just sure that she would like to be a teacher when she grows up…or a dancer, or a surgeon, or an ambulance driver, or a diva, or a pilot….

The Mouse That Jack Built

By Cyndy Szekeres
Published by Scholastic Inc., 1997

An endearing, cumulative, wintry tale featuring a delightful bunny named Jack, the very special snowmouse that he builds, and a surprise ending.

Mouse Views: What The Class Pet Saw

By Bruce McMillan
Published by Holiday House, Inc.; 1993

McMillan's camera—this time at a mouse's-eye view—has readers guessing what that little mouse could possibly be getting into. A class pet makes the ideal tour guide through this curious book.

Nice Mice: Max And Maggie In Winter

By Janet Craig
Illustrated by Paul Meisel
Published by Troll Associates, Inc.; 1995

Max and Maggie are the best of mouse friends who share all sorts of good times together. Join the snowy fun as you read about the lively winter antics of this thoroughly entertaining duo.

The Story Of Jumping Mouse

By John Steptoe
Published by Lothrop, Lee & Shepard Books; 1984

Steptoe's black-and-white illustrations chronicle the journey of a little mouse whose spirit of hope and compassion leads him to the far-off land. This retelling of a Native American legend encourages the reader to dream the impossible dream.

Use with *Do You Want To Be My Friend?* on page 60, *First Snow* on page 61, and *Lunch* on page 63.

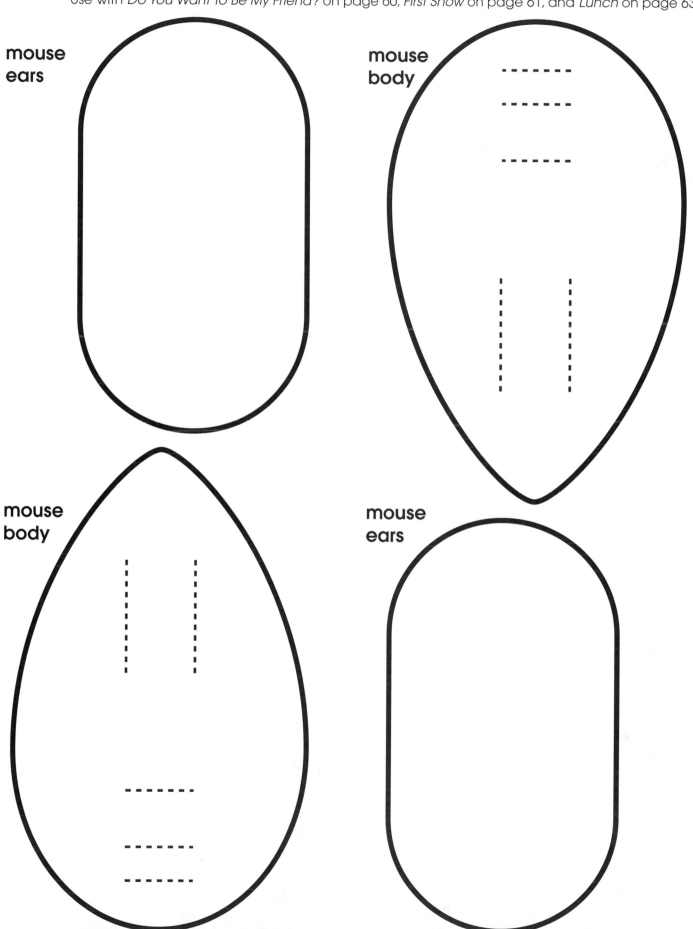

mouse ears

mouse body

mouse body

mouse ears

Holiday Bookshelf

When it's time to gather the children around you for a story, pull one of these fine holiday books from the shelf. But just so you'll know—your children *will* ask for more! Make sure your classroom library is stocked with several of these holiday titles.

by Joe Appleton

The Borrowed Hanukkah Latkes
By Linda Glaser
Illustrated by Nancy Cote
Published by Albert Whitman & Company, 1997

Rachel's mama tells her that Mrs. Greenberg, their next-door neighbor, has "a heart of gold, but she's as stubborn as an ox." On the last night of Hanukkah, neighbors grow closer, and it becomes obvious that Rachel and Mrs. Greenberg have a lot in common.

Harvey Slumfenburger's Christmas Present
By John Burningham
Published by Candlewick Press, 1993

Poor Santa! He's worn out from his long Christmas Eve journey, but then discovers that he has one undelivered present. Santa goes to heroic lengths to deliver Harvey Slumfenburger's gift. For children eagerly anticipating Santa's arrival, this is a reassuring story.

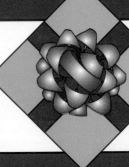

The Magic Dreidels: A Hanukkah Story
By Eric A. Kimmel
Illustrated by Katya Krenina
Published by Holiday House, Inc.; 1996

A scheming busybody tricks young Jacob out of two magic dreidels. But in the finest tradition of folktales, little Jacob outwits her—then forgives her in the end. This story is rich in Hanukkah traditions, from latkes to gelt.

The Mouse Before Christmas
By Michael Garland
Published by Dutton Children's Books, 1997

Perhaps no other creature is stirring, but this little mouse is busy preparing a snack for Santa. When the adventurous mouse is snatched up along with Santa's toy bag, he's in for the ride of his life! Michael Garland portrays the night flight with intriguing illustrations that will captivate your children time and again.

Mr. Willowby's Christmas Tree

By Robert Barry
Published by Bantam Doubleday Dell Books For Young Readers, 1992

In this classic tale, Mr. Willowby's tree is a little too tall for his parlor, so Baxter the butler snips off the top. The upstairs maid uses the top for her own tree, but it's a little too tall for her table, so she snips off the top. The tree is used and passed along by a whole troupe of characters—all totally unaware that the single tree brightens many, many Christmases.

What Could Be Keeping Santa?

By Marilyn Janovitz
Published by North-South Books Inc., 1997

Santa's reindeer are like eager children anticipating Christmas. But where is Santa? Silly reindeer. It's only December 23! This book has great possibilities for teaching calendar skills, for choral reading, or even for creative dramatization.

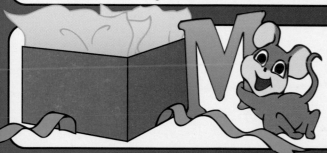

AlphaZoo Christmas

By Susan Harrison
Published by Ideals Children's Books, 1993

It's a zoo! Whimsical animals, from caroling crocodiles to skating swine, celebrate the holiday in style—alliterated style, that is.

A Kwanzaa Celebration Pop-Up Book

By Nancy Williams
Illustrated by Robert Sabuda
Published by Simon & Schuster Children's Division, 1995

A strong sense of pride in Black-American history and culture comes to life in this day-by-day celebration of Kwanzaa. Vibrant colors and inventive pop-ups draw readers in and hold their attention.

Night Tree

By Eve Bunting
Illustrated by Ted Rand
Published by Harcourt Brace & Company, 1991

The true spirit of the season is poignantly portrayed as a family engages in its yearly Christmas tradition. It is an unpretentious reminder to remember all creatures—both great and small—during the holiday season.

Seven Days Of Kwanzaa: A Holiday Step Book

By Ella Grier
Illustrated by John Ward
Published by Viking, 1997

Questions about Kwanzaa? This book can help students learn the fundamentals. Poetry, chants, recipes, and stepped pages with kente-cloth border designs make this book a special addition to your classroom library.

Lyrical Literature

Your students will break out in song—and smiles—when you tune in to this medley of sing-along stories filled with a chorus of curriculum-related ideas.

by Anne Bustard and Mackie Rhodes

The Itsy Bitsy Spider

As Told & Illustrated by Iza Trapani
Published by Whispering Coyote Press, Inc.; 1993

This popular little spider not only treks up the familiar waterspout, but persists throughout the house, then back outdoors again! Readers are bound to get wound up in this fresh retelling of a childhood favorite.

What other adventures could an itsy bitsy spider encounter? After reading this singsong tale, the stage is set to reinforce rhyming. So challenge youngsters to create additional rhyming adventures for their own little eight-legged friends. Have each child create a construction-paper spider with a yarn dragline. Then invite each child to explore the room with his spider, experimenting with items a spider might climb. Ask him to think of a rhyme patterned after the first two lines of this popular song. Then have him write/dictate his rhyme on a large sheet of paper and illustrate it. Stack and staple all the finished pages behind a construction-paper cover titled "Our Itsy Bitsy Spiders." Encourage each child to share his page with the class during a group reading time.

The itsy bitsy spider
climbed up a stack of blocks
Down fell the spider
And landed on my socks.

The Hokey Pokey

Words by Larry La Prise, Charles P. Macak, & Taftt Baker
Illustrated by Sheila Hamanaka
Published by Simon & Schuster Books For Young Readers, 1997

The Hokey Pokey's universal appeal is delightfully depicted in Hamanaka's energetic illustrations and multicultural characters. That's what it's all about!

After a first reading of this book, page through the lively illustrations again with your students. Guide them to determine which body part is being sung about on each two-page spread. Then explain that to do this dance, each child must distinguish between the right and left sides of her body. After a little right-and-left practice, give each child a sticker to place on her right hand. Using the sticker as a cue, invite each child to dance the Hokey Pokey as you read the book one more time!

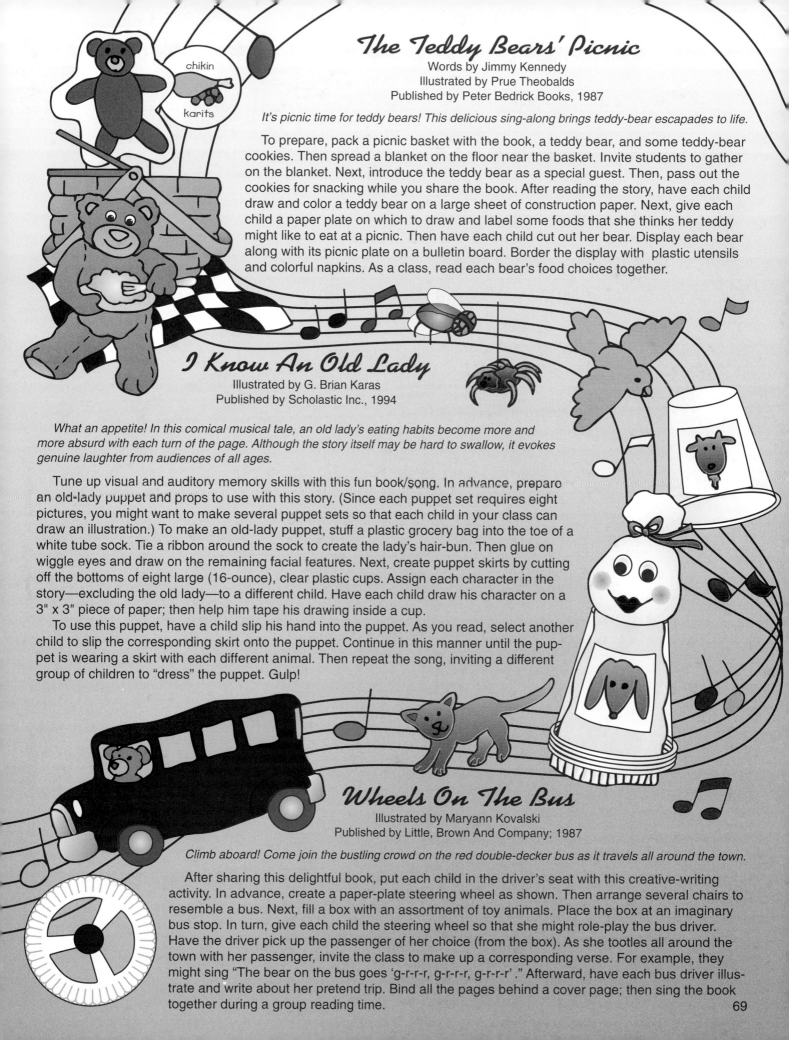

The Teddy Bears' Picnic
Words by Jimmy Kennedy
Illustrated by Prue Theobalds
Published by Peter Bedrick Books, 1987

It's picnic time for teddy bears! This delicious sing-along brings teddy-bear escapades to life.

To prepare, pack a picnic basket with the book, a teddy bear, and some teddy-bear cookies. Then spread a blanket on the floor near the basket. Invite students to gather on the blanket. Next, introduce the teddy bear as a special guest. Then, pass out the cookies for snacking while you share the book. After reading the story, have each child draw and color a teddy bear on a large sheet of construction paper. Next, give each child a paper plate on which to draw and label some foods that she thinks her teddy might like to eat at a picnic. Then have each child cut out her bear. Display each bear along with its picnic plate on a bulletin board. Border the display with plastic utensils and colorful napkins. As a class, read each bear's food choices together.

I Know An Old Lady
Illustrated by G. Brian Karas
Published by Scholastic Inc., 1994

What an appetite! In this comical musical tale, an old lady's eating habits become more and more absurd with each turn of the page. Although the story itself may be hard to swallow, it evokes genuine laughter from audiences of all ages.

Tune up visual and auditory memory skills with this fun book/song. In advance, prepare an old-lady puppet and props to use with this story. (Since each puppet set requires eight pictures, you might want to make several puppet sets so that each child in your class can draw an illustration.) To make an old-lady puppet, stuff a plastic grocery bag into the toe of a white tube sock. Tie a ribbon around the sock to create the lady's hair-bun. Then glue on wiggle eyes and draw on the remaining facial features. Next, create puppet skirts by cutting off the bottoms of eight large (16-ounce), clear plastic cups. Assign each character in the story—excluding the old lady—to a different child. Have each child draw his character on a 3" x 3" piece of paper; then help him tape his drawing inside a cup.

To use this puppet, have a child slip his hand into the puppet. As you read, select another child to slip the corresponding skirt onto the puppet. Continue in this manner until the puppet is wearing a skirt with each different animal. Then repeat the song, inviting a different group of children to "dress" the puppet. Gulp!

Wheels On The Bus
Illustrated by Maryann Kovalski
Published by Little, Brown And Company; 1987

Climb aboard! Come join the bustling crowd on the red double-decker bus as it travels all around the town.

After sharing this delightful book, put each child in the driver's seat with this creative-writing activity. In advance, create a paper-plate steering wheel as shown. Then arrange several chairs to resemble a bus. Next, fill a box with an assortment of toy animals. Place the box at an imaginary bus stop. In turn, give each child the steering wheel so that she might role-play the bus driver. Have the driver pick up the passenger of her choice (from the box). As she tootles all around the town with her passenger, invite the class to make up a corresponding verse. For example, they might sing "The bear on the bus goes 'g-r-r-r, g-r-r-r, g-r-r-r'." Afterward, have each bus driver illustrate and write about her pretend trip. Bind all the pages behind a cover page; then sing the book together during a group reading time.

Roll Over! A Counting Song

Illustrated by Merle Peek
Published by Houghton Mifflin Company, 1981

A little boy's crowded imagination conjures up a crowded bed. But one by one, the imaginary animals roll out of bed and the little boy finds himself alone—at last! The gentle blues and yellows, the expressive characters, and the warm humor make this an inviting book.

After reading this musical countdown, invite youngsters to play a one-less counting game. Create a bed by placing a nap mat on the floor. Then cover the bed with a blanket. Arrange a specific number of stuffed animals on the bed; then ask your students to count the animals. Next, ask children what *one less* would be. Then sing the song beginning with the number in the bed, causing one animal to fall out of the bed on cue. Ask youngsters to chorally count the remaining animals. Did they guess right? Repeat the process until you reach zero. Then invite youngsters to sing the last verse of the song. Ah—alone, at last!

I've Been Working On The Railroad

Illustrated by Nadine Bernard Westcott
Published by Hyperion Books For Children, 1996

All aboard! Chug across the landscape and right up to Dinah's Cafe with this well-known travel tune. Westcott's vibrant, dynamic illustrations add character and charm to this lively American folk song.

An imaginary cross-country train trip—and geography lesson—awaits readers of this delightful book. After sharing the book, revisit the illustrations. Ask each child to notice all the different kinds of landscapes. Then have students close their eyes and encourage them to visualize all the different types of land they have seen, such as mountains, rivers, farms, and fields. Then give each child a sheet of white art paper. Ask him to paint one type of landscape that he likes. When the pictures are dry, mount them on larger sheets of black paper to resemble the frame of a window. Then display the pictures around your classroom to resemble views from the window of a train. Oooh, the scenery is beautiful!

A You're Adorable

Words by Buddy Kaye, Fred Wise, and Sidney Lippman
Illustrated by Martha Alexander
Published by Candlewick Press, 1994

Adorable characters and zippy illustrations make this alphabetical self-esteem booster a charming addition to your musical books collection.

Sing through this book several times with your class. Then use the following idea to strengthen phonics skills and enhance self-esteem. Give each child a sheet of construction paper. Write (or have the child write) her name vertically on the page (as shown), leaving lots of space between each letter. Then, for each letter in her name, encourage the child to write a corresponding word or phrase that describes herself. (For a younger child, you might suggest that she use just the first letter of her name.) Then provide a variety of art supplies and invite each child to decorate her sheet. Bind all the pages alphabetically behind a cover titled "A We're Adorable!" After sharing the completed book with your class, put this on your home-traveling schedule. Parents will love reading about their children and their children's classmates.

C – cute
H – helpful
L – laughing
O – obeyful
E – extra good

Old MacDonald Had A Farm

Illustrated by Holly Berry
Published by North-South Books Inc.; 1994

Head down to this farm for a genuine country hoedown! In a rollicking, rhythmic version of this old-time favorite, Old MacDonald arranges a musical masterpiece.

After sharing this lively book with your students, help them organize their own Old MacDonald hoedown band. To begin, assign a different instrument to go with each animal in the book. For example, you might assign sticks for the pigs, bells for the chicks, etc. Divide your class into eight small groups—one for each animal in the book. Assign each group an animal; then give each group member the corresponding instrument. Lead students in a rambunctious round of the song, inviting members of each group to play their instruments, as well as to make the corresponding animal noise, when that animal is named. E-I-E-I-OOO!

Five Little Ducks: An Old Rhyme

Illustrated by Pamela Paparone
Published by North-South Books Inc.; 1995

While Mother Duck is busy doing chores, one by one her five little ducks are disappearing! Young readers will join in this tune's repetitive text and rejoice with Mother Duck when the little ones return.

Rub-a-dub-dub—there's a duck in the tub! This idea provides hands-on counting practice and also offers a home-school connection. In advance, use the duck pattern shown to make several tagboard tracers. After sharing the book, have each child trace a duck pattern on a piece of craft foam (or a sponge), then cut it out. Invite groups of five children at a time to take their ducks to your water table. Encourage them to sing the song and act out the story with their ducks. Afterward encourage each child to take his duck home to remind him to share the song with his family—and to have as a bathtub buddy!

Duck Pattern

Use with *Five Little Ducks: An Old Rhyme.*

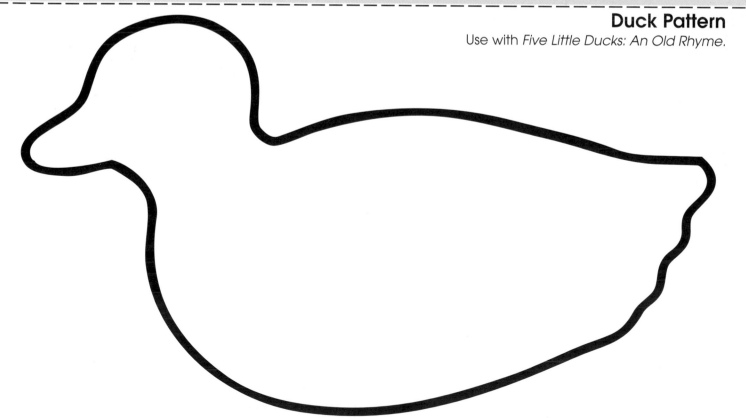

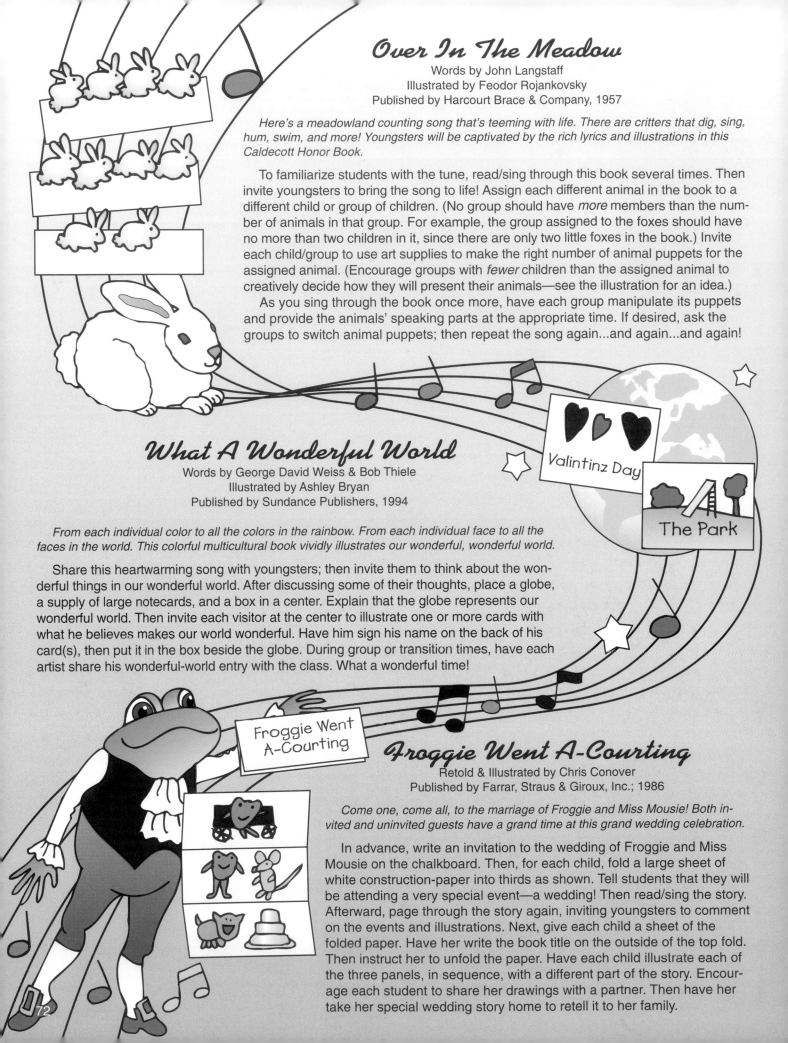

Over In The Meadow

Words by John Langstaff
Illustrated by Feodor Rojankovsky
Published by Harcourt Brace & Company, 1957

Here's a meadowland counting song that's teeming with life. There are critters that dig, sing, hum, swim, and more! Youngsters will be captivated by the rich lyrics and illustrations in this Caldecott Honor Book.

To familiarize students with the tune, read/sing through this book several times. Then invite youngsters to bring the song to life! Assign each different animal in the book to a different child or group of children. (No group should have *more* members than the number of animals in that group. For example, the group assigned to the foxes should have no more than two children in it, since there are only two little foxes in the book.) Invite each child/group to use art supplies to make the right number of animal puppets for the assigned animal. (Encourage groups with *fewer* children than the assigned animal to creatively decide how they will present their animals—see the illustration for an idea.)

As you sing through the book once more, have each group manipulate its puppets and provide the animals' speaking parts at the appropriate time. If desired, ask the groups to switch animal puppets; then repeat the song again...and again...and again!

What A Wonderful World

Words by George David Weiss & Bob Thiele
Illustrated by Ashley Bryan
Published by Sundance Publishers, 1994

From each individual color to all the colors in the rainbow. From each individual face to all the faces in the world. This colorful multicultural book vividly illustrates our wonderful, wonderful world.

Share this heartwarming song with youngsters; then invite them to think about the wonderful things in our wonderful world. After discussing some of their thoughts, place a globe, a supply of large notecards, and a box in a center. Explain that the globe represents our wonderful world. Then invite each visitor at the center to illustrate one or more cards with what he believes makes our world wonderful. Have him sign his name on the back of his card(s), then put it in the box beside the globe. During group or transition times, have each artist share his wonderful-world entry with the class. What a wonderful time!

Valintinz Day

The Park

Froggie Went A-Courting

Froggie Went A-Courting

Retold & Illustrated by Chris Conover
Published by Farrar, Straus & Giroux, Inc.; 1986

Come one, come all, to the marriage of Froggie and Miss Mousie! Both invited and uninvited guests have a grand time at this grand wedding celebration.

In advance, write an invitation to the wedding of Froggie and Miss Mousie on the chalkboard. Then, for each child, fold a large sheet of white construction-paper into thirds as shown. Tell students that they will be attending a very special event—a wedding! Then read/sing the story. Afterward, page through the story again, inviting youngsters to comment on the events and illustrations. Next, give each child a sheet of the folded paper. Have her write the book title on the outside of the top fold. Then instruct her to unfold the paper. Have each child illustrate each of the three panels, in sequence, with a different part of the story. Encourage each student to share her drawings with a partner. Then have her take her special wedding story home to retell it to her family.

More Books To Sing About

America The Beautiful
By Katharine Lee Bates
Illustrated by Neil Waldman
Published by Atheneum, 1993

Coat Of Many Colors
By Dolly Parton
Illustrated by Judith Sutton
Published by HarperCollins
Publishers, Inc.; 1994

**If You're Happy
And You Know
It, Clap Your Hands!**
By David A. Carter
Published by Scholastic Inc., 1997

Mary Had A Little Lamb
As Told & Illustrated by Iza Trapani
Published by Whispering Coyote
Press, Inc.; 1998

On Top Of Spaghetti
By Tom Glazer
Illustrated by Rob Barber
Published by GoodYearBooks, 1995

Raffi's Top 10 Songs To Read®
Published by Crown Publishers, Inc.; 1995

Sitting On The Farm
By Bob King
Illustrated by Bill Slavin
Published by Orchard Books, 1991

Take Me Out To The Ballgame
By Jack Norworth
Illustrated by Alec Gillman
Published by Four Winds Press, 1993

Today Is Monday
Illustrated by Eric Carle
Published by The Putnam & Grosset
Group, 1993

Twinkle, Twinkle, Little Star
As Told & Illustrated by Iza Trapani
Published by Whispering Coyote
Press, Inc.; 1994

Yankee Doodle
Illustrated by Steven Kellogg
Published by Simon & Schuster Books
For Young Readers, 1996

A Flurry Of Flowers

Here's a bouquet of flower-related books that have been handpicked especially for you and your students. Arranged with an assortment of ideas, this unit is designed to bring kindergarten learning into full bloom!

by Anne Bustard and Mackie Rhodes

Counting Wildflowers

By Bruce McMillan
Published by Mulberry Books, 1986

In this wildflower wonder, McMillan creatively combines essential number and word concepts with his fantastic floral photographs.

Convert your math center into a floral fantasy land with this sorting, counting, and sequencing activity. In advance, collect up to 20 sets of small artificial flowers, with each set consisting of a different quantity of flowers from 1 to 20. Combine all the flowers in one basket; then place the flowers, blank paper, sticky notes, and crayons in your math center. After sharing *Counting Wildflowers* with your class, invite student pairs to visit the center. Encourage each pair to sort the flowers onto separate sheets of paper. Have the students count the flowers in each set, then label a sticky note with the appropriate numeral for that set. After each set is labeled, have the pair numerically sequence the flower sets. Math skills are bound to blossom here!

Planting A Rainbow

By Lois Ehlert
Published by Harcourt Brace & Company, 1988

Simple text and bold, bright graphics spring from these pages as a mother and child nurture bulbs, seeds, and seedlings into mature plants. The results? A glorious garden filled with every color of the rainbow!

Invite youngsters to create their own classroom rainbow garden with this activity. To prepare, collect an assortment of packaged flower seeds. (Choose packages that have clear illustrations on them.) Pour the seeds from each package into a different clear, plastic tumbler. Tape each seed package to a craft stick; then rest each craft stick in the appropriate cup. Arrange these cups in your art center. After reading the story, open this center. Instruct each child to choose a seed and glue it near the bottom of a sheet of art paper. Then have her write that flower's name under the seed, referring to the package as necessary. Ask her to paint the flower that will grow from the seed, using the seed package as a reference if desired. After the pictures dry, display them rainbow-style on a classroom wall with the title "Growing A Rainbow."

Wildflower ABC
An Alphabet Of Potato Prints
By Diana Pomeroy
Published by Harcourt Brace & Company, 1997

Exuberant wildflowers spring from the pages of this alphabetical bouquet. The name of each flower provides the text while the intricately carved potato prints steal the show. Interesting tidbits about each flower appear at the end of the book.

After sharing this alphabetical beauty with your youngsters, explain that the pictures were created with potato prints! Then examine the pictures again together. Next invite each child to create her own potato-print flowers. To prepare, cut several large potatoes in half. Cut a different shape into the flat side of each potato; then cut away about 1/2 inch of the surrounding potato (as shown). To make a potato-print flower, arrange several layers of paper towels or newsprint in a tray. Stretch a piece of muslin across the tray; then tape it securely in place. Dip one of the potato printers into a color of paint. Press the potato onto the fabric several times to create a flowerlike design. With a paintbrush, paint a stem and leaves onto the flower. Mount each dried flower print on a sheet of construction paper. After each child shares his print with the class, display the finished potato-print flowers along a classroom wall or in the hallway. Pretty!

Alison's Zinnia
By Anita Lobel
Published by Mulberry Books, 1996

"Alison acquired an Amaryllis for Beryl." Thus begins this gloriously illustrated alphabet book of floral favorites. Colorful blooms burst off each page as the story comes full circle when Zena zeroes in on a Zinnia for Alison!

Cultivate letter sequencing with this alphabet activity. In advance, program a sheet of paper with "_____ made a flower for _____." Duplicate a class supply of the programmed page on construction paper. After reading the book, have students help you list their first names alphabetically on a sheet of chart paper. (If desired, ask youngsters to make up a name for any letter not represented by a classmate's name.) Next give each child a programmed page, glue, and an assortment of paper scraps, such as gift wrap, tissue paper, wallpaper, and sandpaper. Invite each child to use the supplies to create a flower on his programmed page. Then have each child write his own name in the first blank. Next instruct him to refer to the chart to find the name that follows his name. Then have him write that name in the other blank on his page. During group time, invite each child to share his page with the class. Then compile the pages in alphabetical order, bind them between a front and back cover, and then make the book available for free-choice reading. (For paired reading fun, invite one child to read the book aloud while another child uses a pointer to point to each corresponding letter on your alphabet chart.)

Ben made a flower for Carlos.

Abby	Dana
Adam	Everitt
Alex	Haley
Anna	Indigo
Ben	Jamal
Carlos	Kim
Corrine	Levi
Cory	Marta

What We Value Most

The Legend Of The Bluebonnet

By Tomie dePaola
Published by G. P. Putnam's Sons, 1983

This tender retelling of a Comanche legend highlights a young girl and her selfless act that saved her People. And even today, some people still say that the beautiful blue-bonnets that cover the Texas hills each spring are given as an annual tribute to this heroine's miraculous sacrifice.

Help students take inventory of their values with the making of this class mural. In advance, cut lengths of green bulletin-board paper to resemble rolling hills. Also gather a supply of various shades of blue tissue paper. After sharing this tender tale with your class, discuss the difficult decisions She-Who-Is-Alone must have faced. Then invite each child to tell about one of his most special possessions. Would he ever part with it? Why or why not? Is his family more important than that possession? Afterward, give each child a half-sheet of construction paper. Ask him to illustrate and label what or who is *most* important to him. Then have him cut out his drawing. In turn, invite students to glue their illustrations on the green, rolling hills. Then have groups of children take turns gluing torn, scrunched tissue-paper bluebonnets onto the hills. Display this mural with a title, such as "What We Value Most."

Miss Rumphius

By Barbara Cooney
Published by Viking, 1982

Little Alice dreams with her grandfather of traveling to faraway places and living by the sea. But Grandfather always says there is one thing more that Alice must do. She must do something to make the world more beautiful. "All right," says Alice—but she has no idea what that one thing will be.

Encourage youngsters to project their thoughts into the future with this idea. After reading this inspiring tale to your class, prompt students to name some things that people have done to make our world more beautiful. Then ask them to think of something they might do in the future, when they are older, to add to the beauty of the world. Have each child write about her idea on a construction-paper thought cloud. Then have each child draw and color a picture of what she thinks she might look like when she is older. Have each child label the picture with [Miss/Mr.] and [Child's last name]. Display each child's illustration near her thought cloud. Title the display "Beautiful Thoughts For A Beautiful World."

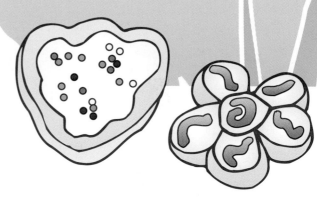

The Gardener

By Sarah Stewart
Illustrated by David Small
Published by Farrar, Straus & Giroux, Inc.; 1997

During the time of the Depression, Lydia Grace Finch is sent to the city to live with her uncle, who never smiles. Can Lydia's determined spirit and passion for gardening yield a surprise that will sprout a smile on her uncle's face? Written as a series of letters, this Caldecott Honor book is sure to brighten any reader's day.

These baked blossoms will help youngsters appreciate both the baker and the gardener in this story, as well as the special workers in your school. After sharing this book with your class, ask students to share their ideas about why Uncle Jim didn't smile. After the discussion, invite your class to bake up a batch of flowery cookies. To prepare, have each child flour his clean hands; then give him several slices of refrigerated sugar cookie dough. Have him form each portion of dough into a flower shape. Bake all the flower cookies according to the package directions. Then invite each child to decorate his cooled cookies with icing or gel and cake decorations. As a class, deliver batches of these floral cookies to selected workers in your school. Watch the smiles appear! It feels good to do good!

Jack's Garden

By Henry Cole
Published by Greenwillow Books, 1995

This bouncy, cumulative text invites readers to visit Jack's garden during its various stages of growth. But readers aren't the only visitors! Follow the pages of this book to discover the many delightful guests that are attracted to Jack's garden.

Read this book the first time to introduce it to your class; then read it again, taking time to discuss the progression of the plants' growth and the many changes that take place in Jack's garden. Afterward, invite youngsters to create some tasty floral treats. To prepare, give each child a small plastic plate and have him choose a sheet of colorful construction paper. Ask him to lightly trace the upside-down plate in the center of his paper. Next, using the circle as a flower center, have him draw a large flower around that circle, then cut it out. Instruct each child to glue his flower cutout to the back of his paper plate. To make a flower snack, have a child scoop pudding (or yogurt) onto his plate. Then encourage him to get creative! Provide a variety of small snack items that you have on hand. Encourage each child to use the supplies to create a garden visitor to position somewhere on his flower snack. This is sure to be a floral "flavor-ite"!

black jelly bean
vanilla wafer
red frosting
chocolate chips

Flower Garden

By Eve Bunting
Illustrated by Kathryn Hewitt
Published by Harcourt Brace & Company, 1994

What a perfect surprise! With help from her dad, a young girl makes a window box of flowers for her mom's birthday. Rhythmic text and bold illustrations make this a cheery, upbeat story of love.

Before sharing this story, ask each child to bring a shoebox to school. Then share this warm, tender story with your students. Afterward invite children to share the names of the special people in their lives. Next, encourage each child to make a garden box in honor of these people. To make one garden box, randomly cut several half-inch slits in the bottom of a shoebox. Then paint the outside of the shoebox. While the paint dries, invite each child to make a different flower for each person she wants to be represented in her special garden. To make a flower, cut a construction-paper flower and a few leaves; then glue them onto a craft stick. Label the back of the flower with the name of the person for whom it was made. Insert each flower into a different slit in the box. Then invite each child to show off her flower garden and to tell the class something special about each person represented in it. Encourage each child to take her garden home to share with her family. It's a garden of love!

Miss Emma's Wild Garden

By Anna Grossnickle Hines
Published by Greenwillow Books, 1997

*Rather than being planted in neat little rows, the flowers in Miss Emma's garden grow any crazy way they want. And her wild, crazy garden attracts an assortment of wild creatures, including the **best** wild creature of all.*

Use these "scent-sational" sachets to bring your home-school connection into full bloom. After reading this story, show your class some *potpourri.* Explain that many different flowers—some of which might be found in Miss Emma's garden—are used to make this colorful mixture of dried, scented flowers. Then spread some potpourri on a sheet of paper in your science area. Provide magnifying glasses and encourage students to examine the mixture. Then give each child a square of fabric (approximately 8" x 8"). Have him place a small scoop of potpourri in the center of the fabric; then help him tie a ribbon around the fabric to create a sachet. Encourage each child to take his scented sachet home and retell the story of Miss Emma's wild garden.

More Bloomin' Good Books

City Green

By DyAnne DiSalvo-Ryan
Published by Morrow Junior Books, 1995

With vision and vibrant enthusiasm, a young girl launches a neighborhood project to convert a grim and garbage-filled city lot into a green and growing wonder.

In My Mother's Garden

By Melissa Madenski
Illustrated by Sandra Speidel
Published by Little, Brown And Company; 1995

It's so hard to keep a secret—especially from Mom! But Rosie does. And when the time is right, Rosie proudly presents her mom with the best birthday surprise Mom has ever had.

The Red Poppy

By Irmgard Lucht
Published by Hyperion Books For Children, 1994

The simply beautiful text and illustrations make this gem the perfect resource to introduce youngsters to the terminology and life cycle of a flower. Breathtakingly gorgeous!

Backyard Sunflower

By Elizabeth King
Published by Dutton Children's Books, 1993

In the spring, Samantha carefully plants a handful of sunflower seeds. Then she tenderly cares for her small crop throughout the summer, carefully observing the growth cycle of the special beauties.

The Legend Of The Indian Paintbrush

By Tomie dePaola
Published by G. P. Putnam's Sons, 1988

This Native American tale recounts how the brilliant flower known as the Indian Paintbrush came to be. This story is also a lesson in persistence, believing in oneself, and pursuing one's special gifts and dreams. A beautiful legend with a powerful message.

The Butterfly Seeds

By Mary Watson
Published by Tambourine Books, 1995

Jake anxiously awaits the appearance of the butterflies that were to come with the butterfly seeds that were given to him by his grandfather. Then, after a hot summer rain, the flittering, fluttering guests arrive!

Ocean Notions

Plunge into this unit swelling with ocean-related literature and ideas. These creative cross-curricular activities will generate a wave of learning excitement in your classroom. So come on—dive in!

by Anne Bustard and Mackie Rhodes

Out Of The Ocean
By Debra Frasier
Published by Harcourt Brace & Company, 1998

Walk along the shore with a mother and daughter as they discover the marvelous treasures that the ocean brings. It's a wonderful journey that readers will eagerly take again and again.

These sandy masterpieces will serve as special reminders of the gifts that come to us out of the ocean. To prepare, stock your art center with a supply of tagboard, an assortment of colorful papers, water-thinned glue, paintbrushes, scissors, and clean play sand. After sharing the story, page through the book again encouraging students to examine the illustrations and speculate about how each one was created. Then invite each child to make his own seashore picture modeled after the art style in the book. To begin, have the child paint a layer of glue on a sheet of tagboard where he'd like his beach to be. Then instruct him to sprinkle sand over the glue and gently shake off the excess. Next, invite the child to cut out paper shapes to represent gifts from the ocean, such as a shell, the sun, a plant, or an animal. Instruct him to glue his cutouts onto his sandpaper beach. During group time, invite each child to describe his masterpiece; then encourage him to take it home to share with his family.

A Swim Through The Sea
By Kristin Joy Pratt
Published by Dawn Publications, 1994

Just what would a seahorse exploring beneath the sea see? Find out with this award-winning alphabet book abounding with assorted ocean creatures.

This lyrical piece of literature naturally leads into a lighthearted lesson on letter sounds. The first time you share this book, read only the large text. (If desired, read the book again later, allowing student interest to dictate the additional text that you read or paraphrase. You might even like to read this deep-sea treasure over several days so that you can share all the interesting information provided.) As you read the large text, invite children to identify the words beginning with the same letter. Afterward, write the name of each featured creature alphabetically on chart paper. Invite each child to select a different creature from the list. Help her write/dictate a simple alliterative sentence about her creature, such as "The angelfish ate an acorn." (Silly sentences are just fine in this activity!) Then have the child illustrate her sentence. Sequence and bind the completed pages between construction-paper covers. Title the class book "A Swim Through The Sea From *A* To *Z*." Then invite each child to share her page during storytime.

Blue crabs blow bubbles.

An angelfish ate an acorn.

Moving Day

By Robert Kalan
Illustrated by Yossi Abolafia
Published by Greenwillow Books, 1996

Young readers will chant right along with the cumulative refrain in this humorous tale about a hermit crab's search for a new home. The repetitive rhyme and charming illustrations make this story a perfect fit for kindergartners!

When youngsters conduct their own search for a perfect fit, they'll gain a new appreciation for this hermit crab's dilemma. To prepare, collect a class supply of containers in different sizes and shapes, such as boxes, plastic eggs, and margarine tubs. After sharing the story, discuss the problems the crab encountered while searching for the perfect home. Then give each child a container. Challenge him to search the room for an item that fits perfectly into his container—not too snug, not too tight, but something that fits just right. Then call students back to the group. Did anyone find an item that was just right? What problems did they encounter in their searches? Afterward, share the story again, inviting youngsters to read along.

Octopus' Den

By Deirdre Langeland
Illustrated by Steven James Petruccio
Published by Soundprints, 1997

After a long night of hunting, Octopus heads toward home only to find that his den is occupied by another larger octopus. So this eight-armed wonder begins his search for a new place to call his own. This factual storybook, from the Smithsonian Oceanic Collection, can be used alone or with its companion read-along tape and/or stuffed toy.

After sharing this story, return to page 26 of the book. Explain that an octopus can squeeze into small spaces, such as the apple-sized opening, because it doesn't have any bones in its body. This flexibility helps the octopus protect himself and escape from enemies. Then offer a hands-on experience of this concept. Give each child in a small group a container of play dough. Have her empty the container, then use the entire amount of play dough to create an octopus. Ask her if her octopus will fit into the original container. Why or why not? Then have the child mold her octopus into the container. Guide children to summarize that, like Octopus, the amount of play dough never changed, but it could be molded into different shapes and sizes.

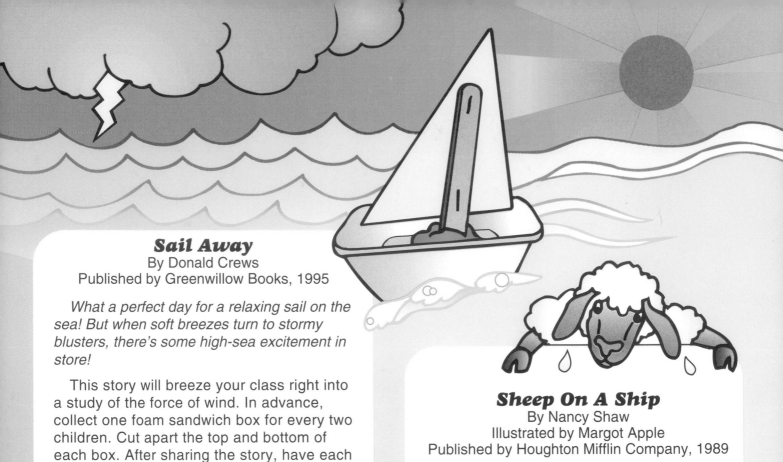

Sail Away
By Donald Crews
Published by Greenwillow Books, 1995

What a perfect day for a relaxing sail on the sea! But when soft breezes turn to stormy blusters, there's some high-sea excitement in store!

This story will breeze your class right into a study of the force of wind. In advance, collect one foam sandwich box for every two children. Cut apart the top and bottom of each box. After sharing the story, have each child create a sailboat. To make one, staple a construction-paper sail onto a craft stick. Press a small ball of clay into the bottom of a sandwich-box half; then anchor the sail in the clay. Next, discuss the different wind conditions that the family in the story might have experienced. Then invite student pairs to sail their sailboats across a water table ocean. Encourage them to create different wind conditions by blowing. Perhaps your students would also like to experiment with different wind forces made from a moving object, such as a cardboard fan. Encourage children to compare and report how each type of wind affected their sailboats' movement and speed.

Sheep On A Ship
By Nancy Shaw
Illustrated by Margot Apple
Published by Houghton Mifflin Company, 1989

Sheep ahoy! This rollicking, rhyming sequel to Sheep In A Jeep finds those lovable sheep posing as seafaring pirates. And although their sail begins rather smoothly, a sudden storm sinks their plans, leaving the sea-tossed sheep to seek a happy ending to their deep-sea trip.

Invite youngsters' imaginations to sail away as they use their creative problem-solving skills to rescue these sheep from the ship. Read the story aloud up through page 20. Then give each child a sheet of paper and ask her to write and illustrate an ending to the story. Bind all the pictures together; then have each child share her page with the class. After all of your classroom authors have shared their stories, continue reading the book to find out how Nancy Shaw chose to end her story of these six soggy sheep.

They could yell and shout for a helicopter.

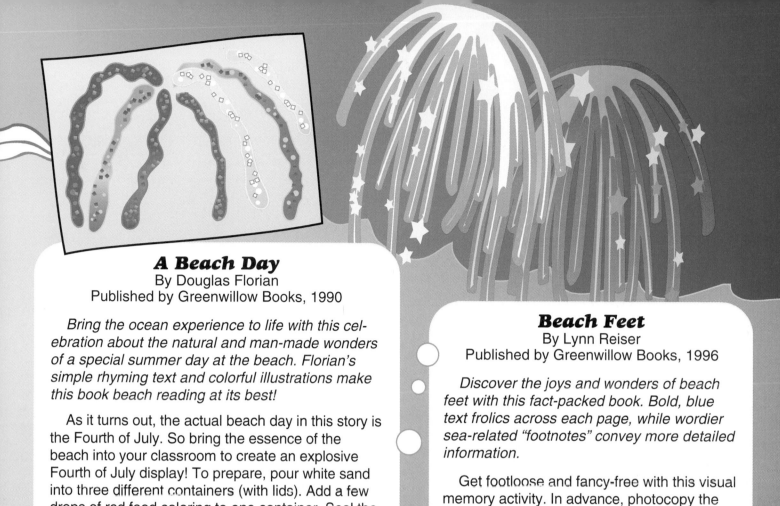

A Beach Day
By Douglas Florian
Published by Greenwillow Books, 1990

Bring the ocean experience to life with this celebration about the natural and man-made wonders of a special summer day at the beach. Florian's simple rhyming text and colorful illustrations make this book beach reading at its best!

As it turns out, the actual beach day in this story is the Fourth of July. So bring the essence of the beach into your classroom to create an explosive Fourth of July display! To prepare, pour white sand into three different containers (with lids). Add a few drops of red food coloring to one container. Seal the container and shake it until the sand is tinted red; then mix in some red glitter. Using blue food coloring and blue glitter, dye the second container of sand in the same manner. Then mix clear glitter into the third container. Arrange the sand in a center along with a variety of seashell scoops. After reading the story, invite each child to visit the center to create a fireworks display. To make one, draw a spray of fireworks with glue. Use a shell to scoop up some sand; then sprinkle it on the glue. Gently shake the excess sand back into the container. To add more color, draw more lines of glue; then sprinkle another sand color on the glue. Repeat this process as desired. When the glue is dry, display these fabulous fireworks high up on a classroom wall.

Beach Feet
By Lynn Reiser
Published by Greenwillow Books, 1996

Discover the joys and wonders of beach feet with this fact-packed book. Bold, blue text frolics across each page, while wordier sea-related "footnotes" convey more detailed information.

Get footloose and fancy-free with this visual memory activity. In advance, photocopy the beach foot patterns (page 86) four times on construction paper; then cut them apart. Color the patterns if desired. After reading and discussing this book, ask each child to remove his shoes and socks. Working in pairs, have each child trace his partner's bare feet on tagboard. Then instruct each child to cut out his foot shapes. Glue one pattern to each foot shape. If you have extra foot cutouts, write "Keep walking!" on each one. Use these foot cards to play a traditional Memory game. If a child turns over a card that says "Keep walking!", he may turn over an additional card. If he happens to turn over two "Keep walking!" cards, he treats those two cards as a pair and play continues accordingly.

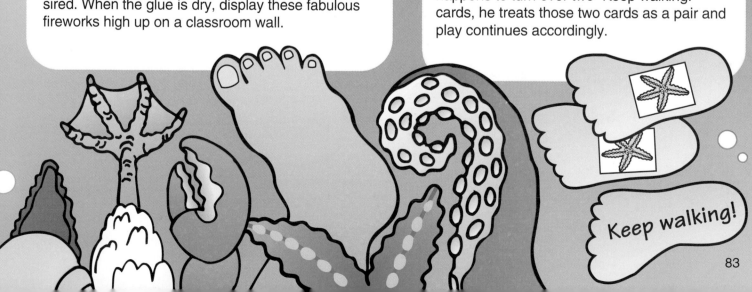

Keep walking!

See The Ocean
By Estelle Condra
Illustrated by Linda Crockett-Blassingame
Published by Ideals Children's Books, 1994

Fog-covered mountains block the view as two brothers compete to be the first to catch a glimpse of the ocean. But Nellie, their sister who is blind, wins the competition when she "sees" the ocean with her sensitive heart and imaginative mind.

Set up this ocean-related discovery center to encourage exploration of the senses. In advance, bury a variety of seashells in your sand table. Also prepare a pitcher of salty water and get a class supply of paper cups. If available, have a recording of ocean sounds on hand too. After reading this touching tale to your students, review the five senses. Explain that the sand table center is set up to help children explore a pretend ocean with all of their senses. Then invite small groups of students to visit the ocean center. As you play the ocean music, instruct children to close their eyes and feel for items in the sand. Can they identify their findings without looking? Invite students to smell and taste the water. Have them listen to the recorded sounds. Encourage youngsters to share their discoveries and experiences with other group members.

My Life With The Wave
Translated & Adapted by Catherine Cowan
Illustrated by Mark Buehner
Published by Lothrop, Lee & Shepard Books; 1997

When a boy brings a stray wave back to his home, he soon discovers that his new companion can really make waves with its many unpredictable moods! After a few trials and errors, the family devises a clever plan to catch the wave and return it to its own home.

After reading this amusing tale, invite youngsters to look carefully at the last picture in the book. Ask them to share their ideas about whether a cloud is really always "soft and cuddly and would never act like a wave." Ask how a stray cloud might behave in their everyday lives. Would it display some of the same moods that the wave did? Then invite each child to create a cloud with cotton balls. Encourage her to show the mood of the cloud in her creation. Then have the child arrange and glue the cloud onto a sheet of construction paper. If desired, have her paint colors onto her picture. Then ask her to write/dictate the cloud's mood onto a sentence strip. Bind the completed pages between construction-paper covers titled "Many Moods." During a discussion about emotions, have each child share her page.

More Ocean Books To Explore

A B Sea
By Bobbie Kalman
Published by Crabtree Publishing Company, 1995

Journey under the sea from A to Z in this fact-filled, photo-illustrated delight, complete with a vocabulary-building section of "Words To Know."

Baby Beluga
By Raffi
Illustrated by Ashley Wolff
Published by Crown Publishers, Inc.; 1990

Raffi's endearing song about a little whale splashes to life in this joyful tribute to an endangered species. Invite your class to sing along!

I Swim An Ocean In My Sleep
By Norma Farber
Illustrated by Elivia Savadier
Published by Henry Holt And Company, Inc.; 1997

This story about a child's dreamy underwater world will prompt readers to anticipate their own sea-slumber adventures.

The Magic School Bus® On The Ocean Floor
By Joanna Cole
Illustrated by Bruce Degen
Published by Scholastic Inc., 1992

Join the zippy and zany Ms. Frizzle as she and her class venture down to the ocean floor. This deep-sea treasure is sure to be asked for time and again.

The Ocean Alphabet Book
By Jerry Pallotta
Illustrated by Frank Mazzola, Jr.
Published by Charlesbridge Publishing, Inc.; 1986

Discover some of the zillions of fish in the North Atlantic Ocean. Bold illustrations and a touch of humor complement this child-friendly, conversational book filled with factual information.

Winter Whale
By Joanne Ryder
Illustrated by Michael Rothman
Published by William Morrow And Company, Inc.; 1991

Come! Imagine and explore the life of a humpback whale—even if it's just 'til storytime is over.

Beach Foot Patterns
Use with *Beach Feet* on page 83.

Thematic Units
And Special Features

The Kingdom Of Kindergarten

Castles and kings and dragons with wings! The goings-on associated with royalty have appealed to boys and girls throughout the ages. So use the regal ideas in this unit to welcome your new court of kindergarten kids to a kingdom full of learning and fun!

ideas by Joseph Dawes Appleton and Jan Trautman

Classroom Castle

This comely castle will decorate your room in majestic style as well as draw in some of your more reluctant newcomers. To make the castle, cut off three intact panels from a large appliance box. Then cut out a crenellated castle piece from poster board. Tape the crenellated piece to the middle box panel (as shown) using strong tape. Then use a craft knife to cut a door in the middle panel. Paint the castle as desired; then use a permanent marker to add details on the dry paint. Further embellish the castle by gluing on construction-paper windows and other details. Top off your castle creation with colorful construction-paper or fabric flags that have been taped to plastic straws. To use your castle, choose from the ideas below.

- Use the castle to designate the borders of a center area.
- Have children decorate the inside of the castle as an art option (see "Deck The Halls!" on page 91).
- Use the castle for a backdrop to photograph children individually.
- Post the letter you are studying on the castle door.
- As you study shapes, add shaped construction-paper windows or decorations to the castle.
- Change your castle flags to reflect the color you are studying.

Hear Ye! Hear Ye!

Jackson _____ is cordially invited to join The Kingdom Of Kindergarten!

I can't wait to see you on August 14th at 8:00!

Sincerely,

Ms. Leggett

Please come ready to tell us:
- your favorite colors
- your favorite animal
- your favorite foods
- who is in your family

Come One! Come All!

To help your new students transition smoothly into kindergarten, let them know that you're looking forward to their arrival and you're anxious to get to know them. In advance, photocopy a class supply of the invitation on page 93. Personalize each invitation; then sign it. A few days before school starts, mail an invitation to each child. This special invitation from you will help begin a home-school connection and will also do wonders for making each child feel like royalty!

Royal Door Decor

New kindergartners will know just where they belong when they see this royal door decor. To begin, cut out a butcher-paper castle tower that will fit on your classroom door. Add colorful construction-paper flags and a large paper window. Next enlarge and trace the friendly dragon (page 94) on sturdy paper. Color and cut out the dragon; then mount it in the castle window. To complete the display, mount any desired room information on the lower part of the castle. Ah, this is right where I belong!

The Crowning Touch

This activity gets your new students involved as soon as they walk in the door. And its crowning benefits include name recognition, fine-motor skills, creativity, and nametags—just to name a few! In advance, duplicate a class supply of the crown pattern (page 93) on construction paper. Cut out the patterns; then write a different child's name on each crown. Arrange the crowns on worktables along with a variety of art supplies, such as crayons, stickers, sequins, jewels, and craft glue. Also have a class supply of sentence strips (to make headbands) and a stapler on hand. As each child arrives on the first day of school, encourage her to find her name and then use the art supplies to decorate her crown. When each child's crown is finished and dry, staple it to a headband. Encourage each child to wear her crown to serve as a nametag throughout the day.

Look Who's In The Castle Today

Each child on your royal roster can participate in making this thematic attendance chart. Then, when your youngsters get in the routine of using it, attendance-taking for you will require only a quick glance at the castle! To make the chart, glue a crenellated, titled cutout to the top of a sheet of poster board. Then tape on toothpick flagpoles and colorful construction-paper flags. For each child, glue a labeled library pocket on the poster board. Next duplicate an attendance card (page 95) for each child, and write his name on the emblem. Then invite each child to color his card to resemble himself. If desired, back the cards with poster board for durability; then laminate them. Display all these cards near your attendance chart. To take attendance, instruct each child to find his card and slide it into his pocket on the chart.

Royal Trappings

Lure youngsters to stretch their imaginations to majestic, faraway places by stocking your dramatic play area with all the royal trappings. Young ladies-in-waiting will enjoy wearing their royal hats (see illustration), while your boys try out their Robin Hood–style versions. Remnants of richly colored or brocaded fabric can instantly be donned as royal robes. Collect a supply of crown jewels by asking for donations of old costume jewelry. In addition, many stores have Halloween supplies for sale early in the traditional school year. These can be great sources for dress-up supplies.

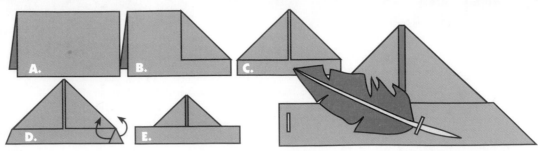

A. B. C.

D. E.

Boys:

To make this hat, fold a 16" x 20" sheet of construction paper as shown in Steps A through E. Then fold under the corners of the brim on one end, and staple them to make a pointed brim. Staple the sides together on the other end. Embellish this hat with a real craft feather or a feather cut from construction paper.

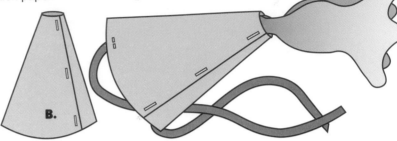

A. B.

Girls:

For a girl's hat, begin by cutting a quarter-circle from a 16-inch square of construction paper as indicated in Step A. Then roll the paper to form a cone that will fit the child's head (Step B). Before stapling the cone, tape a filmy scarf to the inside of the pointed end and allow it to trail out. (If scarves are not available, substitute crepe-paper streamers.) Next staple pieces of ribbon to opposite sides of the wide end of the cone to allow the child to tie the hat on.

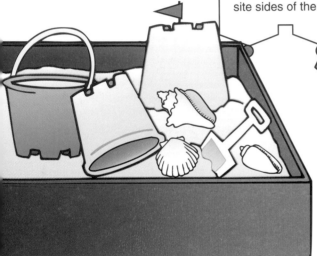

Kindergarten Castles

All you do is provide a few simple supplies, and youngsters will transform your sand table into a kindergarten kingdom landscape. If you don't already have sand-castle molds, take advantage of those end-of-the-summer bargains and purchase a few at your local discount store. Place these molds in your sand table along with a bucket of water, a plant sprayer, plastic shovels, seashells, and other decorative objects such as Unifix® cubes or small blocks. Invite children to visit the sand table and use the supplies to explore mixing sand with water to create their own sand-castle kingdom.

Brick By Brick

What better place for building castles than in the block center? Merge your block area with your kindergarten kingdom theme by displaying castle pictures nearby. (These pictures can often be found in books or magazines or could be donated by local travel agents.) Also supply other castle-related toys, such as kings, queens, knights, and horses. Encourage your youngsters to examine the pictures for inspiration, then get building!

To promote castle-building enthusiasm, have your camera ready to photograph each completed project along with its builders. Display these photos near the block area. When you have a few pictures collected, surprise children by posting an award ribbon next to each photo. Sometimes children will even invent their own award categories, such as "Tallest Castle Without Falling" or "The Castle With The Most Windows." You never know what those castle-building kids will come up with!

Deck The Halls!

If you made a classroom castle (see page 88), enlist the help of your little interior decorators to design the royal decor. Position the castle in your art center near a variety of supplies, such as fabric and wallpaper scraps, crayons, paper, craft sticks, craft glue, and a brush for the glue. Encourage each child who visits this center to creatively use the supplies to decorate the inside of the castle. Perhaps one child will draw and frame a portrait of a queen while another child hangs the royal wallpaper. Little hands will get lots of fine-motor practice while creatively working with colors, shapes, sizes, and textures to deck these royal halls.

Graphing Towers

Use these tall towers to make a graphing poster that you can use throughout your castle theme—or even longer. To make the poster, use the tower patterns on page 95. For each tower, photocopy one tower top and as many tower bottoms as you need to have one square for each child in your class. Mount the towers on a sheet of poster board, leaving a little space at the bottom of each tower. Color the towers; then laminate the poster. Whenever you'd like to do a graphing activity, write a corresponding title on the poster; then paper-clip a label to the bottom of each tower to indicate the categories that you are graphing. Have each student indicate his response by using a dry-erase marker to write his first initial in a space on the appropriate tower. After discussing the graphing results, simply wipe off the laminated surface and you're ready for your next graphing activity.

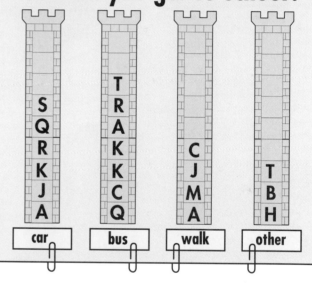

Hang In There!

Promote positive self-esteem and get to know your new students as they make these coats of arms. In advance, cut out a large, simple construction-paper shield for each child. Use a marker to divide the shields as shown. Working with small groups of children, have each child write her name at the top of the shield. Then prompt the child to design her coat of arms according to the directions below. (If you sent home the invitation in "Come One! Come All!" on page 88, your students will have been thinking about this information already.) When all of the projects are done, invite each child to share her coat of arms with the class. Then mount these informative displays on a bulletin board or along a classroom wall.

Section One: Color in this section using your favorite colors.

Section Two: Draw your family.

Section Three: Draw (or cut out and glue) your favorite foods.

Section Four: Draw (or cut out and glue) your favorite animal.

The Age Of Chivalry

"Yes, sir"; "yes, ma'am"; "please"; and "thank you." Sounds from the chivalrous past? They don't have to be! Use your castle theme to promote good manners in your classroom. Make a castle tower by taping a crenellated construction-paper strip around a clear, plastic cylindrical container. Use permanent markers to draw on bricks, windows, and perhaps a few vines. Then collect a supply of counters, such as marbles or jelly beans.

After an introductory conversation about manners, encourage children to use good manners. Each time you catch a child using good manners, drop one of the counters in the tower. When the tower is full, reward your chivalrous class with a special treat. After your youngsters experience initial success with this reward system, vary it by adding counters for other events, such as an entire circle time or lunch period with good manners. And if, by chance, someone should happen to compliment your class on using good manners—that ought to be worth a handful!

Wasn't That A Dainty Dish...

These colorful castles make a perfect thematic snack during your first days of school.

You will need:
- several boxes of flavored gelatin (the number based on your class size)
- hot water (according to the package directions)
- enough clean sand-castle molds to hold the prepared gelatin
- one bowl for each castle mold
- lettuce
- speckled jelly beans
- whipped topping

Divide students so that you have one group for each castle mold. Help each group prepare a box of gelatin; then pour it into a castle mold and chill it. (If your molds do not stand independently, nestle them in a container full of rice, beans, or packing pieces.) Unmold the chilled castles onto beds of lettuce to resemble grass. Then scatter speckled jelly beans on the lettuce to resemble rocks. When you're ready for a snack, have each child scoop a serving of castle into a bowl and top it with a dollop of whipped topping.

Pam Crane

Once Upon A Time

Here's a selection of kingdom-related literature that you can use as read-alouds or to stock your reading center.

Dragon For Breakfast
By Eunice & Nigel McMullen

Into The Castle
By June Crebbin

Kate's Castle
By Julie Lawson

The King At The Door
By Brock Cole

King Bidgood's In The Bathtub
By Audrey Wood

Knee-High Norman
By Laurence Anholt

The Little Prince And The Great Treasure Hunt
By Peter Kavanagh

Nora's Castle
By Satomi Ichikawa

The Paper Bag Princess
By Robert Munsch

The Prince Who Wrote A Letter
By Ann Love

The Princess And The Pea
Retold by Harriet Ziefert

The Story Book Prince
By Joanne Oppenheim

Hear Ye! Hear Ye!

_____ is cordially

invited to join

The Kingdom Of Kindergarten!

Please come ready to tell us:
• your favorite colors
• your favorite animal
• your favorite foods
• who is in your family

Sincerely,

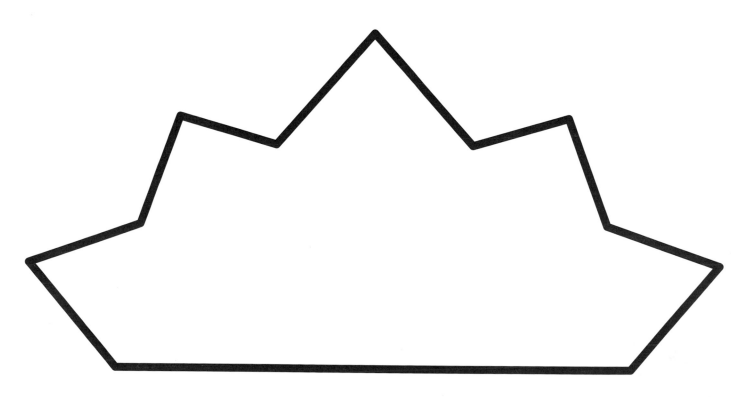

Dragon Pattern
Use with "Royal Door Decor" on page 89.

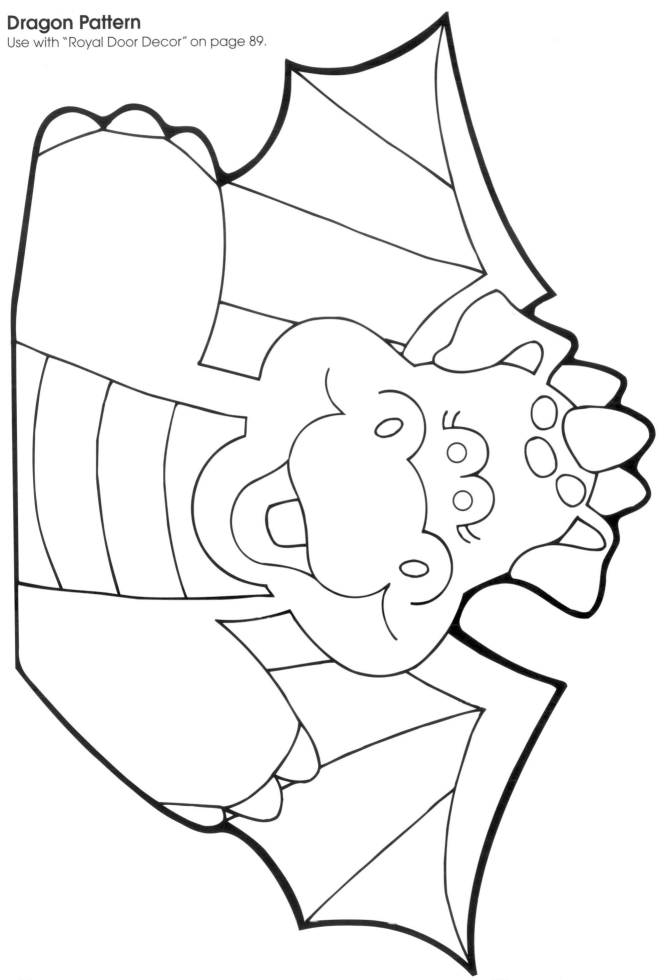

tower top

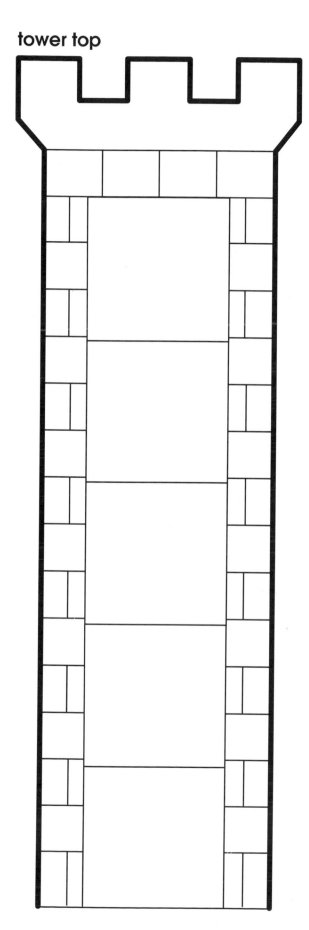

Use with "Look Who's In The Castle Today" on page 89.

attendance card

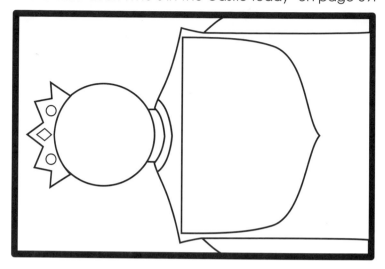

tower bottom

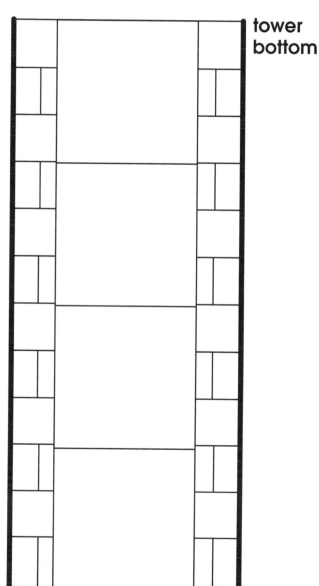

TEDDY & COMPANY

Armed with their favorite teddy-bear buddies and their greatest grizzly growls, your youngsters will be ready for this unit's "un-bear-ably" fun curriculum-related activities.

ideas contributed by Lucia Kemp Henry and Mackie Rhodes

TALKING TEDDIES

Lend a warm-and-fuzzy tone to your beginning-of-the-year circle times by including everyone's best buddies. In advance, ask each child to bring his favorite teddy bear to class during the first week of school. (You might want to have extra bears on hand for those children without bears of their own, and one for yourself.) During a group time, model giving your teddy bear a talking voice and have the bear introduce himself and you to the class. Perhaps your teddy bear could also interact with other teddies in the circle, asking them questions to get the conversations rolling. Then invite each teddy to introduce himself and his owner. Your youngsters won't be nearly as bashful when they let their teddies do the talking!

Hi! My name is Max. This is my friend Mrs. Henry. We like to cuddle and read good books.

Kimberly Richard

TAKING INVENTORY

Once all the introductions have been made, invite youngsters to share a little bit more about their bears. Prompt each child with questions relating to her bear's color, texture, size, or general shape. Guide children to summarize that each teddy has some characteristics that are the same and some that are different from the other bears. Afterward engage youngsters in some "paws-on" classification work. To prepare, enlarge and duplicate the teddy-bear pattern (page 101) in three different sizes. Label each cutout according to its size: "small," "medium," or "large." Then tape each label to a separate basket (or box). Have each child describe her bear using one of the size words, then place it in the corresponding basket. At another time, set up the activity to reflect another characteristic, such as bear colors or clothing accessories. After your group sessions, place the bears and baskets in a center; then challenge youngsters to sort the bears according to their own creative classifications.

Large

Medium

Small

COLOR-CODED CHILD AND CHUM

Each child and her teddy-bear chum can be easily paired and organized into groups when you use these color-coded necklaces. To prepare, program a reduced copy of the bow pattern (page 101) with "I belong to_____." Then duplicate a class supply of both the original bow and the programmed bow onto construction paper, using equal numbers of each color of paper that you use. Ask each child to cut out a color-matched set of the patterns, then write her name on each cutout. Help her use a hole puncher and yarn to create a separate necklace from each cutout. Throughout the day, call children and chums by necklace color to center time, circle time, and anytime activities. (See page 98 for some teddy-bear center ideas.)

WHERE, OH, WHERE IS DEAR LITTLE TEDDY BEAR?

Youngsters' prepositional knowledge will come out of hiding with this "paws-on" activity. In advance, display each of five cards labeled with "on," "in," "under," "beside," or "behind." While students are out of the classroom, hide their teddy bears so that each one is *on, in, under, beside,* or *behind* an object. When children return, tell them that their bears are playing hide-and-seek. Ask each child to search the room to find—*but not move*—his bear. When a child locates his bear, have him stand near it, making a soft growling sound with motions. When all students are softly growling, invite each child to describe his bear's hiding place using one of the words on the cards. Then have him place his bear under the corresponding label. When all the bears are placed, you've got a "gr-gr-great" setup to amble on into some concrete graphing!

HOMEWARD BOUND

This homeward-bound bear partners parents and children for phonics fun. Nestle a teddy bear in an overnight bag. Also include a note explaining that the child and bear are to find up to five items from home that begin with the same sound as *bear.* Have the child place the items and teddy bear in the bag, and return the bag to school the following day. During group time, ask the child and bear to show off their phonetic finds. Then invite a different child to take the bag home to complete the same exercise. Extend this activity throughout the school year by challenging youngsters to find items beginning with different sounds. And watch out— these homebound bears have been reported to sniff out the most creative of phonics finds!

TEDDY-BEAR CENTERS

When you add these teddy-bear touches to your centers, youngsters—and their teddy-bear buddies—will be more than eager to get their little paws on the basic skills.

HONEY HUNTING

Counting skills will be climbing high for just a bit of honey. To create a tree, make a crayon rubbing of a tree trunk on a large sheet of light brown construction paper (or simply use a simulated wood-grain adhesive covering). Glue the decorated paper to an empty, lidded oatmeal canister; then cut a hole in the side. Program a supply of large honey-pot cards like the one shown with dot sets. (If abilities permit, program the other side of each card with a numeral. In this case, have students do the activity as described below, but use the dot-set side of the card for self-checking.) Place the tree trunk in a center along with a supply of counting bears, the programmed cards, and a bowl of Bit•O•Honey® candies.

When you introduce this center, prompt children to remember some storybook bears that *love* honey. In fact, weren't some of those honey-loving bears willing to climb tall trees to get some? Next have a child choose a honey-pot card and place a counting bear on each dot on that card. Then invite the child to "climb" each of these bears up the tree and into the hole—hunting for honey, of course. As a reward for a job well done, offer each child a Bit•O•Honey® candy.

TEDDY'S COLORFUL CLOTHES

Youngsters will develop plenty of teddy-bear fashion sense with this color-matching activity. Make construction-paper copies of the teddy-bear outfit (page 101) in a variety of colors. Also duplicate one brown teddy bear (page 101) for each different clothing color that you chose. Cut out all the patterns; then cut the shirts apart from the pants. Glue each bear to a different tagboard card; then laminate all the pieces. Use a spring-type clothespin to attach each shirt along the rim of a shoebox. Then put the pants inside the box. To use this center, have a child pick a pair of pants from the box, then place it on one of the bears. Next have her find the matching shirt, unclip it, and place it on the corresponding bear. Continue in this manner until each bear is dressed. Afterward have the child practice those fabulous fine-motor skills by setting up the center for the next child.

PATTERNING PALS

Patterning these textured teddies will call on each youngster's sense of touch as well as his patterning skills. Create a tagboard tracer using the teddy-bear pattern on page 101. Trace several of the bear onto a variety of textured fabrics, such as corduroy, felt, and wool; then cut out each shape. (If desired, add wiggle eyes and a pom-pom nose to each bear.) Glue some of the bears onto several tagboard strips to create pattern cards, similar to the one shown. To do this activity, instruct a child to complete each pattern card, guiding his selections with his sense of touch. Extend this activity by inviting each child to create his own teddy-bear patterns with the loose cutouts. Would anyone like to try it blindfolded?

TEDDY-BEAR RHYME TIME

In the charming *Where's My Teddy?* by Jez Alborough (Candlewick Press), young Eddie finds his teddy just in time—with comical rhyme. After sharing this tale with youngsters, write the name of each child's teddy bear on chart paper. Then write each child's real or made-up rhyming word next to his teddy's name. Encourage each child to dictate a rhyme using his teddy's name and the rhyming word. Then have him illustrate his rhyme. Stack the student pages between two construction-paper covers. Title the class book "Teddy-Bear Rhyme Time." During a group time, invite each child to read his rhyme to the class. Then place the book in your reading center for all to enjoy during free times.

Bill	hill
Jane	rain
Booboo	Yoohoo
Ted	bed
Pooky	spooky
Mel	bell
Cuddles	puddle

Look at poor Buddy.
He's all wet and muddy.

BIG BEAR PAINTINGS

Use *Where's My Teddy?* to inspire this enchanting oversized artwork. Invite each child to paint a big bear on a large sheet of sturdy art paper. While the paint is still wet, have the child sprinkle cornmeal or whole-wheat flour over the damp surface to simulate a furry texture. When the paint is dry, have the child cut out the bear. Then ask her to draw, color, and cut out a small teddy bear for her big bear. Have the student glue the small teddy to the paw of her big bear. Display these projects on a woods background along a classroom wall. The finished display lends itself to lots of opportunities for size vocabulary as you encourage youngsters to dictate their own teddy-bear stories into a tape recorder.

COULD THIS BE REAL?

Help youngsters sort fact from fiction with this critical-thinking activity. Ask youngsters to name all the things in *Where's My Teddy?* that could be true about a real bear. For instance, a real bear might be very large, live in the woods, and be frightened by a human. Then talk about the things that are not true about a real bear. *(A real bear could not talk, have a teddy bear, or sleep in a bed.)* Then share some fascinating bear facts from pages 4–14 of *Bears* by Bobbie Kalman and Tammy Everts (Crabtree Publishing Company). Guide students to discuss what they know about bears, listing their responses on chart paper. Then invite each child to illustrate a real bear to display with the student-generated list and the title "The Bear Facts."

The Bear Facts
1. Bears can be big or small.
2. Do NOT touch a real bear!
3. Bears have very sharp teeth.
4. Bears are very strong.
5. Some bears can climb trees.

Walk on all fours!

GRIZZLY BEAR SAYS...

This "bear-ly" modified game of Simon Says will reinforce youngsters' bear knowledge. To play, students will perform an action mentioned by Grizzly Bear—but *only* if the action is preceded with "Grizzly Bear Says." And Grizzly Bear will only give permission to act out real bear actions, such as *walk on all fours, growl, climb a tree,* or *catch a fish.* If a child performs an action without Grizzly Bear's permission, have him sit down with his teddy until Grizzly Bear invites him to join the group of grizzlies again.

BEAR BOOKS

Your children will have very special books to share with their own teddy-bear buddies when they create these cute concept books. For each child, duplicate pages 102–106 on white construction paper. To make the manipulative teddy, have each child color and cut out the pattern on page 103. After laminating each child's bear, help him tape a length of yarn to the back of it. Next have each child color the rest of his pages, then cut out each book page and glue on the corresponding pattern. Instruct students to sequence their pages. Then help each child staple the free end of the yarn between the pages along the left edge of the book. Read the books together, encouraging each child to manipulate his own bear. When your little ones share these books with their families, you're sure to hear about some awfully proud mama and papa bears at home!

BEAR BOOKS: FACT AND FICTION

Now I Know Bears
By Susan Kuchalla
Illustrated by Kathie Kelleher
Published by Troll Associates

Every Autumn Comes The Bear
By Jim Arnosky
Published by G. P. Putnam's Sons

We're Going On A Bear Hunt
By Michael Rosen
Illustrated by Helen Oxenbury
Published by Margaret K. McElderry Books

The Bear Who Didn't Like Honey
By Barbara Maitland
Illustrated by Odilon Moraes
Published by Orchard Books

The Three Bears
By Byron Barton
Published by HarperCollins Publishers, Inc.

Teddy Bear, Teddy Bear: A Classic Action Rhyme
Illustrated by Michael Hague
Published by Morrow Junior Books

Teddy-Bear Pattern
Use with "Taking Inventory" on page 96, and "Teddy's Colorful Clothes" and "Patterning Pals" on page 98.

Teddy-Bear Outfit Pattern
Use with "Teddy's Colorful Clothes" on page 98.

Bow Pattern
Use with "Color-Coded Child And Chum" on page 97.

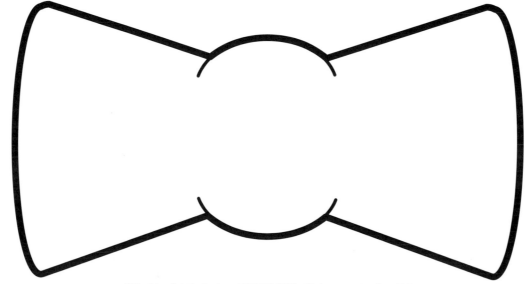

Bear Book Title Page

Use with "Bear Books" on page 100.

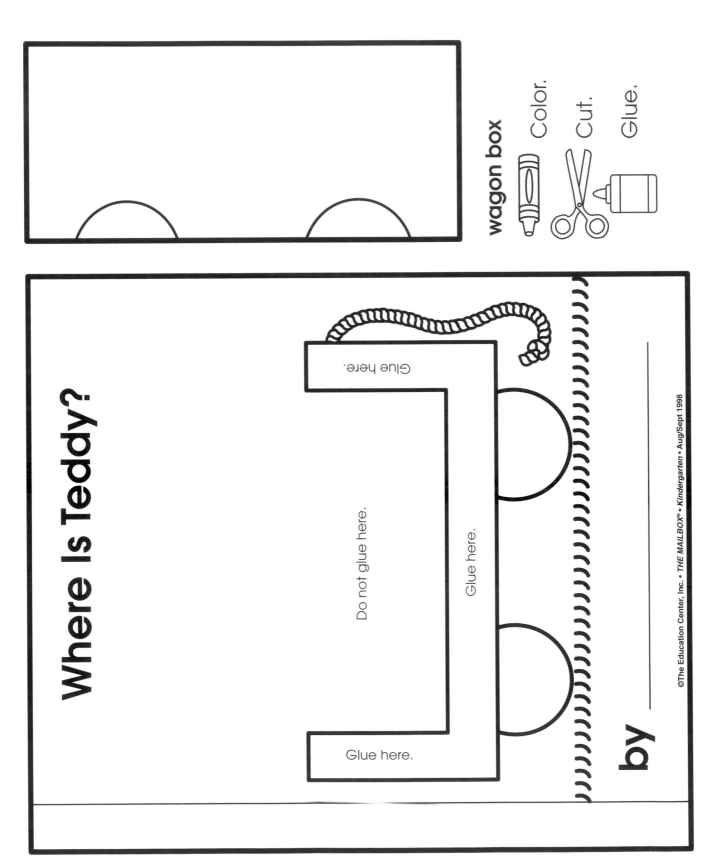

wagon box

Color.

Cut.

Glue.

Where Is Teddy?

Do not glue here.

Glue here.

Glue here.

Glue here.

by _____

manipulative teddy

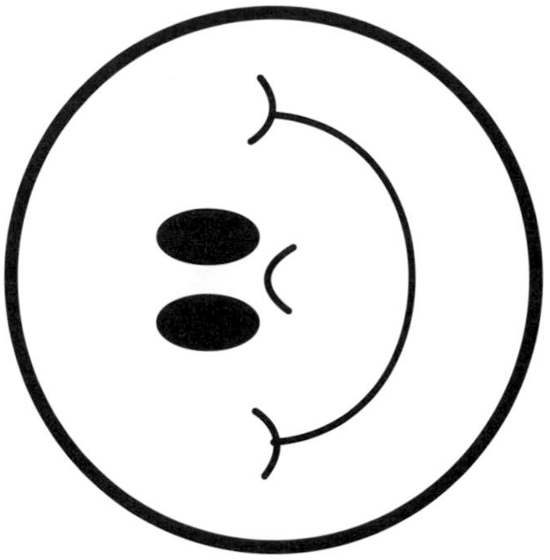

sun

Page one

Teddy's **under** the yellow sun!

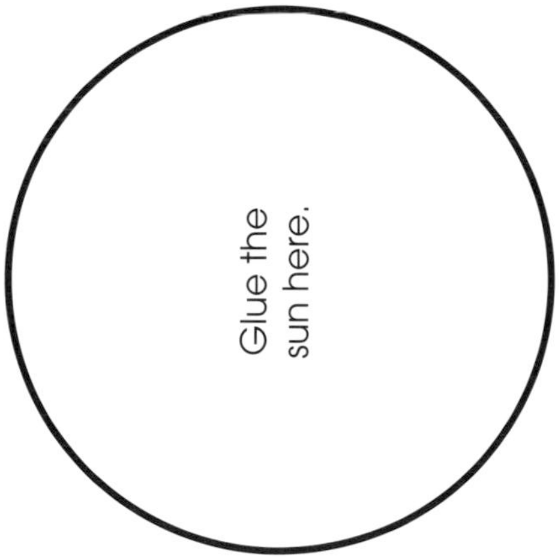

Glue the sun here.

What shape is the sun?

1

Bear Book Patterns

Use with "Bear Books" on page 100.

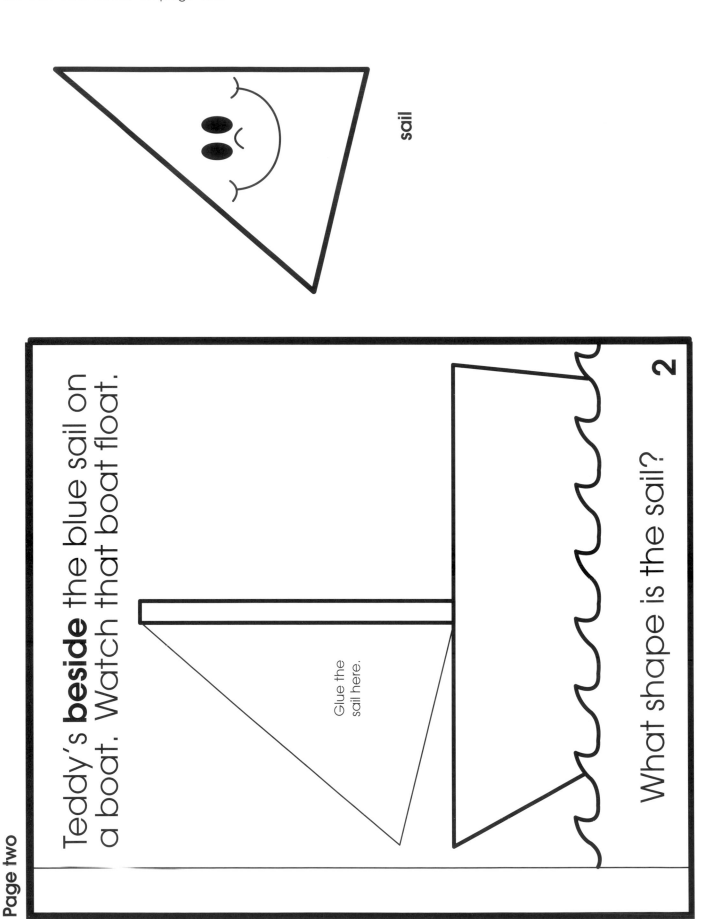

sail

Teddy's **beside** the blue sail on a boat. Watch that boat float.

Glue the sail here.

What shape is the sail?

2

Page two

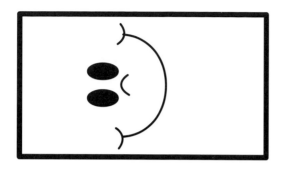

tree trunk

Page three

Teddy's **behind** a green and brown tree. Can you see?

Glue the tree trunk here.

What shape is the tree trunk? **3**

Bear Book Patterns

Use with "Bear Books" on page 100.

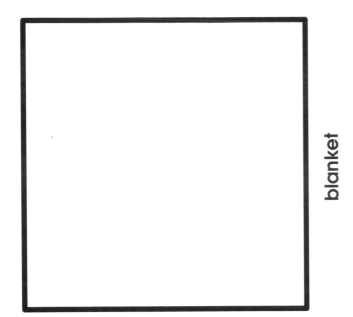

blanket

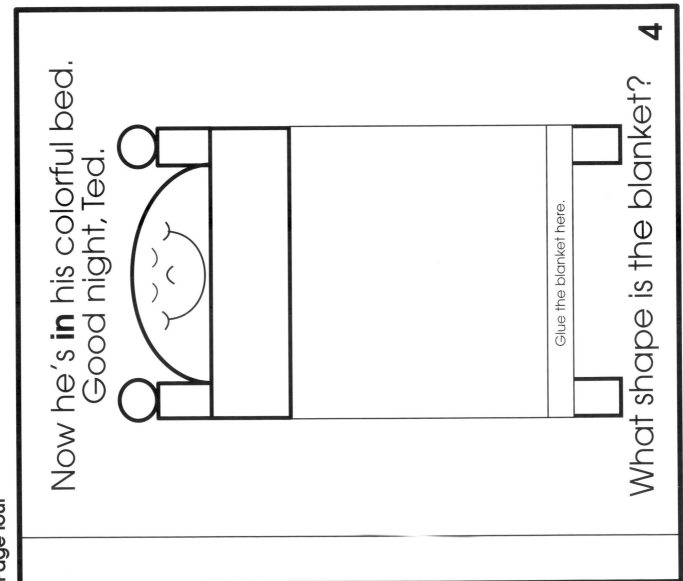

Now he's **in** his colorful bed.
Good night, Ted.

Glue the blanket here.

What shape is the blanket?

4

Page four

WIGGLE IN, WIGGLE OUT, WIGGLE, WIGGLE ALL ABOUT!

Your little ones will be squirming to learn with Wiggle the worm as he wriggles youngsters in and out of a bushelful of positional-word activities.

ideas by Susan DeRiso

INTRODUCING WIGGLE THE WORM!

To begin your exploration of positional words, cut a worm shape from pink felt. Glue on wiggle eyes, and use a fabric marker to add details. From appropriate colors of felt, cut several apples, a tree trunk, a treetop, and a section of grass. Cut out a hole from the center of the tree trunk; then arrange the scene (as shown) on a flannelboard. Next introduce Wiggle to your youngsters. Invite one student at a time to manipulate Wiggle according to your directions. Have students put Wiggle *in* the tree trunk, *on* the treetop, *behind* the grass—just about anywhere you can describe using positional words. Wriggle Wiggle all about!

WORM OBSTACLE COURSE

Reinforce positional words by inviting your little ones to wriggle through a classroom obstacle course. In advance transform old pillowcases into your worm wardrobe. For each pillowcase, cut a neck opening at the top; then cut an armhole in each side. Next set up an obstacle course using items available in your classroom. For each obstacle, duplicate the Wiggle pattern on page 108. Create a direction card by gluing a copy of Wiggle on a large index card. Then draw a dialogue balloon on the card and write a positional word in it. Post each card on the appropriate obstacle. For example, post the word *under* on a chair, the word *in* on a box, or the word *around* on a trash can. Encourage each child to take a turn wearing a worm costume and following Wiggle's directions to worm her way through the course.

WIGGLE ON THE GO!

You never quite know exactly where Wiggle will show up in this song. In advance, enlarge and duplicate the Wiggle pattern (right). Provide each child with a Wiggle cutout and a craft stick. Have him color his cutout; then glue it to one end of the craft stick. When the glue dries, encourage your little ones to demonstrate each positional word as they sing the song. When children catch on to the song, encourage them to repeat it substituting their own positional words each time.

WIGGLE ON THE GO!

(sung to the tune of "The Farmer In The Dell")
Wiggle's **on** my head.
Wiggle's **on** my head.
Oh no, he's on the go!
Wiggle's **on** my head.

Wiggle's **behind** my knee.
Wiggle's **behind** my knee.
Oh no, he's on the go!
Wiggle's **behind** my knee.

Wiggle's **under** my arm.
Wiggle's **under** my arm.
Oh no, he's on the go!
Wiggle's **under** my arm.

©The Education Center, Inc. • THE MAILBOX® • Kindergarten • Aug/Sept 1998

RED, YELLOW, GREEN: WHICH IS IN BETWEEN?

Line up for positional-word learning with this hands-on apple activity. Provide several red, green, and yellow apples; and the felt Wiggle from "Introducing Wiggle The Worm!" on page 107. Arrange the apples in a row or in other configurations on a table. Ask students questions, such as:

Which apple is *beside* a green apple?
Which apple is *behind* a red apple?

Add Wiggle to the fun by encouraging students to wriggle the felt Wiggle among the apples—*on, behind, between, under*—anywhere and everywhere!

APPLE STAMPING

Don't eat those apples just yet! Use this apple art activity to reinforce the positional words your students have been practicing. Set up a center with a supply of white construction paper and three wide, shallow containers, such as aluminum pie pans. Pour a thin coat of red acrylic paint into one container, yellow paint into another, and green into the third. Make apple printers by sticking a different fork securely in the backs of three apple halves. Place one apple printer in each paint container. Encourage each youngster using the center to create apple art by dipping the apples into the paints and stamping the paper. When the paint dries, encourage the child to cut out construction-paper worms and glue them among the apple prints. Then write as the child dictates the position of each worm. Encourage youngsters to take their apple art home and share what they've learned with their parents.

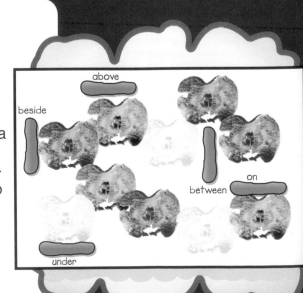

IN AND OUT

Let Wiggle the worm help reinforce the concepts of *in* and *out* with this simple sewing activity. Prepare a sewing apple for each child by tracing a large apple pattern onto heavy tagboard. Cut out each apple shape; then punch holes around its edge. Provide one-half of a pink chenille stem (worm) for each child. Twist a loop at one end of each worm and thread a piece of yarn through the loop. (The yarn should be long enough to go once around the apple.) Knot the ends of the yarn together. Give each child an apple and a threaded worm. Guide the children as they thread Wiggle *in* and *out* of each hole. For extra reinforcement, encourage them to recite the words "Wiggle goes *in*. Wiggle comes *out*" as they sew.

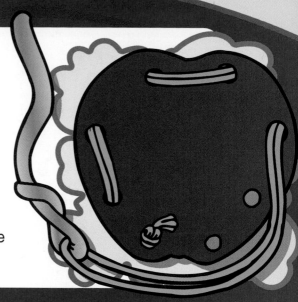

BOOKWORMS

Your youngsters are sure to giggle when they see Wiggle the worm appear on each page of these positional word booklets. On construction paper duplicate a class supply of "Wiggle's Apple Book" (page 110). Trim the edges of each page. To make one booklet, have a child color his booklet pages. Then fold along the vertical line on the page (as shown). Next, starting at the top, accordion-fold along the horizontal lines. (The booklet's cover page should end up on top. If page 1 is on top, re-fold your booklet.) With the booklet folded, hole-punch the black dot through all the pages. Unfold the booklet, cut apart the pages, stack them in order, and staple them along the left edge. Give each child his booklet and a pipe-cleaner worm. As you read the booklet together, encourage each child to insert Wiggle in the hole on the first page so that he appears in the picture. Stress Wiggle's position in relation to the apple(s) on each page. Then have each child remove Wiggle and turn to the next page, continuing in the same manner throughout the booklet. That ole Wiggle is wriggling up all over!

Wiggle is **in** the apple.

Wiggle is **over** the apple.

Wiggle is **between** the apples.

Wiggle is **in** the apple.

Wiggle is **over** the apple.

Wiggle is **between** the apples.

Wiggle's Apple Book

Wiggle's Apple Book

BOOKS ABOUT WHERE

All About Where
Written & Illustrated by Tana Hoban
Published by Greenwillow Books, 1991

Behind The Mask: A Book About Prepositions
Written & Illustrated by Ruth Heller
Published by Grosset & Dunlap, Inc.; 1995
(Although this book contains some more advanced concepts, your youngsters will glean prepositional knowledge from the parts that you choose to share.)

Over-Under
Written by Catherine Matthias
Published by Childrens Press®, Inc. 1984

Elephants Aloft
Written by Kathi Appelt
Illustrated by Keith Baker
Published by
Harcourt Brace & Company, 1993

BARRY SLATE

Wiggle's Apple Book

©The Education Center, Inc. • *THE MAILBOX®* • *Kindergarten* • Aug/Sept 1998

Wiggle is **in** the apple.

1

Wiggle is **out** of the apple.

2

Wiggle is **over** the apple.

3

Wiggle is **under** the apple.   4

Wiggle is **between** the apples.

5

FABULOUS FALL FOLIAGE!

Get a running start and jump right into this pile of autumn-themed activities. Nestled among these layers of lovely leaves, you'll find learning opportunities in language skills, math, science, and more. So get ready…get set…JUMP!

ideas contributed by Lucia Kemp Henry

Dear Parent,
Your child has custom-designed this bag to hold lots of lovely leaves!
Please help your child search your yard, neighborhood, or local park for colorful leaves to bring to school.
We will use the leaves at school in a variety of learning activities.

Thanks for your help!

A GATHERING TIME

Plunge into your leaf studies by launching children on a leaf-gathering expedition. For each child in your class, you'll need a copy of the parent note (page 115) and a medium-sized paper bag. Also provide a variety of leaf-shaped sponges and bright fall colors of tempera paint. (If you need to make leaf-shaped sponges, patterns are provided on page 115.) Invite each child to sponge-paint his bag as he likes. When the paint is dry, help the child staple the parent note to his bag. Read the note together; then foster the home-school connection by encouraging each child to take his bag home and partner with a parent to accomplish the task at hand. (You might also like to have a reserve supply of leaves handy for those children who do not return their bags. And if real fall leaves are not available, cut out an abundance of colorful construction-paper leaves for use in the activities in this unit.)

LOADS AND LOADS OF LOVELY LEAVES

Set the stage for leaps in learning with this simple fall display. Title a board as shown; then staple a large sheet of chart paper to the center. When each child brings his leaf-filled bag back to school (see "A Gathering Time"), tack each bag to the board and add the child's name. As you continue your studies, record your discoveries on the chart paper. This is not only an attractive way to store the leaves, but the board also serves as a focal point as you leaf your way through the rest of your unit.

LOTS AND LOTS OF LOVELY LEAVES!

 Jess

 Josh

 Rick

 Eliza

 Zach

 Eric

 John

 Teri

 Lori

- leaf (one)

- leaves 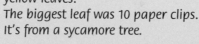 (more than one)

- Lots of leaves change color in the fall.
- Our class had the most of yellow leaves.
- The biggest leaf was 10 paper clips. It's from a sycamore tree.

 Wendy

 Malinda

 Courtney

 Angie

 Bobby

 Carolyn

 Coltrane

 Davis

 Miles

On the leaf words (decorative leaves):
lovely
lots lucky
leaves
lion love
loads lake
Laura lost leak
lemon lip left

L IS FOR...

Don't miss this thematic opportunity for phonics fun! Post a large leaf cutout near your bulletin-board display (see "Loads And Loads of Lovely Leaves"). After reading and discussing the title of the board, ask youngsters to be thinking of and watching for additional words that begin with L. Throughout your leaf unit, each time a child suggests an L word, write it on the cutout. When you fill the first cutout with L words, start on another one. Challenge children to see how many leaves they can fill up around the display. Can you think of *loads* and *loads* of L words?

A LEAFY LANGUAGE LESSON

Little ones will beam with pride as they drift through this little language lesson and emerge with some impressive new knowledge. After discussing the phonemic aspects of the word *leaf,* give each child a sheet of construction paper. Instruct her to glue one leaf (from her bag) to the page. Have her label that leaf. Next ask children what we call more than one leaf—the *plural.* Once you arrive at the plural *leaves,* invite each child to glue more than one leaf to another place on her page. Have her label that clustering of leaves with the plural form. Encourage each child to take her page home to share with her family.
Look, Mom—I know what the plural of leaf is!

Jason
leaf
leaves

LEAVES ARE FALLING

Imaginations, body movements, and sign language come together to make this action autumn poem a seasonal winner. In advance write the poem on a large sheet of chart paper. Practice reading/reciting the poem together, interacting with the print as your students are able. Then have youngsters recite the poem again, adding the motions as they do so.

① Leaves are falling all around—

② Red, yellow, orange, and brown.

③ Twirling, swirling to the ground—

④ Look how many leaves I've found!

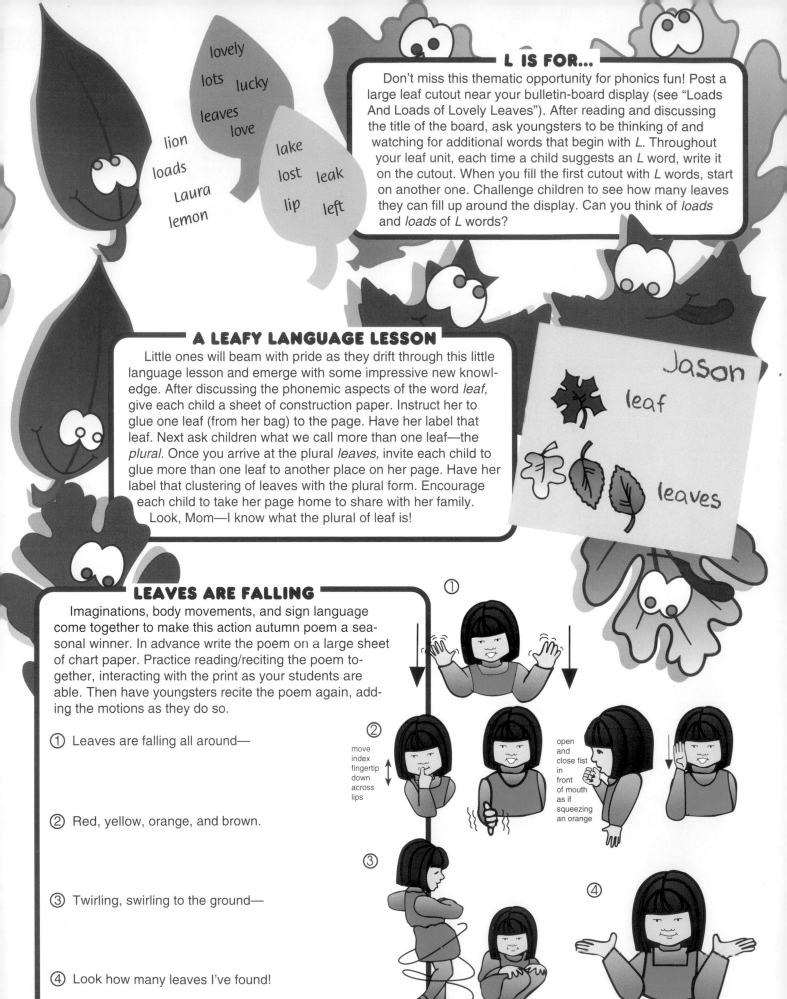

move index fingertip down across lips

open and close fist in front of mouth as if squeezing an orange

Each child's collection of leaves (from "A Gathering Time" on page 111) serves as the hands-on tools for the following investigative studies. So let your little ones loose with these leaves-of-learning; then stand back and watch what happens!

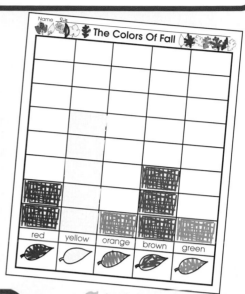

THE COLORS OF FALL

In advance photocopy a class supply of the graph on page 116. Invite each child to take a copy of the graph and his bag of leaves to a workspace. Encourage the child to sort his leaves by color. Then have him color one block on the graph for each corresponding color of leaf. During a group time, discuss what the graphs reveal. If desired, use each child's information to make one large class graph.

HOW BIG, HOW SMALL?

For this activity, each child will need her leaf collection and nonstandard units of measure, such as paper clips. (Have each child or group of children use the same unit of measure.) Ask each child to sort through her collection of leaves to find the biggest and the smallest leaf. Then encourage her to measure those two leaves with the chosen unit of measure. Have each child record the results of her investigation as shown. Next have each child label her measuring lengths with an initialed piece of tape. Then, as a whole class or in small groups, have students sequence all their lengths of measurement. In addition to discussing concepts such as *biggest* and *smallest,* you'll find perfect opportunities here for ordinal-number reinforcement. For example, whose leaf is the *fifth* smallest?

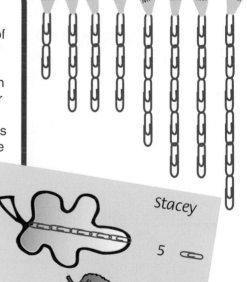

Stacey

5

2

THE SHAPES IN ALL

This activity reinforces visual discrimination and shape recognition, and also stimulates some very creative describing words. To begin, give each child a large sheet of construction paper and glue. Have each child place 10 to 15 leaves on his workspace. Encourage him to sort his leaves by shape. Then have him glue the leaves to his paper according to shape classification. Next ask the child to draw dividing lines to distinguish each grouping. Then encourage each child to write/dictate about the shape of each category of leaf on his paper. During a group time, invite each child to share his work. Then display the projects along with the title "The Shapes Of Fall."

Cori

kind of like an oval

These have points like little triangles.

It looks like a hand but not really.

These are from my yard. They are called tulip leaves.

113

MY BOOK OF LEAVES

Your little ones will display the brilliant colors of accomplishment and pride when they make these books that they can read on their very own! For each child, duplicate pages 117 and 118 on construction paper and cut five 9" x11" sheets of blank paper. Have each child cut out his cover and text strips. Instruct him to glue each text strip to a different page. Have him sequence his pages, then staple them behind his cover page. Encourage each child to creatively illustrate his book according to the text or follow the suggestions below. If you'd like to make leaf tracers or stencils for student use, patterns are provided on page 115.

Cover
Make a crayon rubbing of a real leaf on thin, colored paper. Cut out the picture; then glue it to the cover. Color the rest of the page.

Page 1
Sponge-paint a green leaf on the page. When the paint is dry, add crayon details; then write the numeral 1.

Page 2
Cut out two construction-paper leaves. Paint each cutout with a coat of water-diluted glue. Then press on pieces of fall-colored tissue paper, overlapping the pieces to achieve the desired effect. When the leaves are dry, glue them to the page. Write the numeral 2.

Page 3
Use a large leaf stencil and chalk to create three leaves on the page. Add marker details as desired; then seal the chalk by spraying it with a thin coat of hairspray. Write the numeral 3.

Page 4
Cut out four small leaves from wrapping-paper scraps. Glue the leaves to the page; then write the numeral 4.

Page 5
Draw five leaves on the page. Color the leaves in the colors of fall; then write the numeral 5.

LEAF TREATS

Take your favorite sugar-cookie recipe, add an autumn flair, and you'll have a colorful treat fit for one and all in the fall. Give each child a piece of waxed paper and a portion of cookie dough. Encourage him to mold his dough into the shape of a leaf. Then have him sprinkle on colorful sugar sprinkles to resemble the colors of a fall leaf. Use a permanent marker to write each child's name on his waxed paper. After baking the cookies, invite each child to enjoy his leaf as you share one of the literature selections below.

LEAFY LITERATURE LINKS

Fresh Fall Leaves
By Betsy Franco • Illustrated by Shari Halpern
Published by Scholastic Inc.

Red Leaf, Yellow Leaf
By Lois Ehlert
Published by Harcourt Brace Jovanovich, Publishers

Ska-tat!
By Kimberly Knutson
Published by Macmillan Publishing Company, Inc.

Dear Parent,

Your child has custom-designed this bag to hold lots of lovely leaves! Please help your child search your yard, neighborhood, or local park for colorful leaves to bring to school. We will use the leaves at school in a variety of learning activities.

Thanks for your help!

Leaf Patterns
Use with "A Gathering Time" on page 111 and "My Book Of Leaves" on page 114.

Name _____

red	yellow	orange	brown	green

My Book Of Leaves

by
_____

©The Education Center, Inc. • *THE MAILBOX*® • *Kindergarten* • Oct/Nov 1998

Text Strips

Use with "My Book Of Leaves" on page 114.

Here is **one** leaf that's as **green** as can be.

Here are **two** leaves changing colors, you see.

Three leaves so **big**.

Four leaves so **small**.

And **five** leaves that show all the colors of fall.

1

2

3

4

5

Did Somebody Say "Halloween"?

Does just the mere mention of the word *Halloween* immediately catch the undivided attention of your kindergartners? Is it that feeling of being just a tiny bit scared, but knowing all the while that they're completely safe? Or perhaps it's just the chance to do what they do best—pretend! For whatever reasons, you have their attention. So seize those teachable moments with this harvest of Halloween activities designed for learning fun. By the way—*did* somebody say "Halloween"?

Mood Music

Who better to set just the right Halloween mood for children than Hap Palmer! In his song "Have A Good Time On Halloween Night," Hap highlights the fun and fancy associated with Halloween. The lyrics of the song gently encourage creativity with a strong emphasis on goodwill. An instant sing-along line will have you and your youngsters hooked from the minute you first hear it. So turn it on, sing along, and "have a good time on Halloween night!"

"Have A Good Time On Halloween Night" is on Hap Palmer's cassette titled Holiday Songs & Rhythms. *It is available from Educational Activities, Inc. (1-800-645-3739).*

Halloween Countdown

This house is haunted all right—but not with anything that would make your students want to run away. In fact, it is filled with seasonal delights and educational fun! To prepare, you'll need two sheets of poster board for the steps below: one of yellow and one of another color. Ten days before your classroom party, display this haunted house. Each day, have a different student fold back the window that is programmed with the appropriate date. Help her read the message inside, then follow through on it. Afterward have children compare the number of days to wait with the number of days they have already waited. And the countdown continues!

Steps:

1. Decorate the nonyellow sheet to resemble a haunted house (use the Halloween characters on page 122, if desired). Using a craft blade, slit three sides on each of 11 windows (and/or doors).

2. On one of the windows, draw a brightly colored jack-o'-lantern. Then, beginning with the date that is ten days before your school Halloween party, write a date on each of the remaining windows.

3. Place the haunted house over the yellow sheet. Gently lift each window and trace that opening onto the yellow poster board. Behind the jack-o'-lantern window, write an invitation for your whole class to come to your Halloween party. In each remaining space on the yellow sheet, write a clue leading your students to a location of a treat or seasonal item (suggested ideas are listed below). Then staple the yellow sheet to the back of the haunted house. (Be sure each clue is visible when each window is opened.)

- Write a clue leading children to:
  — a bag of edible treats to be saved for your Halloween party
  — a bag of treats for right then and there!
  — a class pumpkin
  — seasonal classroom decorations
  — seasonal erasers, pencils, or stickers
  — plastic spider rings
  — a seasonal greeting or joke
  — a seasonal literature recommendation (see the list in this unit)

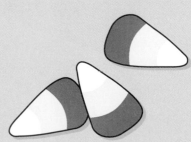

Bonnie McKenzie—Grs. Pre-K and K, Cheshire Country Day School, Cheshire, CT

Bats In The Bat Cave!

Here are the perfect projects to capture the creative interest of your lively little learners. You won't have any trouble finding helpers to assist in the construction of this Halloween hideaway and its residents!

To make the bat cave:

1. Cut apart a large appliance box so that you have three attached sections (or fold a long sheet of cardboard similarly).

2. Stand the cardboard on its edge; then use duct tape to tape chicken wire over the open top.

3. Create a cavelike texture by taping torn newspaper over the top and sides of the cave. Make rocks by taping on wads of scrunched-up newspaper.

4. Then paint the cave.

To make a bat:

1. Cut out two construction-paper bat wings and ears; then glue them on a small pinecone. (Use the wing patterns on page 122, if desired.)

2. Peel the backing off two self-adhesive paper reinforcements; then stick them on the bat to resemble eyes.

3. Tie clear fishing line around the middle of the bat; then hang the bat from the roof of the cave.

Trish Draper—Gr. K
Millarville Community School
Millarville, Alberta, Canada

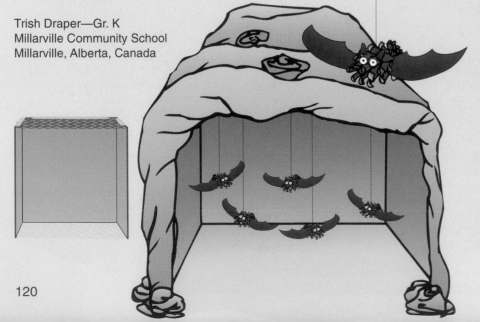

camel in a car
Jody

B-B-B-Bats In A B-B-B-Book!

Use your bat cave to start a little phonics fun that results in classroom publishing! Begin by asking your students what sound they hear at the beginning of *bat* and *bat cave*. Then ask children to think of other animals and places that begin with the same sounds (these can be real or imaginary). Encourage each child to illustrate his animal and place, then label his page. After each child shares his drawing with the class, sequence the pages in alphabetical order; then bind them between two decorated covers. Title the book "Bats In A Bat Cave"; then place it in the bat cave for children to read independently.

dinosaur in a donut shop
Tad

120

Here's the letter [*H*]

To make our potion bubble.

We know the sound.

We'll say it on the double: [sound of the letter].

Drop this letter in

Our Halloween brew.

Letters are magic—

Alakazam! Alakazoo!

Alphabet Brew

Invite each child to chime in with this chant to reinforce letter recognition, oral language, and phonics. To prepare, place a class treat, such as a bag of Smarties®, in a black cauldron (or black pot). Cover the treat with an overturned plastic bowl. Then write the poem on chart paper. Next cut out a supply of laminated construction-paper pumpkins—one or more for each letter that you'd like to reinforce. Write a different letter on each pumpkin, making duplicates as desired.

Seat your children in a semicircle; then place the cauldron in front of the group. Stack the lettered pumpkins facedown. In turn, call each child to select a pumpkin from the stack, then show it to the class. Encourage the group to chant the rhyme together using the letter on the pumpkin to fill in the blanks accordingly. At the end of each verse, invite the child to drop that pumpkin into the cauldron. When the last letter has been added to the brew, pretend to stir it up with a wooden spoon. Then (using a pot holder, of course!) pull out the hidden treat. Alakazam! Alakazoo!

Nancy Richmond—Gr. K
New Martinsville School
New Martinsville, WV

A Patch Of Seasonal Book Selections

Halloween Day by Anne Rockwell • Illustrated by Lizzy Rockwell • Published by HarperCollins Publishers, Inc.

Halloween Mice! by Bethany Roberts • Illustrated by Doug Cushman • Published by Clarion Books

The Hallo-Wiener by Dav Pilkey • Published by The Blue Sky Press

The Thirteen Hours Of Halloween by Dian Curtis Regan • Illustrated by Lieve Baeten • Published by Albert Whitman & Company

This Is The Pumpkin by Abby Levine • Illustrated by Paige Billin-Frye • Published by Albert Whitman & Company

When The Goblins Came Knocking by Anna Grossnickle Hines • Published by Greenwillow Books

Patterns

Bat Wings
Use with "Bats In The Bat Cave!" on page 120.

Halloween Characters
Use with "Halloween Countdown" on page 119.

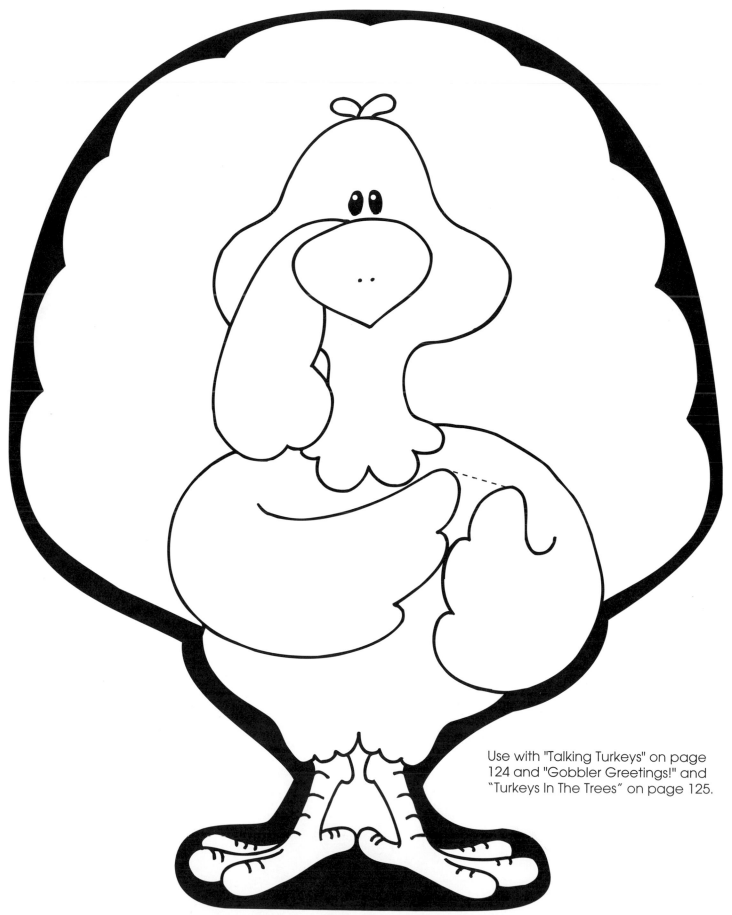

Use with "Talking Turkeys" on page 124 and "Gobbler Greetings!" and "Turkeys In The Trees" on page 125.

It's Turkey

Well, it's the time of year when these "gobbly" little guys come waddling along. Your youngsters will have a grand time with these turkey ideas that tickle the tummy as well as foster phonics fun, reinforce counting capabilities, and enhance lots of language skills.

Thanksgiving Riddle

Your little ones will have a gobblin' good time with this turkey rhyme. To introduce your tots to the topic of turkeys, sing the first stanza of the song below. After youngsters have responded to the first stanza, sing the second one. A gaggle of giggles will greet you as children begin to get this "kid-sized" joke. Have fun with it! (Then waddle right into the next activity on this page.)

(adapt to the tune of "I'm A Little Teapot")

I am not a drumstick.
No, not yet!
I need to eat more
So fat I'll get.
Corn is what I like and
Lots of grain.
Sometimes I gobble.
Can you guess my name?

If you guessed my name
On your first try,
You know I have a problem.
I don't have to tell you why!
If you would be so kind,
I have one wish:
Help me out
And eat some fish!

Rick Sanderford
Greensboro, NC

Talking Turkeys

Classification practice and lots of language skills are tucked into this fanciful idea that is guaranteed to wile a smile or two. In advance, collect one large craft stick per child; then duplicate a class supply of the turkey pattern on page 123. Next read aloud your choice of the turkey literature recommended in "Turkey Tales." After sharing the book(s), prompt children to think of what a turkey might recommend that people eat for Thanksgiving dinner—if, of course, he could *talk!* Then give each child a sheet of construction paper and encourage her to illustrate it as if it were a sign for a turkey to carry—if, of course, he could *write!* Next have the child color and decorate her copy of the turkey. Help the child cut a slit on the dotted line; then have her tuck the craft stick in the slit and glue it to the turkey. Next have the child tape her sign to the craft stick. Encourage each child to share her project with the class; then staple each turkey and sign to a board titled "Talking Turkeys." Passersby are sure to be tickled by these unique turkeys.

Turkey Tales

'Twas The Night Before Thanksgiving
Written & Illustrated by Dav Pilkey
Published by Orchard Books

A Turkey For Thanksgiving
Written by Eve Bunting
Illustrated by Diane de Groat
Published by Clarion Books

Gracias The Thanksgiving Turkey
Written by Joy Cowley
Illustrated by Joe Cepeda
Published by Scholastic Press

T Is For *Turkey*

Tap into this totally terrific idea for phonics fun. For each child, duplicate a construction-paper copy of the turkey-head patterns on page 126. Also cut out, or have each child cut out, a large construction-paper *T*. To make a *turkey-T,* use craft items—such as markers, wiggle eyes, and tissue paper—to decorate both the turkey heads, leaving the tabbed ends undecorated. Then fold the tabbed ends out, and glue the turkey heads together, leaving the tabbed ends free. Next glue the opened tabbed ends to the *T*. Then encourage each child to top his *T* with colorful construction paper or craft feathers. Display these gorgeous gobblers along a classroom wall. And if you wish, challenge each child to name his turkey with a *T* name!

Sharon Schmidt—Gr. K
Theresa Learning Community
Theresa, WI

Gobbler Greetings!

Making this gorgeous gobbler reinforces letter formation, fine-motor skills, and patterning. In addition, you'll have a beautiful display for your door, classroom, or hallway. In advance enlarge and duplicate the turkey pattern on page 123 on construction paper. Color and cut out only the body and head of the turkey; then laminate it. Cut out a class supply of construction-paper feathers; then write a different child's name on each one. Give each child her personalized feather and a supply of colored popcorn kernels. Encourage the child to glue the popcorn kernels along the letters of her name according to a pattern or color design of her choice. When the glue is dry, mount all the feathers behind the turkey's body. If desired, add a title to this display by gluing on a craft stick and labeled sign.

Terri Strong—Gr. K
Santa Paula, CA

Turkeys In The Trees

This manipulative turkey rhyme waddles right into counting and beginning subtraction skills. Make ten copies of the pattern on page 123, reduced 50 percent. Then color, cut out, and laminate them. Prepare these cutouts for flannelboard or magnetboard use, or make stick puppets by taping a craft stick to the back of each one. Then copy the poem below on chart paper. As you read the poem together, encourage selected students to manipulate the turkeys according to the poem. When you get down to zero little turkeys, use the last verses to bring all the turkeys back again!

[Ten] little turkeys
Were sitting in the trees.
They were sleeping very soundly
When up blew a breeze!

Hang on, little turkeys!
Hang on to each feather!
There's nothing to fear.
It's just a little windy weather.

Turkeys blowing here.
Turkeys blowing there.
Then one little turkey
Blew away in the air!

(Repeat the poem, substituting the new number of turkeys in the first line, until there are zero little turkeys left; then use the verses below.)

[Zero] little turkeys
Weren't sitting in the trees.
They weren't sleeping very soundly
When up blew a breeze!

Hang on, little turkeys!
Hang on to each feather!
There's nothing to fear.
It's just a little windy weather.

Turkeys blowing here.
Turkeys blowing there.
Then ten little turkeys
Blew back in the air!

Turkey-Head Patterns

Use with *"T* Is For *Turkey"* on page 125.

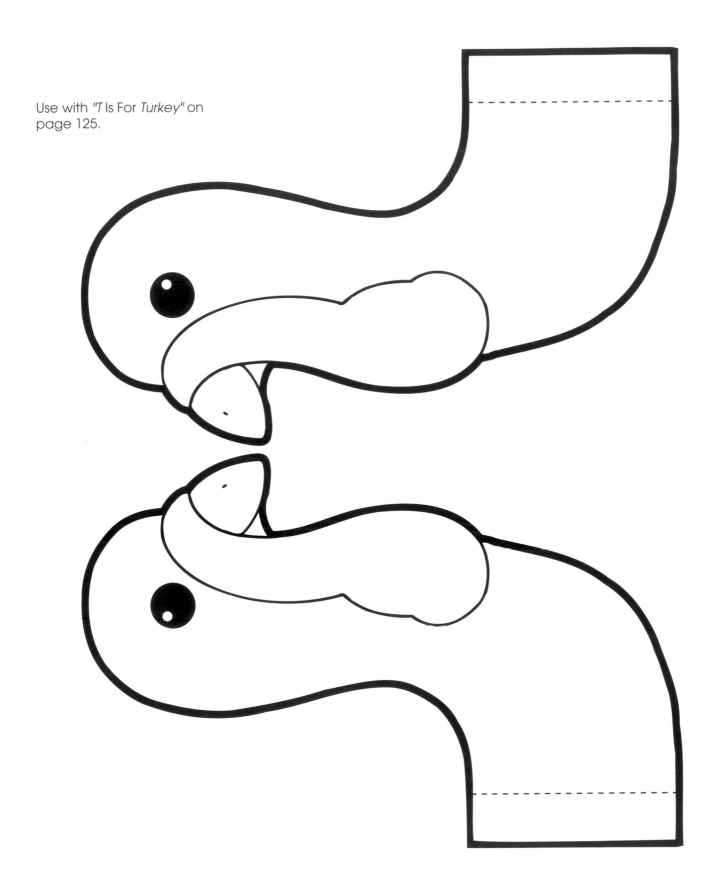

Strengthening The Home-School Connection

Encourage parents to become part of the kindergarten experience with these exciting teacher-ideas for hosting an Open House, creating a parent newsletter, inviting parent visitations, and lots more!

Masterful Invitations

Here's just the touch to spark each parent's interest in Open House. First enlarge and duplicate a class supply of the invitation on page 131. Then encourage each child to color a picture about school in the frame. Several days before Open House, have each child take his invitation home and present it to his parent. Parents will enthusiastically anticipate Open House when they see these invitations embellished with their own children's artistic masterpieces.

Sue De Riso, Barrington, RI

Every day I'm off to school,
And I think that's really cool!
But now it's time for you to see
This very special part of me!

Please come to Open House on
Monday, October 5, 1998

Classroom Walk Of Stars

Prepare your little ones to shine during Open House with this special guide. In advance display a numbered star cutout at each point of interest in your classroom. Then draw a simple map of your classroom, using correspondingly numbered stars. Next write or type a key describing what parents should note at each stop along the way. Then duplicate a supply of the map and key. Before the big night, familiarize your students with the maps so that they'll be able to guide their parents along. As each parent and child arrives for Open House, give the parent a map and a key; then encourage the child to guide her parent through all the points of interest on your classroom walk of stars.

Sue Creason—Gr. K
Highland Plaza United Methodist Kindergarten
Hixson, TN

Housekeeping Dramatic Play Center 3

Library 4

Sign-in Table 5

Writing Center 6

Restroom

Table 1 1   **Table 2** 2

Block Center 10   **Art Center** 11

Math Manipulatives 7

Key

1 2 Tables 1 and 2: Check out our Weather Journals!

3 Housekeeping and Dramatic Play Center: Make your own pizza!

4 Library: Look at all our class-written books. We can read to you!

5 Sign-in Table: We can demonstrate writing our names.

6 Writing Center: Take a peek at our Big Beautiful word books.

7 Math Manipulatives: Watch us demonstrate how talented we are at making patterns.

Familiar-Face Find

Isn't it always nice to see a familiar face? Well, have your little ones create this clever collage to greet parents as they arrive for Open House. In advance have each child cut out a supply of faces from old magazines. Encourage children to include plenty of diversity in the faces they choose. Then give each child a color copy of his school photo and have him cut his face out of it. Next glue a copy of the poem shown in the center of a large piece of tagboard. During a center time, have each child, in turn, glue his face cutouts (including his own) around the poem. Then laminate the poster board and post the finished collage in a prominent position. Watch parents' faces light up as they pick their little ones' smiles out of the crowd. My, you look familiar to me!

Nan Hokanson—Gr. K, Circle Time Preschool, Sheboygan Falls, WI

So many different kinds of faces—
No two are exactly the same.
Find the one that's dear to you
That says, "I'm glad YOU came!"

A Patchwork Quilt Of Teachers

Patch together this crafty introduction to your teaching staff for everyone to enjoy during Open House. Give each teacher, assistant, support staff, or parent volunteer a sheet of white construction paper. Ask her to fill the sheet with pictures (from photos, magazines, catalogs, postcards, or craft books) that reflect her hobbies, interests, experiences, or talents. Mount each finished sheet on a larger sheet of construction paper of a complementary color. (Alternate background colors if desired.) Then staple the finished projects on a bulletin board, adding additional sections with your favorite quotes on education or warm greetings, if needed. Use a marker to add stitches to give it that quilted look. Everyone will enjoy trying to match each teacher to a quilt section.

Taryn Lynn Way—Gr. K
Los Molinos Elementary School
Los Molinos, CA

"Kinder-Days" Photo Craze

Next year's students and parents will look forward to the kindergarten year after thumbing through this memorable album. As you collect photos this year, set aside a few each month that depict typical classroom events. At the end of the year, arrange all the photos in an album. During your visitations of incoming kindergartners, place the album beneath a sign that reads "Take A Look At This Book!" Encourage children and parents to get a feel for what they can expect in the coming year by looking through this special album.

Marlene Baker—Gr. K
Mars Hill Bible School
Florence, AL

Your students literally "make headlines" with this nifty newsletter idea. Arrange your students' school photos along the top of a sheet of unlined paper. Add a title; then photocopy a supply of the page. Use one of these pages as your original each time you create a classroom newsletter. If desired, stamp different seasonal prints along the border of each new newsletter. Write your weekly news on the page; then photocopy a class supply. Your youngsters' cheerful faces will entice their families to read all about it!

Susan Gaffney—Gr. K
Marie Duffy Elementary School
Wharton, NJ

And The Survey Says...

Everybody puts their two cents in with this idea that incorporates beginning keyboarding skills, parent involvement, math, and a whole lot more! First send home a survey with several appropriate questions, such as "What do you like best about school?" or "What is your favorite flavor of ice cream?" Ask each parent to interview her child, record his dictation, and return the survey to school. Set up a computer page to record all the incoming information. Position the cursor for each child (or have a volunteer do this); then have each child type in his own name. If your survey answers lend themselves to graphing, plug that information into a computer program that makes graphs. Give each child a copy of the resulting graph; then have him color each bar a different color. Staple each graph to a copy of the next newsletter; then send it home. Each time you send home a survey, more and more parents will participate because they will want to see their children's names in the news!

Cindy Daoust—Gr. K, Johnson Elementary, Franklin, TN

Our Favorite Things At School	Our Favorite Ice-Cream Flavors
Adam–the playground	Chelsea–chocolate
Cody–stuff with numbers like math	David–just vanilla
Jackson–art	Kelly–chocolate chip
Missy–I like to read.	Ali–strawberry
Callie–I like all of the stuff!	Kristen–chocolate
Ali–Music time	Michael– fudge ripple
David–Circle time	Adam–vanilla with sprinkles
Michael–Lunch time	Cody–chocolate
Kristen–when we read books together	Jackson–vanilla
	Missy–vanilla

Pam Crane

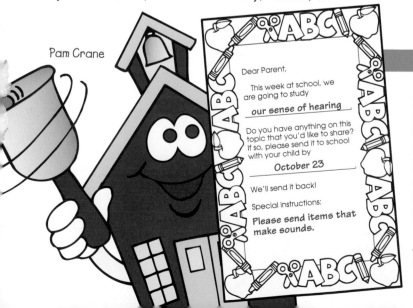

Dear Parent,

This week at school, we are going to study

our sense of hearing

Do you have anything on this topic that you'd like to share? If so, please send it to school with your child by

October 23

We'll send it back!

Special instructions:

Please send items that make sounds.

Topic Trackers

Turn parents and children into topic trackers by asking them to help locate items for upcoming themes or topics. You can do this in your weekly newsletter or use the reproducible on page 131. To use the reproducible, make one copy; then write in the topic and add a deadline for bringing the items to school. Then duplicate a class supply. Parents and children instantly become involved in your school topics. Now that's the track of purposeful parent involvement!

Judy Clifford—Gr. K
Central Elementary, Point Pleasant, WV

Parents Are Teachers, Too!

You'll have more and more participating teachers with this motivating idea. Begin by inviting a parent to share a hobby, career, craft, talent, or story with your little ones. Take several candid photos of each parent as she interacts with your students. Place these photos in a Ziploc® bag that has been stapled to the inside of a file folder. Inside the folder, glue a class-dictated letter explaining what the parent shared with the class and include some anecdotal remarks. Glue a library pocket on the back so students can check out the folders to take home and share with their parents. Once these folders start traveling to each child's home, other parents will see how fun and easy it is to volunteer. (This also serves as a great recruiting device for parents or other volunteers who have special skills or experiences but wouldn't even consider the skills worthy of sharing without your prompting!)

Joan Piela—Gr. K, Woodrow Wilson #5, Garfield, NJ

Mr. Mayworth can play the guitar. He is called a musician but he works on telephones too. He sang a song about a frog. It was really funny.

Mrs. Crane can draw a picture of anything you can think of! She is an artist. Mrs. Crane drew every animal we could say in the alphabet. She is Jackson's mom.

"Deck-orate" The Halls!

When your students partner with their parents, your halls will be decked to the nines—all year round! Near the end of each month, duplicate a class supply of a seasonal shape or an enlarged copy of clip art for each child. Send the shapes/designs home along with a note asking parents to help their children decorate them as desired. They can use buttons, Cheerios®, ribbon, glitter glue, nuts and bolts—anything goes! When youngsters return their projects, display these festive, family-made projects along a hallway. Each time parents visit, they'll know they helped make your hall shine throughout every season.

Judy Clifford—Gr. K, Central Elementary, Point Pleasant, WV

From Parents With Love

Doesn't everyone enjoy receiving a love letter every now and then? Your kindergartners will too—especially when the letters come from their own parents! Ask each parent to write a loving letter to her child, then drop it off at your school office or mail it in care of you. When you feel the time is right, don a construction-paper postal hat and deliver the letters to the addressees. Encourage children to read their letters aloud (or ask you to do it) if they wish. Then store the letters for later. Whenever a child comes down with the blues—or just because—read his letter again!

Latresa Bray—Gr. K, Townview Elementary
Dayton, OH

October 26, 1998

Dear Jessica,

I hope you are having a good day at school. I just wanted to tell you how much I love you. And also, how I love to hear you sing!

Love,
Dad

P.S. I can't wait for our music night together!

Use with "Masterful Invitations" on page 127 and "Topic Trackers" on page 129.

Dear Parent,

This week at school, we are going to study

________________________.

Do you have anything on this topic that you'd like to share? If so, please send it to school with your child by

________________________.

We'll send it back!

Special instructions:

Every day I'm off to school,
And I think that's really cool!
But now it's time for you to see
This very special part of me!

Please come to Open House on

____

SNOW DAYS!

When the temperatures drop and winter is upon us, it seems that the same hope is on each child's mind—SNOW! Whatever your weather happens to be, youngsters will be eager to plow into this indoor storm of snow-themed learning activities. You'll find a load of language skills, a mound of math matters, a flurry of phonics fun, and mountains more!

ideas contributed by Lucia Kemp Henry

Setting The Scene

Set a snowy scene by "literature-ally" burying your little ones in a blanket of snow-related storytimes. To prepare for "Snowball Buddies," see the titles in "Snow Pals." For general snow literature, see "...And Snow On, And Snow On."

Snow Pals
Elmer In The Snow by David McKee
Kipper's Snowy Day by Mick Inkpen
One Snowy Day by Jeffrey Scherer
SnowPaws by Mary Alice Downie
Snow Riders by Constance W. McGeorge
The Snow Whale by Caroline Pitcher
Snowballs by Lois Ehlert

...And Snow On, And Snow On
The First Snow by David Christiana
Ridiculous! by Michael Coleman
Six Snowy Sheep by Judith Ross Enderle &
    Stephanie Gordon Tessler
The Snow Lambs by Debi Gliori
Snip, Snip...Snow! by Nancy Poydar
Snow Angel by Jean Marzollo
Snow Day by Moira Fain
Snow Inside The House by Sean Diviny
Snowed In by Barbara M. Lucas

Snowball Buddies

Shovel up visual-perception skills and mounds of creativity when your youngsters make these snowball buddies. In advance, collect a wide variety of art supplies (such as those shown in the illustration). After sharing some motivating literature* from "Snow Pals," give each child a large sheet of blue, purple, or black construction paper. Then encourage her to use the art supplies to create her own original snowball buddy. (Be sure to keep the books available for inspiration while children are working!) When each child's creation is complete, invite her to add some snowy touches to her project by making white-paint prints with a small piece of sponge, a spool, or a cylindrical block. When the paint is dry, back each project with a larger sheet of tagboard. Display these projects near the title "Snowball Buddies." There's "snow-body" like a snowball buddy!

Snowballs by Lois Ehlert (Harcourt Brace & Company) is a particularly good choice to complement this activity.

Snow, My Darlin'

This snowy song is drifting up with lots of language opportunities! In advance, write the song on chart paper. Sing and act out the song together. When children are familiar with the lyrics, encourage them to interact with the print according to their abilities. (See the suggestions to the right of the lyrics.)

(sung to the tune of "Clementine")

Roll some snowballs.
Roll some snowballs
Just to make a man of snow.
Make a **silly, chilly** snowman.
Make a snowman out of snow.

Suggested Interactions For "Snow, My Darlin' "

- Choose a child to highlight the word *snow*.
  — How many times do you see the word *snow*?
  — What sound do you hear at the beginning of *snow*?
  — What letter(s) make that sound?
  — Can you think of more words that start like *snow*?
  Write (or have children write) their responses on a large snowball cutout. Can they fill up the whole snowball?

- Choose a child to circle the rhyming words. Say the words together.
  — Can you think of other real or made-up rhyming words to replace the boldface words? *(nicey, icy; freezy, breezy; roly, poly; itty, bitty; happy, dappy; funny, sunny; bumpy, lumpy; frowning, clowning; scary, hairy)*
  Ask your budding songwriters to sing the song with their new rhyming words!

My Snow Book

The forecast is for significant accumulations of keen counting, remarkable reading, and imaginative illustrating when each child makes his own book filled with the snowy sights of the season. To prepare, gather the supplies listed below. Then give each child seven blue construction-paper pages and a copy of page 136. Instruct each child to cut apart his sentence strips and then to glue each strip to the bottom of a different page. Next, help each child follow the directions below to complete each page. When the books are finished, seat children in a circle with their books. Read each page together; then encourage each child to show his illustrated page—teacher-style!

Supplies:
scissors
glue
craft batting
toothpicks
stapler
wrapping-paper or wallpaper remnants
snowflake stickers (or snowflake printers and paint)
decorative supplies—such as sequins, small beads, dried beans, colorful pipe cleaners, buttons, fabric scraps, etc.

white paper towels
white foam sheets or trays
fine-tip markers
glitter glue

Page 1 Cut out a snowman from craft batting; then glue it to the page. Use the craft supplies to decorate the snowman as desired.

Page 2 Cut out the angel pattern; then trace it two times on the back of a piece of wallpaper or wrapping paper. Cut on the resulting outlines; then glue the angel cutouts to the book page. Give the angels a frosty glow with glitter glue.

Page 3 Tear three snowdrifts from paper towels; then glue them to the page.

Page 4 Cut out four snowballs from the foam sheets or trays. Glue them to the page.

Page 5 Attach five snowflake stickers to the page. (Or make five snowflake prints on the page.)

Page 6 Use the remaining art supplies to illustrate the page as desired.

Cover Use the remaining supplies to title and decorate the cover however you like! Then sequence and staple the pages behind the cover.

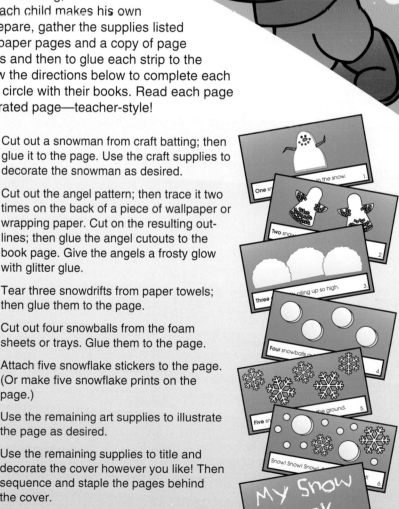

133

Snowed In!

Doesn't everyone like to be snowed in every once in a while? Go ahead—stir up a storm of these snowy activities in your classroom centers. It's fun being snowed in!

To create portable snowdrifts, loosely stuff sturdy, large, white plastic bags with newspaper or foam packing pieces. Then tie the bags closed. Stock a dramatic-play area with these stackable snowdrifts; then encourage children to build snow forts, castles, or whatever they imagine! (They might make a rather comfy reading area, too!)

For some fine-motor sculpting fun, fill a saucer sled with various sizes of foam snowballs. Nearby, provide a supply of plastic straws and a pair of scissors. Invite children to use the straws (or to cut pieces of straws) to connect the snowballs to form interesting snow sculptures. Encourage each child to make a sign to identify his creation on display.

Transform your water table into a snow zone for miniatures! After draining and drying the table, pour a supply of white foam packing pieces into the table. To encourage lots of dramatic play, add a supply of long blocks, and toy trucks, cars, trees, houses, animals, and people. There's snow all over the land!

A Flurry Of Flakes

These snazzy snowflakes will make your classroom glisten with wintertime wonder. And they can also be used as manipulatives in the activities on page 135.

You will need:

1 small paper plate per child	glitter glue
1/2 of a 2" foam ball per child	glue
a large supply of 3" lengths of blue, silver, and white pipe cleaners (sparkly and chenille pipe cleaners work well)	

To make a snowflake, insert several pipe-cleaner pieces around the foam-ball half to resemble the design of a snowflake. (Be sure to leave the flat side completely empty!) Add and twist on more pipe-cleaner pieces as desired. (Remember that no two snowflakes are exactly alike!) Write your name on the back of a paper plate; then punch a hole near the edge. Next, glue the flat side of the foam ball to the front of the plate. Apply the final glistening touch by squeezing a glitter-glue design on the ball. When you're not using these fabulous flurries as manipulatives or props, suspend them from the ceiling as shown. Oooh, in the *classroom,* snow is glistenin'!

Frosty Fellows

These child-made treats will hit the spot with a cup of hot chocolate and a snowy story or two.

For each child, you will need:
1 graham cracker
2 large marshmallows
1 paper plate
1 plastic knife

To share, you will need:
peanut butter
edible decorations, such as
    colorful candies, raisins,
    shaped crackers, and pretzels

To make one frosty fellow, spread a thin coat of peanut butter on a graham cracker. Then cut two marshmallows in half. Arrange three marshmallow circles on the graham cracker to resemble a snowperson. Microwave the cracker for five to eight seconds. Using the peanut butter as "glue," decorate your snowperson as you like.

Snow Graphs

Use the snowflakes made in "A Flurry Of Flakes" with these snowy math activities.

On separate sentence strips, write each color of pipe cleaner that your students used in their snowflakes. Add a sample pipe cleaner to each strip, if desired. (If some children mixed colors, make appropriate labels such as "blue-silver.") Then use each sentence strip to label a different column on a floor graph. Ask each child to place her snowflake on the graph according to color; then discuss what the graph reveals.

If you have a daily yes-no graph in your room, use this wintertime adaptation. First, divide a section of a bulletin board into halves. Label one half "yes" and the other "no." Write a question on a long strip of paper; then staple it above the headings. Put all the snowflakes in a basket near the board, along with a supply of pushpins. Ask each child to read the question, then indicate his answer by posting his snowflake in the appropriate column. What will it be—yes, no, or a dusting of each?

Sing A Song Of Snow

Fluff up these snowy wintertime songs and rhymes by prompting children to use their snowflakes (from "A Flurry Of Flakes") as manipulatives and/or props.

Five Little Snowflakes

Five little snowflakes
Dancing here and there.
Then one little snowflake blew away in the air!

Four little snowflakes
Dancing here and there.
Then one little snowflake blew away in the air!

Continue to repeat the rhyme, replacing the boldface number according to the lyrics. When you get to zero, finish up with the stanza below.

Zero little snowflakes—
Not one to be found—
'Cause five little snowflakes have fallen to the ground!

–by Lucia Kemp Henry

Snowflakes, One By One

One little snowflake with nothing to do.
Along came another, and
Then there were **two.**

Two little snowflakes playing in a tree.
Along came another, and
Then there were **three.**

Three little snowflakes looking for some more.
Along came another, and
Then there were **four.**

Four little snowflakes that finally did arrive.
Along came another, and
Then there were **five.**

Five little snowflakes having so much fun.
Out came the sun, and
Then there were none!

Snowflake, Snowflake
(sung to the tune of "Twinkle, Twinkle, Little Star")

Snowflake, snowflake, fancy free.
Snowflake, snowflake, dance with me.
Touch my **head,** then my **toes.**
Land on my **nose** where the cold wind blows.
Snowflake, snowflake, turn around.
Snowflake, snowflake, touch the ground.

Snowflake, snowflake, fancy free.
Snowflake, snowflake, dance with me.
Touch my **elbow,** then my **shoulder.**
Land on my **chin** where it's a little bit colder.
Snowflake, snowflake, turn around.
Snowflake, snowflake, touch the ground.

Snowflake, snowflake, fancy free.
Snowflake, snowflake, dance with me.
Touch my **ear,** then my **knees.**
Snowflake, I'm about to freeze!
Snowflake, snowflake, fancy free.
Snowflake, snowflake, dance with me.

135

Pattern And Sentence Strips

Use with "My Snow Book" on page 133.

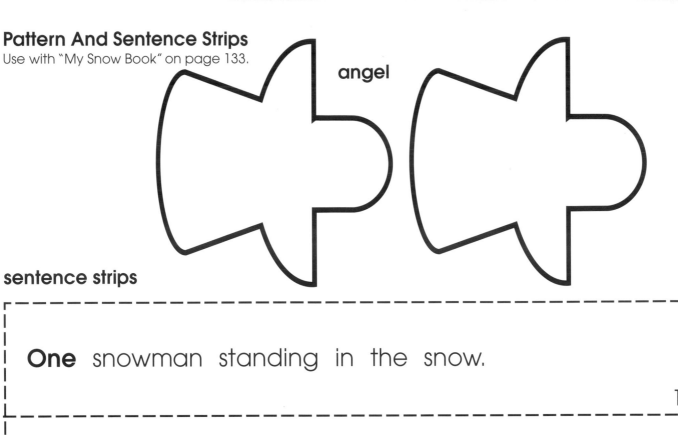

angel

sentence strips

One snowman standing in the snow.

1

Two snow angels with a frosty glow.

2

Three snowdrifts piling up so high.

3

Four snowballs quickly sailing by!

4

Five snowflakes falling to the ground.

5

Snow! Snow! Snow! Snow is all around!

6

Once Upon A Rhyme

Mother Goose is on the loose! So it's the perfect time to reinforce rhyme! Use this unique collection of child-centered ideas in your classroom to reinforce the concept of rhyme.

ideas by Susan A. DeRiso—Kindergarten Teacher

Jack Horner's Corner

Gather 'round and gather in, 'cause the rhyming switch is about to begin! In advance, write the words to "Little Jack Horner" on chart paper, leaving blanks as shown. Attach a piece of Velcro® to each of the blank spaces. Then attach a corresponding piece of Velcro® to each of a supply of sentence strips. On four of the prepared sentence strips, write the missing words from the rhyme. Attach these strips to the chart. Then, if possible, position the rhyme and sentence strips near a corner of your room. Invite children to come with you to Jack Horner's Corner.

To do this activity, read the rhyme together; then remove the original sentence strips. Invite children to "rewrite" the rhyme by thinking of new rhyming words. For each new round of the rhyme, write each suggested rhyming word on a separate sentence strip. Then attach it to the appropriate place on the poem. Encourage your class to read the new rhyme together. Watch those giggles multiply as each child gives this a try!

Little Jack Horner

Little Jack _____ nice

Sat in the _____ rice

Eating his Christmas pie.

He put in his _____ knee

And pulled out a _____ bee

And said, "What a good boy am I!"

Little Red Said

Since Little Red Riding Hood's episode with that pesky old wolf, she has been learning all kinds of interesting things. And now she thinks the time is prime for rhyme! In fact, she will allow *only* rhyming words in her baskets. (After all, can you think of a rhyme for *wolf?*) To prepare for this activity, gather three small baskets. Next, photocopy the rhyming cards on pages 141 and 142 and the pattern for Little Red Riding Hood on page 143. Color the picture of Little Red. Then cut apart the rhyming cards. Back the picture and the cards with tagboard; then laminate them. Next, choose three cards that do not rhyme; then tape each one to a different basket. Stack the remaining cards facedown in front of the baskets.

To do this activity, a child selects a card from the stack, says the name of the picture, and then drops it in the appropriate basket. He continues in this manner until each card that rhymes is in a matching basket. (If you'd like to make this activity self-checking, use a permanent marker to draw matching symbols on the back of the cards in each rhyming set.) It's off to rhyming land you go!

Name Fame Banners

A banner of rhyme reinforcement spreads over your classroom with this rhyming activity. To make each name banner, have each child think of a rhyming sentence using her own name—silly sentences are acceptable! Then write each child's sentence (leaving a blank for her name) on the bottom of a large vertical sheet of construction paper. Next, encourage each child to illustrate her sentence, then write her name on the back of the banner. Fold down the top of each child's banner; then hang it over the bottom part of a hanger, securing it with masking tape.

To use these banners, hang them on a wall, on a bulletin board, or from a ceiling where you've posted the rhyme shown below. Begin the activity by saying the rhyme together. Read each child's banner sentence in turn. Encourage children to complete each sentence by supplying the name of the appropriate classmate. Then read the sentence together, inserting that classmate's name. If you display these banners in your classroom for a while, children will delight in asking visitors to guess a riddle or two every now and then.

Hey, diddle diddle, I've got a riddle.
Who can it be? Look around, and you'll see!

Let's Play Cards!

Here's a rhyming card game for two to four players. In advance, duplicate the spinner wheel on page 141. To make a spinner, slip a paper clip onto a brad; then poke the brad through the center of the wheel and secure it.

To set up, use the rhyming cards from "Little Red Said." Give each player four cards; then stack the remaining cards facedown in the center. To play, the first player spins the spinner and says the name of the picture on which it lands. If he has a card that rhymes with that picture, he may add it to the bottom of the center pile. If he does not have a rhyming card, he draws one card from the center pile. If that card rhymes, he may discard it. If not, he keeps the card, and play continues with the next player. Continue in the same manner until one child has discarded all his cards.

A Wheel Deal

Rhyming is the real deal in this activity. For each child, enlarge and duplicate the "A Wheel Deal" patterns on page 144. Have each child use colored pencils to color the page. Then have him cut out all the pictures and patterns. Next, help each child stack and staple his picture cards to the front wheel where indicated. Using a brad, fasten the front wheel to the back wheel. Then tape a large craft stick to the back of the picture wheel.

To use the wheel, a child flips through the picture cards on the front wheel. For each picture shown, he uses the craft-stick handle to move the wheel until a rhyming picture appears in the opening. That's the deal!

Rhyming Day Matinee!

After all the time you've worked on rhyme, it seems only right that a party's in sight! Use the following ideas and activities to enhance a very special rhyming celebration.

It's A Wrap

A few days before your party, send the parent note below home with each child. As the gift-wrapped boxes begin to arrive at school, stack them in a conspicuous place in your room. During your rhyming celebration, invite each child to choose a box and tear into the rhyming surprises. Then have each child share the contents of her package. For added fun, have children arrange all the pictures and objects according to rhyming families. For each rhyming family in turn, choose one child to be the pointer. As that child points to each object or picture, encourage the class to say its name aloud. And, of course, you'll have to have many subsequent choral rounds in which youngsters try to say the names faster and faster!

Dear Parent,

Have you noticed that we're studying rhyming at school? We're going to have a rhyming party to celebrate all that we've learned!

To prepare for our party, please help your child find a box. Next have him/her find objects or pictures of objects whose names rhyme (such as a hat, a photo of a cat, and a drawing of a rat). Have your child put the objects and pictures in the box. Then help him/her wrap the box. Please send the wrapped box to school no later than _____. On the day of our party, we will exchange gift boxes and share all the rhymes inside!

It is true!
For all you do,
We thank you!

The Brag Bag

These little bags of goodies will tap into your youngsters' sense of rhyme. To prepare for this game, collect a supply of opaque bags. Put a different object in each bag. For each different bag, recite the rhyme below, filling in the blank with a word that rhymes with the name of the object in the bag. (Provide additional clues when appropriate.) When students name the object, choose one child to reveal the contents of the bag. When children are familiar with this game, invite each child to secretly hide an object in a bag. Then encourage each child to recite the rhyme and lead the class in guessing what is in his own brag bag.

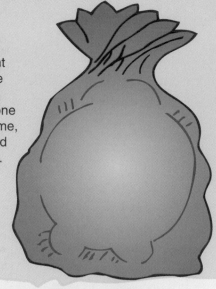

I don't mean to brag,
But I have something in my bag.
And if you listen to this clue,
I bet that you can guess it too!
It rhymes with _____.

The Race Place

Well, it looks like Jack and Jill are still trying to get up that hill! Youngsters will cheer as they play along in this rhyming race. In advance, duplicate one Jack and one Jill (page 145) for each child. Also duplicate the patterns on page 146. (Make two sets of the buckets.) Color the patterns from page 146; then prepare them for flannelboard use. Next, cut out a large green felt hill. Arrange the hill on a flannelboard along with the well (at the top) and Jack and Jill at the bottom, on either side of the hill. Keep the buckets nearby. Next, have each child color his Jack and Jill faces. Then have him glue the two faces back-to-back, inserting a large craft stick in the middle, to make a paddle.

To play the game, tell your students that Jack and Jill are racing up the hill. Then say a word pair. If the word pair rhymes, have the children show the Jill side of their paddles and chant, "Up the hill, Jill!" Then choose a child to place a bucket on the Jill side of the hill. If the word pair does not rhyme, have the children show the Jack side of their paddles and chant, "Take it back, Jack!" Then choose a child to award Jack a bucket. The first character to receive ten buckets is the winner!

Meet, Greet, And Eat!

There's nothing that reinforces a concept like that good old sense of taste! So prepare the foods below; then gather together for a good old-fashioned time of meeting, greeting, and eating. There's just one catch—before eating, your little ones must figure out the rhyme for each neat treat!

Fish In A Dish
Serve Goldfish® crackers in a decorative dish.

Horn Of Corn
Serve Bugles® corn snacks and guide youngsters to realize that these horn-shaped snacks are made from corn.

Mother Goose Juice
Duplicate the Mother Goose pattern on page 143. Color and laminate it. Then tape it to a pitcher of juice.

fan

shell

boat

pear

cat

cake

Spinner

Use with "Let's Play Cards!" on page 138.

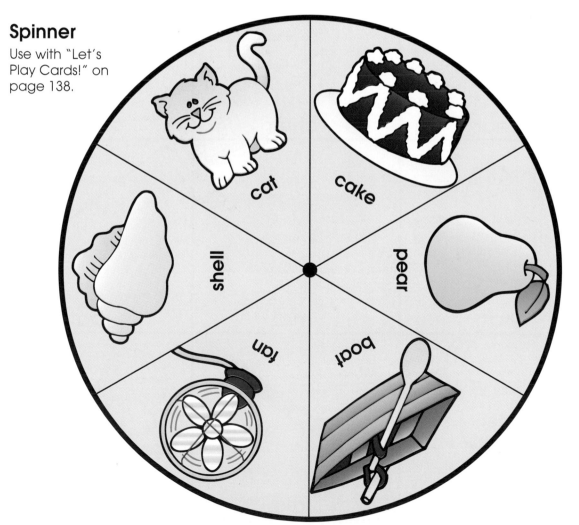

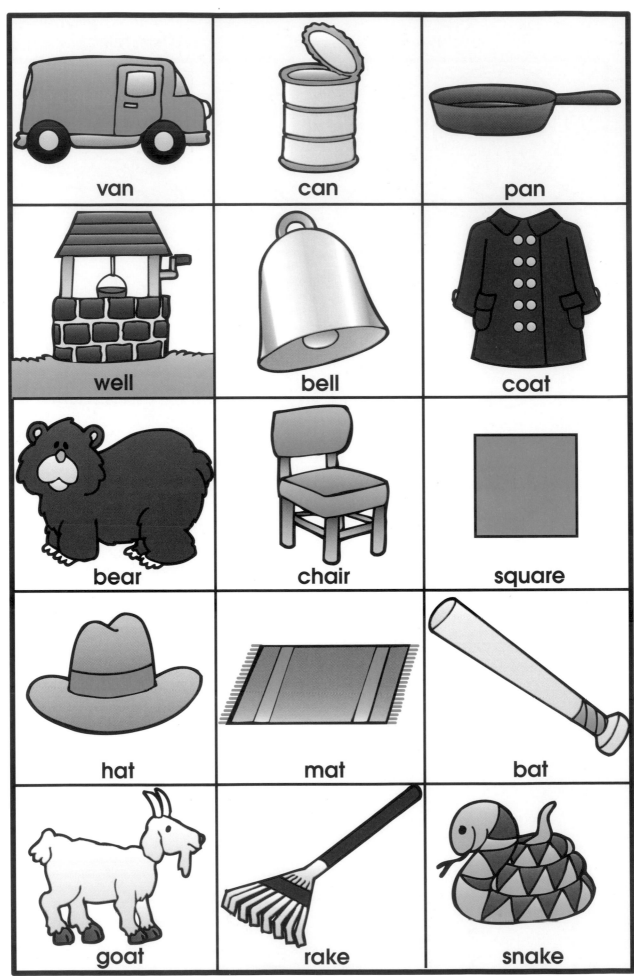

van	can	pan
well	bell	coat
bear	chair	square
hat	mat	bat
goat	rake	snake

Use with "Little Red Said" on page 137 and "Let's Play Cards!" on page 138.

©The Education Center, Inc. • THE MAILBOX® • Kindergarten • Dec/Jan 1998–99

Little Red Riding Hood
Use with "Little Red Said" on page 137.

Mother Goose
Use with "Meet, Greet, And Eat!"
on page 140.

Patterns
A Wheel Deal

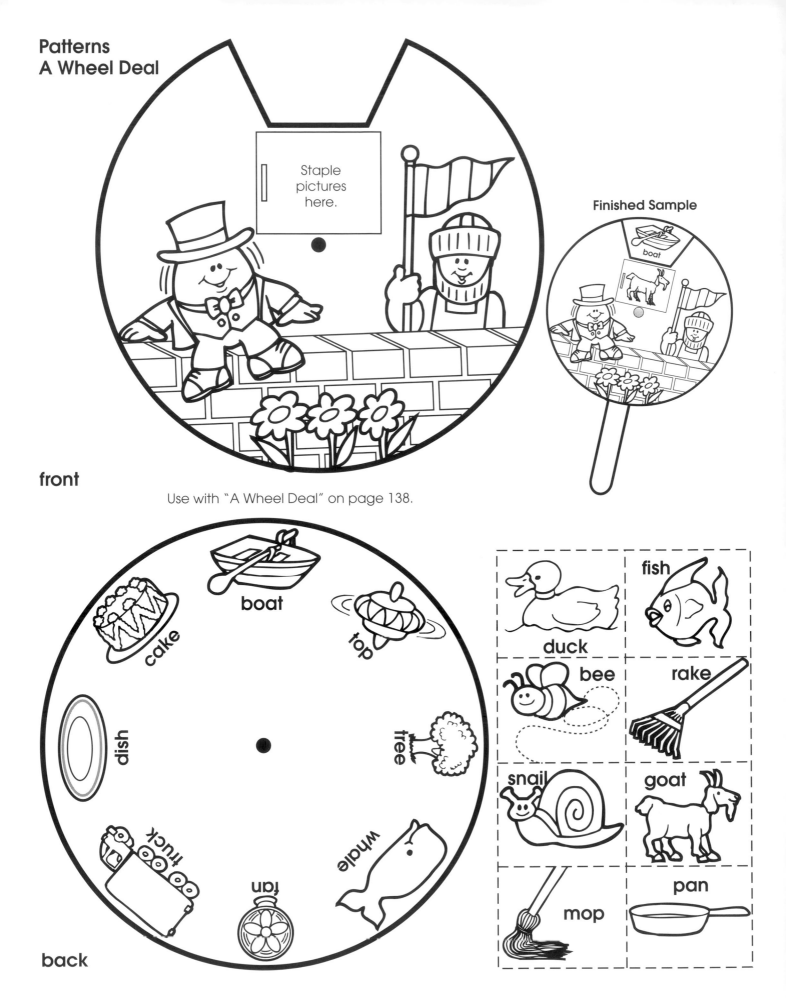

Staple pictures here.

Finished Sample

boat

front

Use with "A Wheel Deal" on page 138.

back

cake

boat

top

dish

tree

truck

whale

fan

duck

fish

bee

rake

snail

goat

mop

pan

Jack

Jill

Jack

Jill

Patterns

Use with "The Race Place" on page 140.

buckets

1 2 3 4

5 6 7 8

9 10

well

Jack   **Jill**

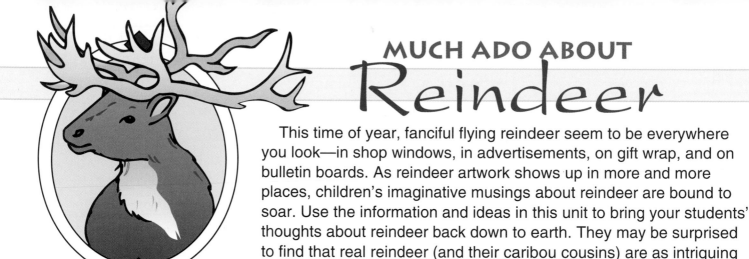

MUCH ADO ABOUT
Reindeer

This time of year, fanciful flying reindeer seem to be everywhere you look—in shop windows, in advertisements, on gift wrap, and on bulletin boards. As reindeer artwork shows up in more and more places, children's imaginative musings about reindeer are bound to soar. Use the information and ideas in this unit to bring your students' thoughts about reindeer back down to earth. They may be surprised to find that real reindeer (and their caribou cousins) are as intriguing and awe inspiring as the fabled ones!

ideas contributed by Joe Appleton and Karen Shelton

REALLY? ARE REINDEER LIKE THAT?

No reindeer in sight? No problem. Use this booklet and the suggestions on page 148 to help children learn some of the characteristics of these deer. For each child, duplicate the booklet pages on pages 150–152 and cut apart the triangular pages. As you introduce each page, discuss it by sharing the corresponding information on page 148. Bring the information to life by sharing illustrations from the books listed (below) and completing the "Try This" activities. Then have each child color his page, drawing in more details if he wishes to. When each page has been discussed and completed, assist students in making booklet covers as described in "Simply Irresistible Booklet Covers."

Fur keeps them warm.

SIMPLY IRRESISTIBLE BOOKLET COVERS

These student-made covers can be used with "Really? Are Reindeer Like That?" to make reindeer science booklets or with blank paper to make journals or other seasonal booklets. To make a cover, begin by folding an eight-inch square of construction paper to create a triangular shape. Sequence the triangular booklet pages, tuck them into the folded paper, and staple them near the fold. To make antlers, trace a partner's hands onto construction paper. Then cut out the hands, and glue them to the back of the booklet for antlers. There you have it! One fine reindeer booklet.

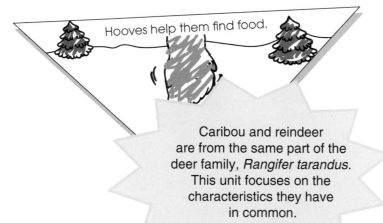

Hooves help them find food.

Caribou and reindeer are from the same part of the deer family, *Rangifer tarandus.* This unit focuses on the characteristics they have in common.

REINDEER AND CARIBOU BOOKS

Reindeer by Emery Bernhard (Holiday House, Inc.)
A Caribou Journey by Debbie S. Miller (Little, Brown and Company)
A Caribou Alphabet by Mary Beth Owens (Farrar, Straus & Giroux, Inc.)
Far North: Vanishing Cultures by Jan Reynolds (Harcourt Brace & Company)

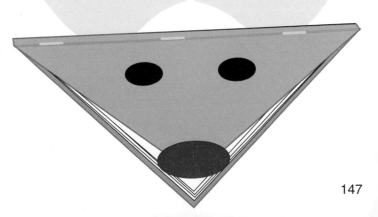

Did You Know?

Use these facts with "Really? Are Reindeer Like That?" on page 147.

All reindeer grow antlers.

BOOKLET PAGE 1—Usually, only male deer have antlers. But both male *and* female *reindeer* have antlers. Reindeer have their antlers for several months; then they fall off. New ones grow back later.

TRY THIS:
Antlers can be very heavy! Have students take turns carrying a heavy book or two on their heads (using their hands to balance the books). After a few minutes, find out what this experience tells your children about reindeer.

Fur keeps them warm.

BOOKLET PAGE 2—Reindeer live where it is cold and snowy. They have special fur that keeps them warm. Next to their skin, reindeer have thick, woolly fur. During the summer, the fur thins out so the reindeer will be cooler.

TRY THIS:
Have students take turns wrapping up in several layers of warm, woolly blankets for a few minutes. If a student becomes too warm, ask him to remove only one blanket at a time. How does it feel after a blanket comes off? Can he imagine wearing woolly blankets all the time?

Hooves help them find food.

BOOKLET PAGE 3—Reindeer have hooves that spread out when they walk on them. They use their hooves like scoops when it's time to find something to eat beneath the snow.

TRY THIS:
Hide a few plastic plants beneath Styrofoam® pieces in your sand table. Have students take turns using U-shaped plastic scoops to uncover the plants. Hey! This is what reindeer do when they are looking for plants in the snow!

Reindeer go to look for food together.

BOOKLET PAGE 4—Reindeer go from place to place looking for food to eat. They travel—or migrate—in large herds.

TRY THIS:
On the playground or in a gym, play follow-the-leader. Have children take turns leading the herd. Reindeer travel together the same way.

Reindeer live near the North Pole.

BOOKLET PAGE 5—Reindeer live near the North Pole.

TRY THIS:
Using a classroom globe, help children find the North Pole. Help them find Greenland, Alaska, Canada, Norway, and Sweden, explaining that this is where reindeer live.

Some reindeer help people.

BOOKLET PAGE 6—Some people follow reindeer herds. They make cheese and butter from reindeer milk! Other people have reindeer pull sleds and sleighs.

TRY THIS:
Attach a rope to a cardboard box (to serve as a harness as children role-play reindeer). Have children take turns loading the box with a few blocks from the block corner. Encourage children to take turns pretending to be reindeer slowly pulling the box from place to place.

TOO MANY TO COUNT?

When they're migrating, reindeer pour over the mountains and into the valleys by the thousands. To represent an ever-growing influx of reindeer in your classroom, you'll need several 8" x 60" strips of brown bulletin-board paper. Accordion-fold each strip at six-inch intervals. Enlarge the reindeer outline on page 150 so that it's about 8" x 6"; then cut it out. Trace it onto each stack of folded paper; then cut out the design, cutting through all thicknesses. (Do not cut along the dotted lines!) When each strip is unfolded, you'll have a set of ten reindeer.

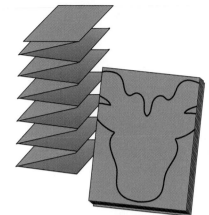

Post the first set of ten reindeer, and ask for several volunteers to color eyes and noses on the deer. Have students count the deer and post the total number nearby. The following day, repeat the process with an additional set of deer. Use all 20 reindeer for more counting practice and have students compare the totals from each day. Continue adding to your herd until all strips are used.

Our herd is ...
large   huge   enormous
big   giant
gargantuan   tremendous

THAT'S AN ENORMOUS HERD!

As your classroom is filling with the reindeer described in "Too Many To Count?", talk about how big—how extremely big—your herd is getting. Ask children to think of or find words that have a meaning similar to that of *big*. As the children contribute words over several days, post them near the reindeer. Periodically reread the words, discussing with the children which words seem to indicate the largest herd.

CLICKING ALONG

During their long, long annual migration, reindeer and caribou move in a wide range of ways. Sometimes they lope, trot, or run along. Sometimes they wheel around to escape a predator. At other times they make their way gingerly down hillsides or stroke strongly against the currents of mountain streams. Ask your students to imagine that they are reindeer and to act out several kinds of movements. After a while, explain that reindeer's hooves click as they walk, and encourage students to snap their fingers or tap rhythm sticks as they move along.

To get your children really prancing and pawing like reindeer, play recordings of several classical instrumentals. As the music plays, ask students to move to the beat as reindeer would.

Pattern

Use with "Too Many To Count?" on page 149.

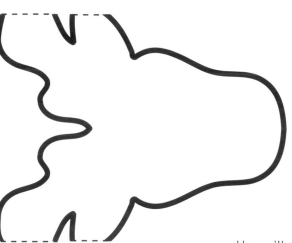

Booklet Pages

Use with "Really? Are Reindeer Like That?" on page 147.

All reindeer grow antlers.

Fur keeps them warm.

Bookmark

Reproduce and distribute during your reindeer unit.

Let's read about reindeer!

Try

A Caribou Alphabet
by Mary Beth Owens
Farrar, Straus & Giroux, Inc.

and

Reindeer
by Emery Bernhard
Holiday House, Inc.

Booklet Pages

Use with "Really? Are Reindeer Like That?" on page 147.

Hooves help them find food!

Reindeer go to look for food together.

Let's read about reindeer!

Try

The Wild Christmas Reindeer
by Jan Brett
G. P. Putnam's Sons

and

*What Could Be
Keeping Santa?*
by Marilyn Janovitz
North-South Books, Inc.

©1998 The Education Center, Inc.

Booklet Pages

Use with "Really? Are Reindeer Like That?" on page 147.

Reindeer live near the North Pole.

Some reindeer help people.

©1998 The Education Center, Inc.

5

6

SIGNING ALL AROUND

When we asked teachers to send us ideas
for using sign language in the classroom, our mailbox overflowed!
So, in this unit, we've compiled a bunch of the great tips and activities that we received
from caring, creative teachers across the country. As you begin to use these ideas
in your classrooms, you'll see signs of learning all around!

*ideas contributed by Marianne Cerra, Barbara Cohen, Sandy Drake, Barb Hartlaub, Rebecca Hughes,
Sherri MacLean, Beverly McNeilly, Vicki Shannon, and Tamara Hofer Voegeli—Kindergarten Teachers*

WHY SIGN?

- Teaching children sign language promotes deaf awareness and helps them become sensitive to the needs of others.

- Sign language enhances learning for kinesthetic learners.

- Sign language can be beneficial for ESL students and students with speech difficulties.

- Sign language builds finger dexterity.

- Signing promotes creative expression.

- Children love it!

CAN YOU TELL ME WITHOUT TALKING?

Before modeling formal sign language, use this idea to introduce your youngsters to the idea of *voiceless communication*. On individual strips of paper, write words, phrases, or ideas that people often communicate through gestures. (See the list at the right for ideas.) Put the strips of paper in a bag; then seat students in a circle. In turn, ask each child to come to the front of the circle, close his eyes, and pull a slip of paper out of the bag. Have him silently read the message on the slip (or whisper it to him). Then encourage him to act out the message until the class guesses it. Hey, you just *told* me something without words!

Pat Piechowski—Gr. K
Annunciation Regional
Bellmawr, NJ

read a book

yes
no
reading a book
drinking
combing hair
brushing teeth
washing hands
hot
cold
sleepy
happy
sad
scared
Be quiet.
Stop.
Come with me!
I don't know.
What time is it?
Yum!
Yuck!
That smells terrible!
That smells good!

SIGN IT ALL AROUND!

To provide lots of opportunities for youngsters to interact with sign language, collect some visual reminders for your classroom. A set of rubber stamps, sign-language alphabet cards, and simple sign-language books and dictionaries are great references to have on hand. The stamp set is particularly useful in a writing center. Simply arrange the stamps and a variety of paper in a center; then invite youngsters to stamp out their names and other words they know.

* *To order the stamps or request a catalog, call Harris Communications at 1-800-825-6758 (voice line) or 1-800-825-9187 (TTY). Or contact them at their Web site: www.harriscomm.com.*
* *Also see the resource list on page 155 to get your book collection started.*

Kristine Petersen—Gr. K
Mounds Park Academy
St. Paul, MN

153

FROM YOUR TEACHER, WITH LOVE

Make one of the signs that you teach your students a very special one! Begin by reading *The Kissing Hand* by Audrey Penn (Scholastic Inc.). Ask youngsters to pay special attention to the last page of the book that shows a raccoon paw making the sign for *I love you*. (Children might even spy this sign on another page in the book!) Then teach your little ones this hand sign. Use this sign daily at dismissal time (or anytime!) to show your youngsters that you're thinking of them and sending love their way.

Geraldine Riemer—Gr. K, Wenonah Elementary, Lake Grove, NY

EASY AS ABC

After teaching your youngsters the sign-language alphabet, try these language activities. Show students a sign-language letter; then have them respond with the phonetic sound (and vice versa). At another time, finger spell short or familiar words (such as *cat* or your students' names*)*. Have each child watch you and write the letters on a sheet of paper as you sign them. Can your students sound out the words? Do they recognize a classmate's name? All the signs here point to language learning!

Darleen Gibbs—Gr. K
Charlotte Christian School
Charlotte, MI

A IS FOR...

Here's a way to link beginning-sound recognition with sign language. As you introduce each letter sign, also demonstrate signs for words beginning with that letter. For example, make the sign for *A* followed by the sign for *apple* and *alligator*. After you teach some signs in tandem with several letters, encourage your students to take over the teaching! Have a good sign-language dictionary available (see page 155) and invite youngsters to find more signs associated with each alphabet letter. During a group time, invite each child to teach the class a sign that he has learned.

SINGING AND SIGNING

Music is an ideal place to weave sign language into your curriculum! Familiar words and repetitive refrains naturally lend themselves to signing. Use a resource book that translates songs into sign or simply pick a favorite song and teach youngsters the signs for some of the words. Good song choices include those that mention color words, days of the week, number words, or animal names.

154

HANDY SIGNS

Sign language is not only a great teaching tool; it's a great management tool, too! Teach youngsters the signs illustrated on this page (and others that you find useful). Then introduce a system whereby you and your students can silently signal each other for these needs or instructions. This is particularly useful when an individual student needs your permission or acknowledgement while you are otherwise engaged. Simply acknowledge the signing student with a nod and keep your lesson or group time going without interruption.

BATHROOM

DRINK

WAIT

LINE UP

STOP

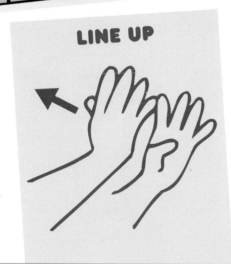

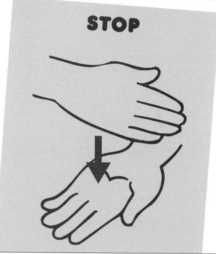

SIGN-LANGUAGE RESOURCES

- *The Handmade Alphabet*
  Written & Illustrated by Laura Rankin
  Published by Viking Penguin

- *Handsigns: A Sign Language Alphabet*
  Written & Illustrated by Kathleen Fain
  Published by Chronicle Books

- *Sesame Street Sign Language ABC With Linda Bove*
  Published by Random House Books For Young
    Readers

- *Simple Signs and More Simple Signs*
  Written & Illustrated by Cindy Wheeler
  Published by Viking Children's Books

- Books in the Handtalk series
  Written by Remy Charlip and Mary Beth Miller or
    George Ancona and Mary Beth Miller
  Illustrated by George Ancona
  Published by Simon & Schuster Children's Division

- *Signs For Me: Basic Sign Vocabulary For Children,
    Parents & Teachers*
  Written by Ben Bahan and Joe Dannis
  Published by DawnSignPress

- *The Gallaudet Survival Guide To Signing*
  Written by Leonard G. Lane
  Illustrated by Jan Skrobisz
  Published by Gallaudet University Press

Additional sign-language materials are available from DawnSignPress.
For more information, call 1-800-549-5350.

Strike It Rich With
Environmental Print!

Yee-ha! Here's a gold mine of ideas for incorporating environmental print into your classroom activities. Your little ones will hoot and holler as they develop a wealth of literacy skills with these hands-on activities. So dig right in!

We Can Read That!

Enlist the help of students to create this classroom display that will have each child exclaiming "I can read that!" To begin, send home a note requesting that parents help their children find samples of environmental print, such as candy wrappers, coupons, cereal-box labels, cookie packages, and familiar logos. When the print samples come in, laminate them. Then have each child attach his samples to a wall or bulletin board. Label the display "We Can Read That!" Encourage each child to include this display in your read-the-room activities. When adult visitors stop by, you will no doubt have loads of little ones ready and able to use this display to show off their reading skills.

Bobbie Hallman—Kindergarten
Burbank School, Merced, CA

Sort It Out

Environmental print and classification skills join forces to offer this valuable learning center. In advance, provide a supply of environmental print sources, such as old magazines, food wrappers and boxes, and newspaper ads. Ask student volunteers to search through the supplies and cut out words they can read. Then scan the collection of print samples, noting each category that is represented among them (such as cookies, candies, chips, restaurants, etc.). Next label a sheet of poster board with each of those categories, adding picture cues if desired. (Use more than one sheet of poster board if necessary.) Each day put a collection of print samples in a basket; then place the basket near the programmed board. To do this activity, have a child sort a few of the samples, then tape them in the appropriate sections on the board. When a board gets filled up, read and discuss the results during a group time.

Lori Kent
Hood River, OR

Pop Points

Pop, pop, fizz, fizz—oh, how refreshing this behavior display is! To create a display that encourages kids to read—and also reinforces good behavior—use an overhead projector to enlarge a soft-drink logo (such as Pepsi® or Coke®) onto a length of bulletin-board paper. Trace the logo; then color and laminate it. Next staple the logo to a background, along with a matching soft-drink cup for each child. Make pop points by attaching white stickers on a large supply of poker chips or milk-jug lids. Store the pop points in a soft-drink cup and keep that cup handy. When you wish to reinforce a child's behavior, simply write your comment(s) on a pop point; then invite the child to drop his pop point in his cup. At the end of each week, read each child's pop points aloud or invite him to take them home to share the good news with his family!

adapted from an idea by Deb Neumann—Kindergarten
Clearwater Public School, Clearwater, NE

Great Listening!

Print Puzzles

Have you been puzzled while pondering a new way to incorporate environmental print in your classroom centers? If so, then this idea is just the right fit for you! Ask your students to bring in empty food boxes, such as cake mixes, crackers, and cereals. Cut the front panel of each box into randomly shaped pieces to create a puzzle. Store each set of pieces in a different resealable bag; then place the puzzles in a center. (For your youngest children, you might want to provide matching box fronts to serve as guides when they reassemble the puzzles.) After completing a puzzle, challenge students to read as many words on the puzzle as they can. Hey, this makes chocolate cake! I can read that!

Lori Kent
Hood River, OR

Recycled Reading

Use these recycled workmats to expose students to print while protecting tabletops from messy craft projects. To make workmats, cut the printed panels from large cereal boxes or soda cartons. Place several of these workmats in your art area. When a child is working with a messy material, have him slip a workmat under his project. With the workmat in place, your students will be practicing reading without even realizing it! And cleanup is a simple toss in the recycling bin!

Deb Neumann—Kindergarten
Clearwater Public School
Clearwater, NE

It's All Zipped Up!

These nifty books are the perfect way to get your little learners reading. To make a book, punch three holes in the bottoms of several Ziploc® bags. Use brads or metal rings to fasten the bags together creating book pages. Then slide a different sample of environmental print into each of the bags. Seal the zipper on each bag, and there you have it—instant books that little ones can read at their leisure. For a variation, program strips of paper with a frame sentence, such as "I see…," "I like…," or "This is…." Tape each programmed strip to the top of a page. Invite youngsters to read the sentence, then complete it with the print in the bag. Maintain students' interest in these books by changing the print samples throughout the year.

Bobbie Hallman—Kindergarten
Burbank School, Merced, CA

Ready-To-Wear Reading

Make a statement—a fashion statement, that is! For each child, make a vest by cutting a paper grocery bag as shown. Invite each child to take his vest home and decorate it by gluing on samples of environmental print. When all the vests are back in school, invite each student to don his ready-to-wear reading apparel. Conduct a fashion show having children read the print on each model's vest. Now that's haute couture reading!

Lori Kent

WONDERFUL 100

There's something special about the number 100. It seems like *so much* to a kindergarten child. So reaching the 100th day of school—well, that's a pretty big deal! Let's celebrate!

100th-Day Attire

You don't have to be a seamstress extraordinaire to create this unique sweatshirt that's perfect to wear on the 100th day of school. All you need to know is how to sew on a button—well, actually *100* buttons! To begin, purchase a solid-colored sweatshirt and gather a collection of 100 buttons. Arrange some of the buttons to form the numeral 100 across the chest of the sweatshirt. Sew those buttons in place; then sew the remaining buttons in a scattered design on the front of the shirt. You can count on this shirt to grab youngsters' attention—and they can count on it, too!

Carolyn Bryant—Pre-K 5s, First Baptist Church Of Powder Springs, Powder Springs, GA

Count-By-Tens Top Hat

Now you've got something to wear, but what about your students? Invite them to create these tagboard top hats that provide practice with counting to 100 by tens. In advance, make a top hat for each child by stapling one long side of an 8 1/2" x 11" sheet of tagboard to the center of a sentence strip. On each hat, draw lines to create ten sections as shown. Then set up ten stations around your room, with directions and materials at each station for students to use in decorating the sections of their hats. For example, at one station a student might glue ten cereal pieces on one section of her hat. At other stations, she might stamp ten designs, write ten alphabet letters, or make ten fingerprints. Once a child has completed all ten stations and any glue or paint is dry, staple the ends of the sentence strip together to fit her head. This fashion statement says, "I can count to 100!"

Jennifer Farneski—Kindergarten
Watsessing School
Bloomfield, NJ

Stamp-A-Mat

For more practice with groups of ten, have youngsters create these festive placemats, perfect for use at snacktime or lunch on the 100th day of school! In advance, draw a design similar to the one shown on a 12" x 18" sheet of white construction paper. (Make sure your design has exactly ten sections around the border.) Duplicate a class supply of the placemat. Then invite each child to stamp a different small rubber stamp or Crayola® MiniStamper ten times in each section. Have each student color the numeral 100 in the center of his placemat. Now you're ready for some mealtime math!

Barbara Cohen—Kindergarten
Horace Mann School
Cherry Hill, NJ

Transformations

This mix of math and art might deliver...well, a *hundred* variations! For each child, die-cut one *1* and two *0's* from construction paper. Invite each child to arrange her die-cut numerals as she chooses to create a unique picture. Have her embellish her design with markers or crayons.

Barbara Cohen—Kindergarten
Horace Mann School, Cherry Hill, NJ

Mystery Math

This color-by-numbers puzzle will have your students showing off their numeral-recognition skills. To begin, give each child a duplicated hundreds chart. Then read aloud the following numbers. Tell youngsters they can reveal a mystery design by coloring in the square containing each number they hear. Ta da!

22	60	28	62	38	72	74
78	54	56	70	66	44	46
52	30	58	40	36	80	48
24	26	32	34	42	50	76
64	68	25	75	79		

Rhonda Chiles   Kindergarten
South Park Elementary, Shawnee Mission, KS

100-Second Snack

Prepare this simple cookie recipe on the 100th day of school (or anytime). It cooks up in 100 seconds. Really!

Beverly McNeilly—Kindergarten
Federal Terrace Elementary
Vallejo, CA

100-Second Cookies (makes approximately 100)

1 1/2 cups softened margarine
3 cups sugar
6 eggs
3 teaspoons vanilla
3 3/4 cups flour
3 teaspoons baking powder
1 1/2 teaspoons salt

Cream together the first four ingredients. Sift together the dry ingredients; then stir them into the creamed mixture. Drop about two teaspoons of batter onto each of the four quarters of a heated waffle iron and cook for 100 seconds.

Counting Cans

If you're going to count all the way to 100, why not count something worthwhile? Sponsor a canned-food drive, and invite little ones to help you keep track of donations. About two weeks before the 100th day of school, send home a note to parents asking them to send in cans of food that will eventually be donated to a local food bank or shelter. Explain your goal: 100 cans of food by the 100th day of school. As the donations come in, have the children sort the cans into groups of ten and keep track of the total on a chart. Once you've gotten 100 cans of food, arrange to drop off the food at your chosen charity. Hey, math makes you feel *good!*

Diana Phillips
—Kindergarten
Washington
Elementary
Jacksonville, IL

How Many Cans?

100!	
90	
80	
70	
60	
50	
40	
30	
20	
10	

btrfli

Spotlight On Black Americans

February is Black History Month—a time to spotlight the achievements and contributions of Black American citizens. The activities in this unit are designed to introduce Black American inventors and to encourage hands-on interaction with each remarkable achievement. So shine the spotlight on center stage and celebrate Black History Month!

ideas by Allison Ward

Tee Time!

In 1899, a Black American named George Grant invented the golf tee. This invention prevents the golf ball from rolling away while the golfer tries to hit it. Can you imagine what golfing was like before Mr. Grant invented this little aid?

Golf tees in the classroom? Sure! They make wonderful math manipulatives and foster fine-motor fun. In advance, collect a supply of multicolored tees. Put the tees in a bowl; then place the bowl in a center. Also provide a supply of the recording sheets on page 163. Instruct students to create color patterns with the golf tees, then record their favorite pattern on the sheet. Vary this activity by programming several recording sheets with patterns for students to copy. Display the finished tee patterns with the title "Tee Up With Patterns."

Kimberly Richard

Super Scoopers

Alfred Cralle invented the ice-cream scoop in 1897. Where would triple-decker ice-cream cones be without him? Gee, thanks a heap, Mr. Cralle!

Clearly, your dramatic-play area is the place to celebrate Alfred Cralle's oh-so-valuable invention! Set up an old-fashioned ice-cream parlor with batches of colored play dough for ice cream, a money drawer, dishes, paper cones, and—of course—an ice-cream scoop or two! You might even inspire students to create signs and a menu board, or even name the ice-cream flavors. Invite children to take turns being clerks and customers. As students learn and play in this center, prompt them to scoop out the play-dough ice cream with an ice-cream scoop and with a spoon. Ask which tool they like better.

It's A "Shoe-In"!

Before the invention of automobiles, many people used horses for transportation. But on rough and rocky terrain, can you imagine how the horses' hooves must have worn out? That's just where Oscar Brown comes into the picture. He invented the horseshoe in 1892!

Recognizing Oscar Brown's invention is an opportunity to flex those gross-motor skills! Obtain a plastic horseshoe set. After demonstrating how to play the game, set it up as a center or free-time choice for your youngsters. To add a math element to this center, teach students to keep score by counting each horseshoe that rings the stake.

That's A Good Point!

Let's suppose you have a brand-new pencil without a point. What do you do? Thanks to J. L. Love—the inventor of the pencil sharpener—you simply sharpen that pencil into a point!

To recognize J. L. Love's contribution to our everyday lives, make a sign similar to the one shown. Then collect a variety of handheld pencil sharpeners. Place this collection near your mounted pencil sharpener, along with a trash can and the sign. When a child needs to sharpen a pencil, invite her to use her choice of the sharpeners available. Get the point?

Writing Made Simple

Have you ever thought about a pen and exactly how the ink gets in it? Long ago, people had to constantly dip their pens in bottles of ink in order to write. But in 1890, W. B. Purvis invented a cartridge for fountain pens. What a difference!

Lots of fine-motor and writing practice will take place with this activity designed to acknowledge the invention of W. B. Purvis. First, demonstrate how a real fountain pen works and compare it to today's ballpoint pens and felt-tipped markers. Then provide a variety of pens for children to use in your writing center. For added interest, also provide a small container of washable ink (or thinned tempera paint) and quill pens (borrowed from your art teacher). Invite students to try all the different pens to write their names, days of the week, color words, etc. Then prompt them to compare the pen choices and state their preferences.

Biscuit Bakery

Have you ever wondered how bakeries and restaurants make all those perfectly rounded biscuits? In 1875, A. P. Ashbourne invented the biscuit cutter—that's how!

In honor of A. P. Ashbourne, set up a biscuit bakery in your cooking center. First, place parchment paper on baking sheets. Then personalize a space for each child. Next mix up a big batch of biscuit dough. Sprinkle flour on your clean work surface; then provide a rolling pin and a round biscuit cutter. Have each child roll out a small piece of dough, then use the biscuit cutter to cut out a biscuit. Instruct each child to place his biscuit by his name on the baking sheet. Bake the biscuits according to your recipe; then serve the warm biscuits with butter. Mmmm—good things come in round packages!

161

Traffic Language

Oh no—two cars are heading in different directions toward an intersection! How will they avoid crashing? Thanks to Garrett Morgan, there's no problem! Mr. Morgan invented the traffic light in 1923.

Teach your little ones about traffic signals with this idea based on the invention of Garrett Morgan. For each child, reproduce the signal pattern (page 164) on white construction paper. Also reproduce the light patterns (page 164) on red, yellow, and green paper. Instruct each child to cut out the signal, then color the outside part yellow or black. Then have him write "stop" in the top circle, "caution" in the middle circle, and "go" in the bottom circle. Next have him cut out the red, yellow, and green lights, then fold them on the line to create flaps. Instruct each child to glue the top of each light onto the corresponding signal. When the glue is dry, have him lift each light and read the meaning of the signal. Encourage each child to take his traffic light home and share it with his family.

Madame Walker's Beauty Shop

Madame C. J. Walker certainly had a hand in the shaping of the hairstylings of today. In the early 1900s, Madame Walker created a line of hair-care products for Black Americans. Because her products were so well loved, Madame Walker was able to rise from her roots of poverty to become the richest black woman in America in her time!

Madame C. J. Walker is an inspiration! Springboard off this inspiration to make a classroom beauty shop. To begin, collect several dolls with washable hair and put them near the water table. Provide brushes, combs, towels, shampoo, ribbons, barrettes, and hand mirrors. Invite the young stylists in this center to select a doll and wash, dry, and style its hair. Simply gorgeous—courtesy of Madame Walker!

Other Nifty Inventions

There are hundreds more inventions by Black Americans that have been developed into products that we use and benefit from daily. Here are just a few more to share with your kindergartners.

- Overgrown grass didn't stand a chance when J. A. Burr invented the lawn mower in 1899.

- Sarah Boone said good-bye to wrinkled clothing when she invented an ironing board in 1892.

- Mail found its home when P. B. Dowing invented the mailbox in 1891.

- Now you can pick up a few things when you ride your bicycle because J. M. Certain invented a bicycle basket in 1899.

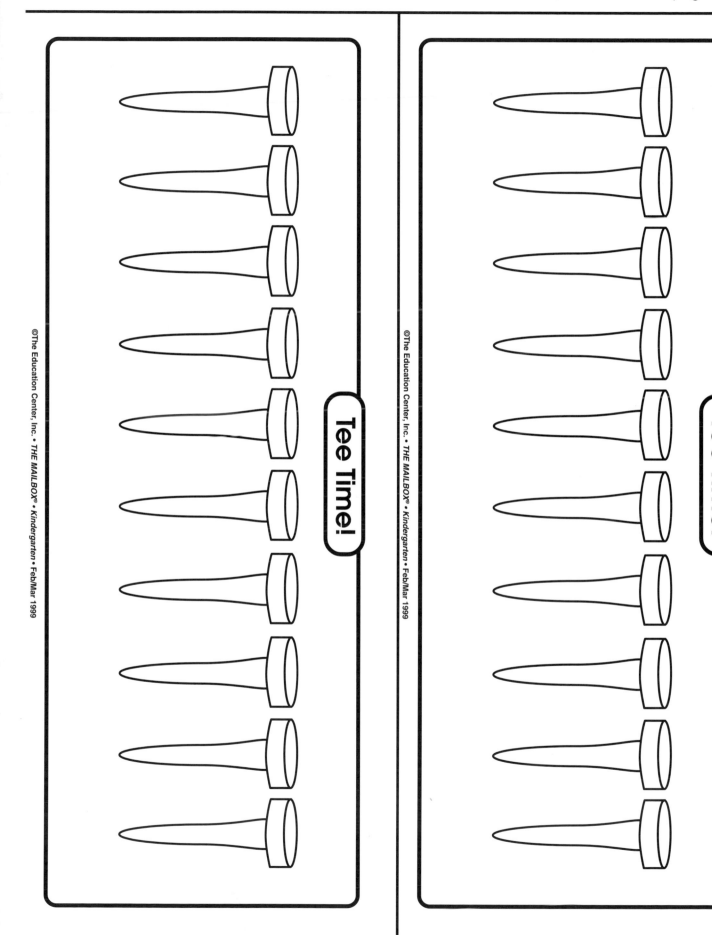

Tee Time!

Tee Time!

Traffic Lights

Use with "Traffic Language" on page 162.

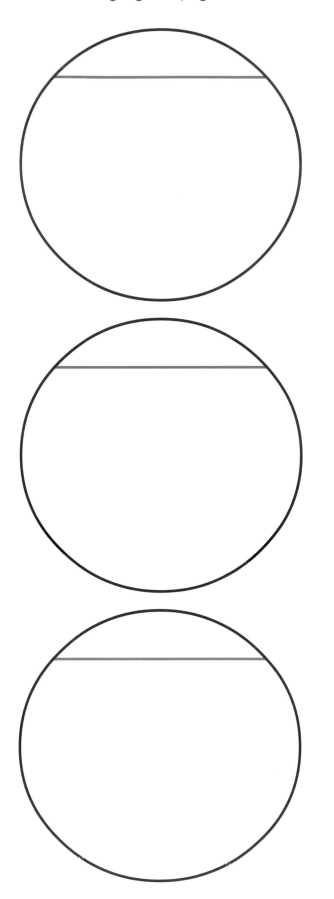

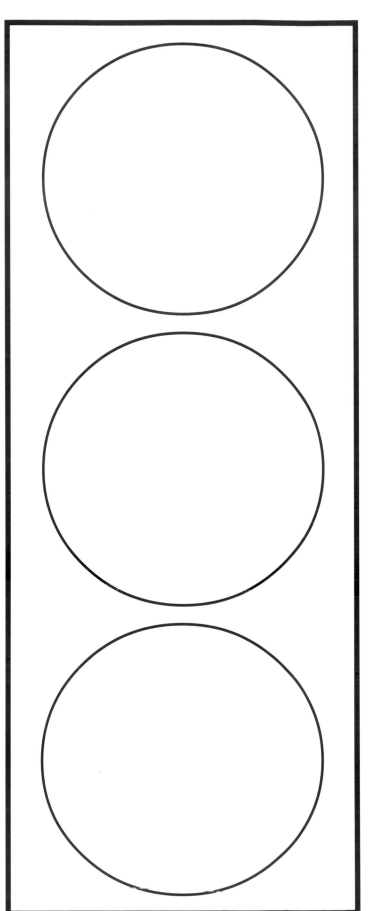

stamps

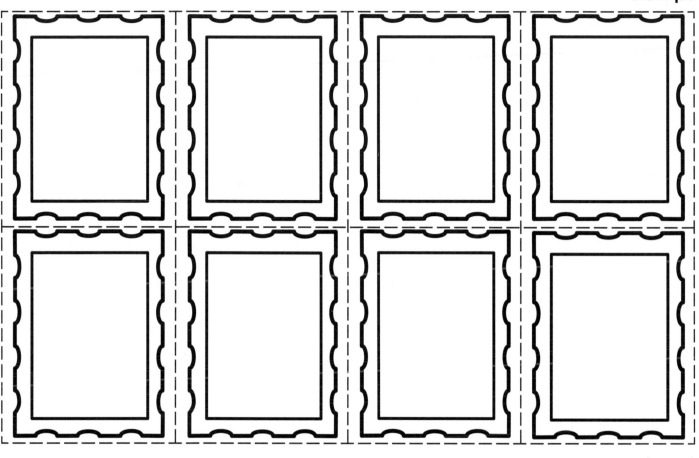

postcard

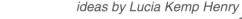

It's In The Mail!

With Valentine's Day on each child's mind, it's the perfect time to learn about the mail! So sign, seal, and deliver each of these mail-related activities designed for February learning fun.

ideas by Lucia Kemp Henry

Postal Possibilities

A familiar tune and a little postal pondering are all you need to reinforce this bundle of mail-related vocabulary. Since the melody is familiar, youngsters will catch on quickly and be eager to supply new lyrics.

What Can We Send In The Mail?
(sung to the tune of "Go In And Out The Window")

What can we send in the mail?
What can we send in the mail?
What can we send in the mail
At the post office today?

Oh, we can mail a **letter.**
Oh, we can mail a **letter.**
Oh, we can mail a **letter**
At the post office today.

(Repeat the second verse prompting youngsters to replace the boldfaced words with their own suggestions, such as *valentine, postcard, package, birthday card, invitation,* and *magazine.*)

Kim Richard

Fun Fact
A long time ago, mail was delivered across certain parts of the United States on horseback! Daring riders would race across the country as fast as they could to deliver the mail.

Let's Send A Letter!

Wrap up the whole process of writing and sending a letter with this child-made book. To prepare, cut a 7-inch length of string for each child. Then photocopy a class supply of pages 169–172. Have each child cut apart and trim his cover and pages 1–4, then sequence and staple them along the left edges. Instruct each child to set aside his pattern pages for later. Then follow the directions below. When all the books are finished, read them together. Then encourage each student to take his book home to share with his family. Let's send a letter!

Cover Write your name on the mailbox pattern piece (from page 171); then color and cut out all the book-cover patterns. Apply glue where indicated on the book cover; then see the illustration below for further details.

Page 1 Read and color the page. Then write a letter on the stationery provided (on page 172).

Page 2 Glue a small envelope to the page, flap facing out. Fold the letter; then slide it into the envelope. Seal the envelope.

Page 3 Write an address in the space provided. Attach a stamp where indicated—use stickers, promotional stamps, or child-made stamps.

Page 4 Cut out the type of mailbox (from page 172) that you are most likely to use. Glue the picture to book page 4; then draw a picture of yourself mailing the letter.

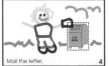

My Mailbox

Each child adds his own creative flair to these personalized mailboxes. For each child, temporarily slide a sheet of cardboard or a clipboard into a large manila folder (for protection). Then slit a mail opening as shown. Encourage each child to use a variety of art supplies to decorate his mailbox as he likes. Then staple only the top of each mailbox along the lower portion of a bulletin board.

*Note: In "Le Petit Post Office," students sort classroom mail according to how the mailboxes are displayed. So, for example, you might group the mailboxes according to the first letter in each child's name, such as *A* or *A–D.* For younger children you might group them by *boys* and *girls.*

Making Mail

Rich writing practice combines with creativity to make this a first-class mail-making center. In advance, decorate a box to resemble a class mailbox. Position this mailbox near the center. Then stock the area with construction-paper copies of page 165, a variety of other paper and/or stationery, stickers, envelopes, markers, colored pencils, scissors, and glue. If desired, display a valentine word bank nearby. Then encourage each child to use the materials to create the mail items as described below.

Valentine Word Bank

love	mine
like	you
be	fun
my	today
valentine	

Stamps In order to reach its destination—of course—every piece of mail must have a stamp! So when a child makes a piece of mail at this station, encourage him to color and cut out one of the stamp patterns. Then have him glue the stamp to his piece of mail. You might even have some children who would like to make a large supply of stamps to have on hand. If so, keep these stamps in a small box or case in the center.

Postcard To make a postcard, have a child cut out a postcard pattern. Then encourage her to decorate the front as she likes. On the back of the postcard, have the child write a short message to a classmate on the left side, then sign her name on the right. And, of course, add a stamp before mailing!

Dear Molly,
I lik yer dres.

Sally Barns

Letters Encourage children to use the supplies at the center to write or design their own original greetings. When they're signed, sealed, and stamped, they're ready for mailing!

Fun Fact
Collecting stamps is one of the most popular collecting hobbies in the world. It has been called "the hobby of kings and the king of hobbies." Some people collect only stamps with pictures of birds or railroads, for example. Other people collect stamps of a certain color or from other countries. The reason for stamp collecting can be anything—as long as it is fun!

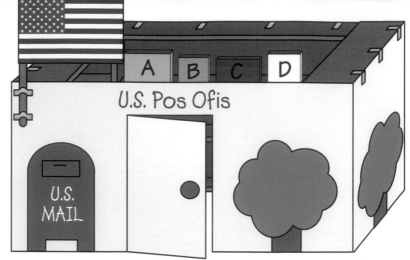

Le Petit Post Office

This kid-sized post office is the perfect place for piles of postal practice. Use a bookcase to designate a section of your room as the post office. Tape bulletin-board paper around the outside of the bookcase; then enlist the help of your students to turn it into a post office! Next arrange a collection of boxes—such as tissue boxes or shoeboxes—on the shelves. Label each box according to your mailbox groupings. (See the note at the end of "My Mailbox.") Also provide a few cloth sacks or tote bags (to resemble mailbags).

Then What?

What happens to the loads of letters that are dropped into mailboxes all over the United States (and classrooms!) every day? That can be summed up in three words: *collection, sorting,* and *delivery!* Involve your class of petite postal people in these three steps with the following activities.

Collection

After each center time (during which children send mail), assign a different child to be the letter carrier. Ask that child to empty the contents of the classroom mailbox into a basket. Then have her bring the basket to your classroom post office (described in "Le Petit Post Office").

Sorting

Ask your selected postal worker(s) of the day to sort the incoming mail into the labeled boxes.

Delivery

When the mail is sorted, choose several mail carriers to each take a mailbag and a group (or several groups) of sorted mail. Then have the mail carriers deliver the mail to the appropriate mailboxes (made in "My Mailbox").

Books About Mail & Mail Carriers

Dear Timothy Tibbitts
By Judith Ross Enderle &
   Stephanie Gordon Tessler
(Marshall Cavendish)

Good–bye, Curtis
By Kevin Henkes
(Greenwillow Books)

Grace And Joe
By Maribeth Boelts
(Albert Whitman & Company)

*Harvey Hare: Postman
   Extraordinaire*
By Bernadette Watts
(North-South Books)

Mailing May
By Michael O. Tunnell
(Greenwillow Books)

Monsters In My Mailbox
By Ellen Jackson
(Troll Associates)

Mr. Griggs' Work
By Cynthia Rylant
(Orchard Books)

Toot & Puddle
By Holly Hobbie
(Little, Brown And Company)

Tortoise Brings The Mail
By Dee Lillegard
(Dutton Children's Books)

Let's Send A Letter!

Glue here.

Glue here.

Glue here.

Glue here.

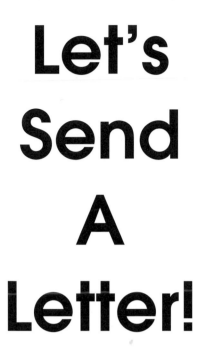

Write a letter.

1

Book Pages 2 And 3

Use with "Let's Send A Letter!" on page 166.

Put the letter in an envelope.
Seal the envelope.

2

Write the address.
Attach a stamp.

3

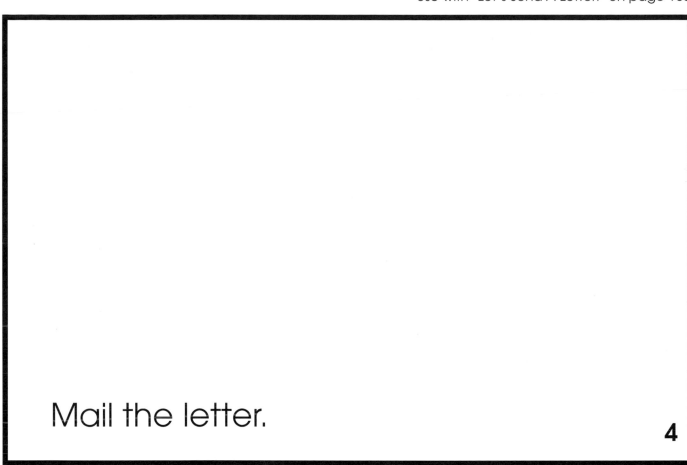

Mail the letter.

4

Book-Cover Patterns

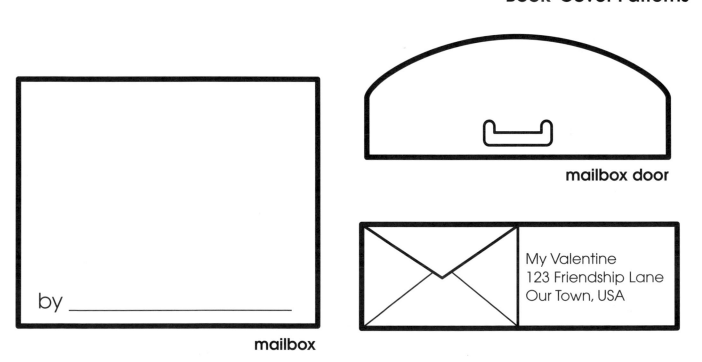

mailbox door

by _____

mailbox

My Valentine
123 Friendship Lane
Our Town, USA

Patterns For Book Pages 1 And 4

Use with "Let's Send A Letter!" on page 166.

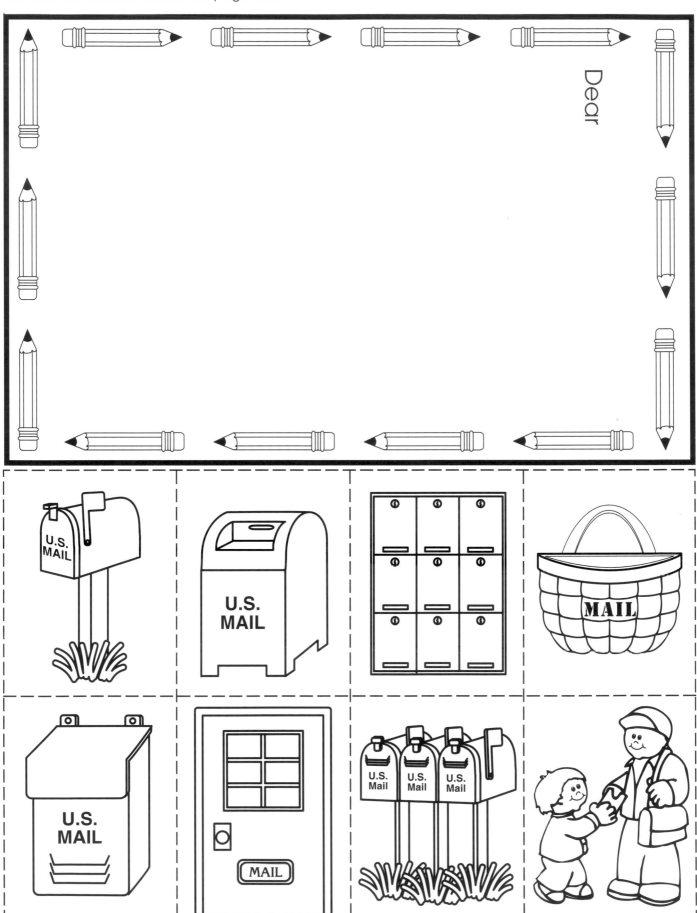

Dear

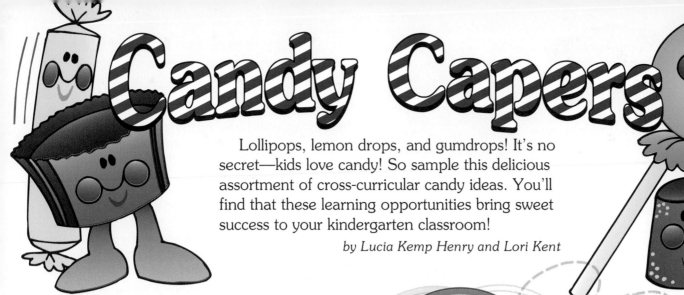

Candy Capers

Lollipops, lemon drops, and gumdrops! It's no secret—kids love candy! So sample this delicious assortment of cross-curricular candy ideas. You'll find that these learning opportunities bring sweet success to your kindergarten classroom!

by Lucia Kemp Henry and Lori Kent

Welcome To Candy Land!

Usher your youngsters into their candy unit with this thematic welcome. To begin, make several lollipop props by painting a supply of cardboard gift-wrap tubes white. When the paint is dry, cut slits on opposite sides of one end of each tube (as shown). Next insert a paper plate into each slit. Cover each paper plate with colorful plastic wrap; then gather it around the top of the tube. Secure the plastic wrap with a length of curling ribbon. Use another longer length of curling ribbon to tie each group of three lollipops together. Then gently spread the tubes until these lollipop bouquets stand independently. Arrange the lollipops along your hallway or around your classroom door. To complete (and personalize) this enchanting entrance, cut out a class supply of construction-paper gumdrops. Write a different child's name on each gumdrop; then spray clear glitter over all of them. Create a delightful stepping-stone path by using clear contact paper to affix each gumdrop to the floor leading up to your door. There's no doubt about it—your little ones are entering Candy Land!

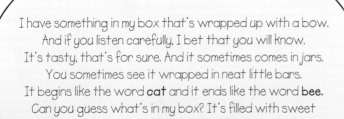

I have something in my box that's wrapped up with a bow.
And if you listen carefully, I bet that you will know.
It's tasty, that's for sure. And it sometimes comes in jars.
You sometimes see it wrapped in neat little bars.
It begins like the word **cat** and it ends like the word **bee**.
Can you guess what's in my box? It's filled with sweet

_____!

A Sweet Mystery

This confection detection will get your classroom candy capers rolling! Prepare by separately covering the top and bottom of a small pizza box with gift wrap. Fill the box with an assortment of wrapped candies, such as cinnamon disks, butterscotch drops, Gummy treats, caramels, and root-beer barrels. Close the box and tape a bow to the top. During a group time, present the box to your students as you say the riddle on the left. When the contents have been guessed, open the box. Then discuss each different type of candy as you write the different names on a sheet of chart paper (in graph style). Wrap up this introductory activity by inviting each child to sample a candy from the box!

A Jar Full Of Favorites

Predicting and graphing come right along with these sweet hands-on activities. To prepare, restock the candy box (from "A Sweet Mystery") with the same kinds of candies. Also glue one of each candy under the corresponding label on the graph referred to in that same idea. Then display the open box alongside a clear jar. After reviewing the candy names on the graph, ask each child to select his favorite candy from the box, then drop it in the jar. When each child has participated, pass the jar around and encourage each child to visually examine the contents, then predict which candy has the most. When all the predictions have been made, place the graph on a flat surface; then ask each child to remove one candy from the jar and place it on the graph. Discuss what the graph reveals. Then drop a new number of candies in the jar and arrange all the supplies in a center. When a child visits this center, encourage her to do the predicting and graphing independently.

caramel | lollipop | peppermint | root-beer barrel | fruit chew

Name Coltrane

I Lik it bkoz it haz gum in the midl.

A Penny For Your Thoughts

The opinions of your little candy connoisseurs are all welcome in this expressive language activity. For each child, duplicate the candy-machine pattern (page 177) on construction paper. Invite each child to use scented markers to draw his favorite kind of candy in the candy chute. Then have him write/dictate about that candy in the large open space. Finally, have him glue a penny to the coin slot. After each child shares his candy report, display all of the finished projects with the heading "A Penny For Your Thoughts."

Candy Container Classification

Environmental print provides the reading material for this classification activity. In advance, send a note home requesting that each child bring in the packaging from one of his favorite types of candy. (Provide some extras for those children who do not bring their own.) Label a large, three-column chart "boxes," "bags," and "wrappers." Then tape this chart to the inside of your classroom door. As each child brings in his candy container, invite him to share it with the class, read the main words aloud, and then glue the container to the chart on your door. Encourage students to "read the door" as part of your read-the-room activities or as they transition from inside to outside times.

boxes | bags | wrappers

Dandy Candy Booklet

When youngsters make this little sweetie of a booklet, you'll see those emergent reading skills unwrapping all over your classroom! For each child, duplicate pages 178 and 179 on construction paper. Have each child cut out her cover, pages, and patterns. Then guide her to complete each page. (See the directions below for your reference.) When each page is complete, instruct each child to sequence the pages behind the cover, then staple the booklet along the left edge. Be sure to read these little treats together during a group time!

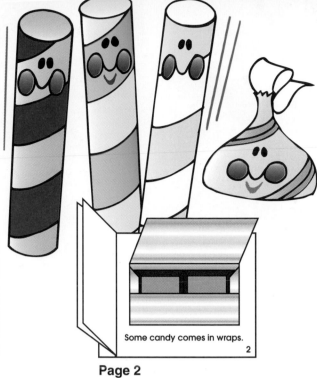

Cover
Write your name. Draw candies in the box. Glue the lid pattern to the box where indicated.

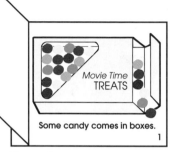

Page 1
Color the box. Use scented markers to draw little candies inside the box window and on the box flap.

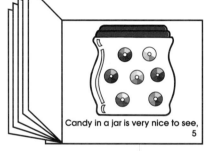

Page 2
Glue the center of a 3 1/2" x 3 1/2" piece of foil or tissue paper to the middle of the page. Color the candy bar pattern, then glue it to the center of the wrapper. Fold the wrapper flaps over the candy bar.

Page 3
Stick colored sticker dots inside the bag.

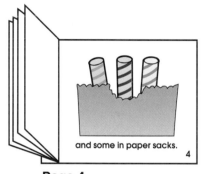

Page 4
Color the candy sticks however you like. Cut a small rectangular shape from a paper bag; then glue it to the booklet page, leaving the top edge open.

Page 5
Glue small craft jewels or sequins to the jar to resemble fancy candies. (Colorful hole-punched dots would work well too, if needed.)

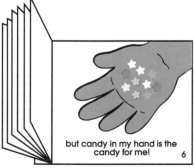

Page 6
Color the hand to resemble your own. Glue cake-decorating candies to the palm of the hand.

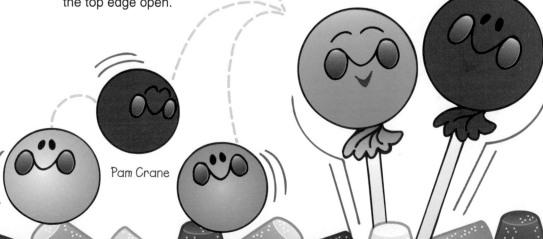

Pam Crane

175

Aromatic Art

Wake up each child's sense of smell as he makes these pleasing projects in your art center. To prepare, sprinkle matching colors of unsweetened Kool-Aid® into a variety of colors of tempera paint. Then pour the same colors of Kool-Aid® into separate (empty) salt shakers. Invite each child who visits this center to paint precut tagboard candy cutouts with the sweet smelling paint. While the paint is still wet, shake on a corresponding color of Kool-Aid®. When the paint is dry, punch a hole in each candy; then tie a length of ribbon through the hole. Suspend the candies from your ceiling to create a deliciously scented display.

Heads Or Tails

This center activity addresses reading, writing, arithmetic—and more! To prepare, stock a center with a class supply of snack-sized bags of M&M's®, napkins, paper cups, paper, and crayons. Working with a small group of children, have each child create a chart on her paper like the one shown. Then instruct her to pour her bag of candy into her cup. Next have her gently pour the cup of candy onto her napkin. Then have her count the number of candies that landed with the *M* side up, and the number that landed with the *M* side down. Ask her to record this information on her chart. Have her repeat the activity several times, recording the information each time. Afterward, encourage her to write the *greater than, less than,* and *equals* symbols appropriately on her chart. When all is said and done, of course, the candy may be eaten!

up		down
7	<	11
9	=	9
6	<	12
10	>	8

Luscious Literature Links

The Candystore Man by Jonathan London
The Chocolate Wolf by Barbara Cohen
Chocolatina by Erik Kraft
The Gumdrop Tree by Elizabeth Spurr
The Gummy Candy Counting Book by Amy & Richard
  Hutchings
The Incredible Jelly Bean Day by Taylor Maw
Jelly Beans For Sale by Bruce McMillan

Name _____

Booklet Cover, Pages, And Patterns
Use with "Dandy Candy Booklet" on page 175.

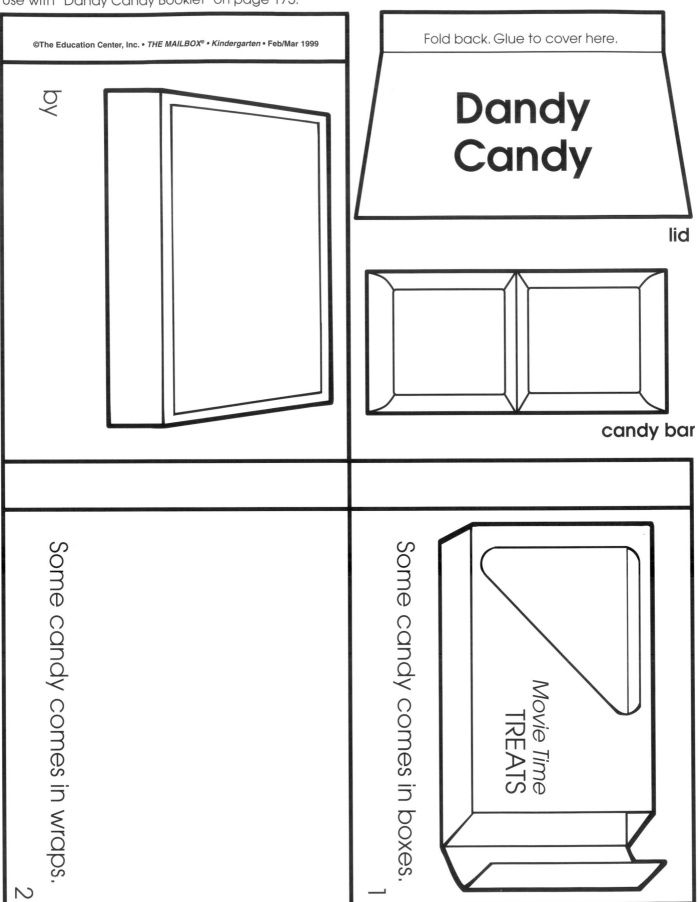

by

Fold back. Glue to cover here.

Dandy Candy

lid

candy bar

Some candy comes in wraps.
2

Some candy comes in boxes.
1

Movie Time TREATS

Candy in a jar is very nice to see,

5

Some candy comes in bags,

3

but candy in my hand is the candy for me!

6

and some in paper sacks.

4

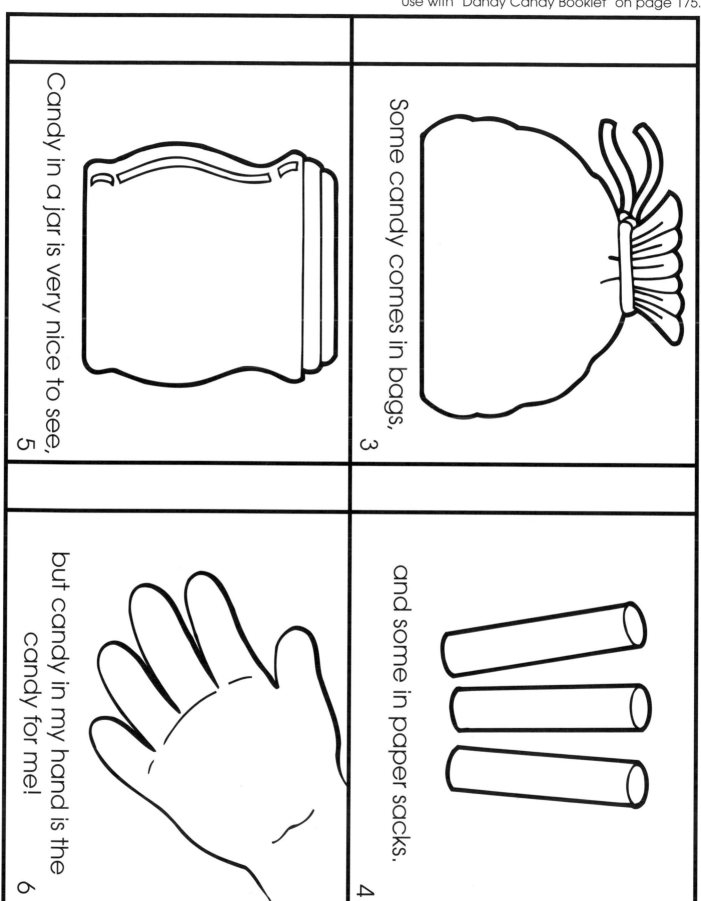

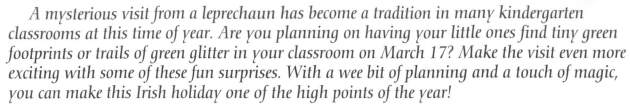

St. Patrick's Day Surprises

A mysterious visit from a leprechaun has become a tradition in many kindergarten classrooms at this time of year. Are you planning on having your little ones find tiny green footprints or trails of green glitter in your classroom on March 17? Make the visit even more exciting with some of these fun surprises. With a wee bit of planning and a touch of magic, you can make this Irish holiday one of the high points of the year!

Paddy's Pudding

Have a friendly leprechaun leave the makings of a yummy treat for your youngsters. To prepare, purchase one 3.4 ounce box of instant pistachio pudding for every six students in your class. Empty the pudding mix into a plain brown bag and label the bag "Magic Mix." Print simplified directions (from the box) for making the pudding on the opposite side of the bag. Then write the note shown on green paper.

Arrange for another teacher or an assistant to leave the note, the bag of pudding mix, and a carton of milk in your classroom while you are out with your students. Upon your return, read the note aloud; then whip up the pudding in a bowl or blender. Wow—it's *green!*

Joe Appleton—Gr. K
Hillandale Elementary
Durham, NC

Patricia Halstead—Gr. K
Chesapeake, VA

Dear children,
I came to visit, but you were out. Enjoy this magic treat!

Your friend,
Paddy
Paddy the Leprechaun

Wee Little Houses

Explain to your students that they might be able to entice a leprechaun to visit by building some tiny little houses just right for a tiny little leprechaun. Provide a variety of scrap materials, such as oatmeal boxes, cardboard tubes, bottle caps, fabric, ribbon, spools, and small plastic containers. Give each

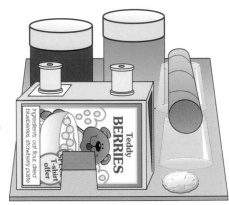

child a square of corrugated cardboard to use as a base. Then have each child glue, staple, or tape together the materials of her choice to create a leprechaun house.

Leave the houses on display in your classroom, and arrange for a colleague to drop in (while you and your students are out, of course) and leave a gold foil–wrapped chocolate coin in each house. Surprise!

Joe Appleton—Gr. K

Leprechaun Storytime

Enlist the help of a parent or other adult to give your kindergartners a storytime they'll always remember. Ask the adult to dress up like a leprechaun in green clothing, a red or white wig, a pointy hat or bowler, and silly shoes. Have your leprechaun look-alike come in to read a St. Patrick's Day story to your students. Faith and begorra—it's a real live leprechaun!

Blarney Stones

If you're looking for an inedible treat for your leprechaun visitor to leave behind, you're in luck! Prepare a class supply of Blarney stones for your little lads and lassies to take home. Collect a small, smooth stone for each child (or purchase a bag of landscaping pebbles from a local home-improvement store). Wash the stones and let them dry. Use glow-in-the-dark paint to paint a shamrock on each stone. Print the poem shown several times on a sheet of copy paper; then duplicate a class supply of the poem on green construction paper. Have your leprechaun visitor leave a stone and a copy of the poem for each child.

Susan Brandeberry—Gr. K
Washington Elementary
Gallipolis, OH

Tuck me in bed.
Turn out the light.
Lay down your head.
Sweet dreams tonight!

Peeking Puppet

Youngsters won't believe their eyes when they see a leprechaun peeking in their classroom window! In advance, purchase or make a small puppet that resembles a leprechaun, and find an adult helper. Ask the helper to scatter gold foil–wrapped chocolate coins on your playground just prior to the leprechaun visit. Once the coins are in place, your helper puts the puppet on her hand and crouches just below your classroom window. At a designated time, she makes the puppet peek in at the children. Announce to the class that you've just seen a leprechaun! Caution the children to sit very still and be very quiet, so that they might see the leprechaun, too. After a couple of peeks, announce that you think the leprechaun is heading for the playground. Encourage the students to line up and walk to the playground (while your helper runs in the opposite direction). They'll be thrilled to find the candy treats awaiting them!

Patricia Halstead—Gr. K, Chesapeake, VA

Magic Beans

For this elaborate but oh-so-fun St. Patrick's Day trick, you'll need a box, some green foods, a class supply of dried beans that you've spray-painted gold, a simple map of your classroom, a class supply of lollipops, and the help of another adult. Have youngsters help you set a trap for a leprechaun by placing the green foods in the box. After the children are gone for the day, remove the green foods and replace them with the map, on which you've drawn a line leading to the classroom location of your choice. Hide the beans in that location.

The next day, when your students discover the map, encourage them to follow the map's directions until they find the gold beans. Invite each child to plant one of the beans in your outdoor sandbox and say a few magic words. Return to the classroom for a while (to give the beans time to grow). Have your adult helper stick the lollipops in the sand where the beans were planted. Then bring the children back out to discover the surprise.

Linda Rasmussen—Gr. K, Donner Springs Elementary, Reno, NV

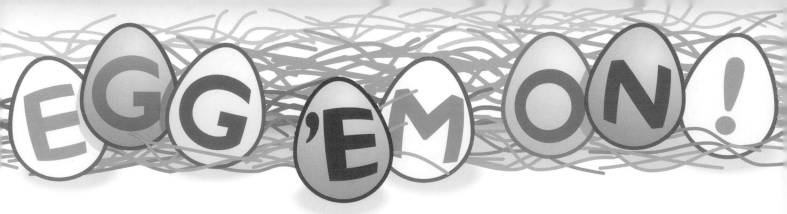

EGG 'EM ON!

Whether they're fried, dyed, made from sugary crystals, or rich, dark chocolate—'tis the season for eggs! Use these Grade-A ideas to hatch a basketful of cross-curricular learning in your springtime classroom.

ideas by Lucia Kemp Henry and Michele Dare

Crackin' Up

A wealth of information—and an impressive new vocabulary word—will feed kids' curiosities as you introduce them to an array of critters and creatures that come cracking out of eggs. To make these introductions, share your choice of the books below. After discussing the book(s), prompt your students to brainstorm a list of *oviparous* animals. Write children's responses on a large egg-shaped cutout. Display this cutout for reference and reading throughout your egg studies. Wow, it's nice to meet *all* of you!

Chickens Aren't The Only Ones
By Ruth Heller
Published by Grosset & Dunlap

Egg: A Photographic Story Of Hatching
By Robert Burton
Published by
Dorling Kindersley Publishing, Inc.

Knock, Knock

"Who's there?" Youngsters will find out when they make this class book! In advance, program a sheet of construction paper as shown; then duplicate a class supply of that page. Also duplicate a class supply of page 186 on white construction paper.

To begin, give each child a blank sheet of construction paper and a copy of the egg patterns. Instruct each child to cut out his eggs, then glue the blank one to the center of his construction paper. Ask him to illustrate one *oviparous* animal on that egg. Next, have each child cut his other egg along the dotted line, then attach those two egg parts to the page with a brad. (Some students might even like to color this top egg to resemble their creatures' egg colors.) Next, read the text page together. Then have each child write/dictate a response on his illustrated page. (To promote ease of reading, encourage each child to follow the text pattern shown.) Assemble the book so that each child's page is behind a text page; then add a cover. During a group reading time, have your class read the text-only pages aloud. Then invite each author to read his page to the class. This just-right reader will be cracked open again and again. (And it's a great home-school traveler to let parents in on your studies, too!)

programmed sheet

Chicken, Chicken, Where's Your Egg?

This oviparous version of Doggy, Doggy, Where's Your Bone? is fun to play and reinforces science concepts as well as new vocabulary. After reviewing the meaning of the word *oviparous*, seat children in a circle. Select one child to be It. Ask her to name an oviparous animal, then turn to face the outside of the circle and cover her eyes. While her eyes are covered, secretly give another child a plastic egg to hide behind his back. Signal It to turn around by having the class chant, "[Turtle, turtle], do not rest. An egg is missing from your nest!" Have the [turtle] guess who has her egg by asking a specific child, "Are you oviparous?" If a child does not have the egg, he replies, "No, I am not," and the [turtle] continues looking. If the child does have the egg, he replies, "Yes, I am!" and hands the egg to the [turtle]. Then the [turtle] chooses the next person to be It. Continue play until each child has had a turn to be an oviparous animal in search of her egg.

Gathering Eggs

Sure, you could simply *hand* each child a plastic egg, but this idea scrambles in learning fun along the way. In advance, collect a class supply of different-colored plastic eggs. Tuck a marshmallow chick, bunny, or some jelly beans inside each egg before securely sealing it. Then hide the eggs in your classroom. To begin, instruct each child to search the room for one egg. When a child finds an egg, have him hold the egg in his hand and sit down near the egg's hiding spot. (Instruct students to keep their eggs sealed until you signal them!) In turn, have each child use positional words to describe where he found his egg, then sit in the circle. When everyone is seated in the circle, ask youngsters to unscramble themselves by grouping according to egg color. Once they're in color groups, take a crack at singing the song to the right.

> Mine was **under** the water fountain.

Scrambled Eggs

All listening ears must be sunny-side up to keep pace with this upbeat song! In advance, write the song on chart paper. (To match your batch of eggs, substitute appropriate color words if necessary.) With children seated and eggs in hand (see "Gathering Eggs"), sing the song. Encourage each child to follow the directions in the song according to the color of the egg that she is holding. Sing the repeated verses as fast as your little group can handle. Are you ready? Let's scramble!

(sung to the tune of "The Muffin Man")

Oh, do you have a special egg,
A colorful egg, a pretty egg?
Oh, do you have a special egg
You're holding in your hand?

Stand if you have a purple egg,
A yellow egg, a blue egg.
Stand if you have an orange egg
And pink and green besides!

Repeat the second verse replacing the boldfaced words with other action words, such as *jump, bow, twirl, whistle, wave,* and *sit down.* For added fun, have children pass their eggs one person to the right each time you repeat the second verse!

*After youngsters eat the treats, save the eggs for other activities in this unit!

—adapted from a song by Lucia Kemp Henry

Graduated Graphing

Since by now your egg theme is rolling right along, keep it up! Use the plastic eggs from "Gathering Eggs" (on page 183) to begin this graphing sequence. Also, cut a matching construction-paper egg for each plastic egg.

Real

To prepare a real graph for the plastic eggs, write each egg color on a separate word card. Align the cards and tape them to a flat surface, such as a table or countertop. In turn, ask each child to choose an egg from the collection, then use a pinch of clay to secure it in the corresponding column of the graph. (For visual clarity, prompt children to position their eggs in the same direction.) When each egg has been graphed, guide your class to discuss what the graph reveals.

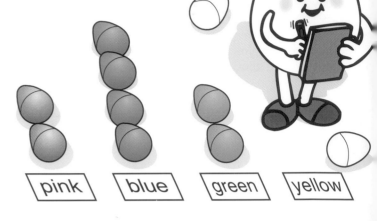

Picture

To create a picture graph, write each egg color on the bottom of a sheet of chart paper. In turn, invite each child to remove an egg from the real graph and place it in a basket. Then instruct her to take a construction-paper egg of that same color and tape it to the picture graph. Continue in the same manner until all the real eggs are in the basket and the picture graph is complete. Does the picture graph show the same information as the real graph? Why? Did your youngsters forget what the real graph revealed? If so, encourage them to set it up again for more discovery learning!

Written

And now…the opportunity to transfer information to print! To prepare, photocopy the graph on page 187. Write each of the colors in your egg collection in a different space on the graph. Then photocopy a class supply of this programmed graph. Arrange all the eggs in a center along with the stack of graphs and crayons. Encourage each child to visit this center and color the graph to correspond to the egg collection. Have each child bring his graph to a group time and discuss the results. (If desired, do this graphing activity several days in a row, varying the number and color of eggs each day. Instruct children to keep their graphs from day to day. Then encourage them to compare the information on all of the graphs.)

"Egg-lettes"

These adorable little booklets can be adapted to address a variety of skills. And they're awfully fun for youngsters to take home and show off to their families! To make one booklet, photocopy the booklet patterns (from page 188) on construction paper. Cut out the patterns along the bold outlines. Then glue the tabbed end of one pattern piece to the back of the other pattern piece. Accordion-fold the booklet as shown. Use the booklets in the ideas that follow.

glue tab to back

Counting Chicks—Before They've Hatched

In this case, counting chicks before they've hatched is definitely recommended—in the form of eggs, of course! In advance, follow the directions in "Egg-lettes" to help each child make a **yellow** booklet. Then, according to each child's abilities, have her write a book title and numerals or number words on the pages of the book. (See the illustration for examples.) Next have each child use paint to make the corresponding number of thumbprint eggs on each page. When the paint is dry, invite her to use fine-tipped markers, colored pencils, and other art supplies to add any desired details on the pages and to the cover.

Sounds Like *Egg*

Fry up some phonics practice with this variation on the egg booklet. Follow the directions in "Egg-lettes" to help each child make a booklet of any color. Have each child title his cover "Sounds Like Egg." Then encourage children to look through old magazines and workbooks and cut out pictures that begin with the short *e* sound. Instruct each child to glue one picture to (or draw a picture on) each page of the booklet. Exceptional!

Designer Eggs

This is the place to emphasize creativity and descriptive vocabulary! Follow the directions in "Egg-lettes" to help each child make a **white** booklet. Have each child use crayons to title and decorate the front cover. Then have her open the booklet so all of the pages are lying flat. Encourage each child to choose from a variety of art supplies to decorate *every other* egg-shaped page. Then have each child write or dictate text to describe each illustrated page. Lastly, fold the book to close it. Have each child paint over the front cover with a thin watercolor wash.

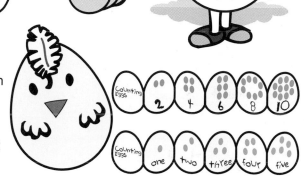

Crack Open An Egg Book

Big Egg
By Molly Coxe
(Random House, Inc.)

Dora's Eggs
By Julie Sykes
Illustrated by Jane Chapman
(Little Tiger Press)

The Great Egg Hunt
By Maggie Kneen
(Chronicle Books)

Little Lumpty
By Miko Imai
(Candlewick Press)

Emma's Eggs
By Margriet Ruurs
Illustrated by Barbara Spurll
(Stoddart Publishing Co., Ltd.)

Egg Patterns

Use with "Knock, Knock" on page 182.

Booklet Patterns

Use with "Egg-lettes," "Counting Chicks—Before They've Hatched," "Sounds Like *Egg,*" and "Designer Eggs" on page 185.

Apply glue here.

Farm Phonics

What's happening down on the phonics farm? Plenty! Take a gander at these farm-related ideas that have been designed to yield a bumper crop of phonemic awareness in your students. See you down on the farm!

by Lori Kent

Everybody's Talking!

Farmyard animals are naturals when it comes to helping youngsters focus on sounds in language. To prepare, cut out a large barn shape from sturdy red paper; then mount it on a bulletin board. To get your children thinking about farmyard animal sounds, read your choices of the titles on page 192. Afterward, ask students to name animals that live on a farm. List each suggested animal on the barn cutout. One by one review the animals on the list, asking children to make the corresponding sound of each animal. Next, invite each child to illustrate the animal of his choice. Then give each child a white construction-paper speech bubble. Encourage him to write the noise his animal makes in the speech bubble. (Prompt invented spelling by reminding children that even adults spell animal sounds many different ways!) Then mount each animal and its sound around the barn cutout. Have each author-illustrator share his picture and sound with the class. Then have the class say that sound together. Boy, oh, boy—everybody's talking on the farm!

horse cat chickens
cow mouse baby chicks
goats dog rat
sheep llama duck
pigs lamb frog
flies

Naaa

Kwak

Moo, moo, moo

Sounds Like This

Your classroom farm will be teeming with the sounds of language with this little tune. Teach your little farmhands the song below. Each time you repeat the song, substitute a different animal from your list (made in "Everybody's Talking!"). According to your youngsters' abilities, challenge them to identify the sound at the beginning, middle, or end of each animal noise. It sounds like *this!*

The Animals On The Farm

(sung to the tune of "The Wheels On The Bus")

The [cow] on the farm goes
[Moo, moo, moo,]
[Moo, moo, moo,]
[Moo, moo, moo.]
The cow on the farm goes
[Moo, moo, moo,]
All through the day.

189

Farmyard Families

These farmyard friends are great for reinforcing the concept of word families. Duplicate and cut out the hen and pig found on pages 193 and 194. Color them. Then duplicate each of the corresponding letter wheels (page 195) on construction paper. Laminate the animals and the letter wheels. Cut out a window along the dotted line on each animal. Then use a brad to attach each wheel to the corresponding animal. Use these farmyard friends with small groups of children. It's all 'round fun!

p ig

h en

Have You Heard The Word?

You won't need to scratch around long to find a whole bunch of rhyming practice in this activity! In advance, write the poem below on a large sheet of chart paper, but draw blanks in place of the bracketed words. Then duplicate, cut out, color, and laminate the worm, bug, corn, and scratch patterns from page 196. As you read the poem aloud, pause at each blank, asking children to identify the picture that completes that couplet with a rhyme. Have a child use reusable adhesive to post the correct picture in that blank. Once youngsters get the hang of this, remove the pictures and store them in a basket near the poem. Then encourage students to use this interactive poem in your read-the-room activities.

worm

Hungry Chicks

Said the first hungry chick, with a funny little squirm,
"I wish I could find a juicy, little [worm]."

bug

Said the second hungry chick, with a funny little shrug,
"I wish I could find a juicy, little [bug]."

corn

Said the third hungry chick, looking so forlorn,
"I wish I could find a juicy piece of [corn]."

"See here!" said their mama from a little garden patch.
"If my little chicks are hungry, come and [scratch, scratch scratch!]"

scratch, scratch, scratch

by Lori Kent

190

What's In Your Barn?

In this activity, your little farmers find exactly what belongs in their own barns. In advance, photocopy a class supply of the barn patterns (page 192) on red construction paper. Give each child a barn cutout and a paper lunch bag. Instruct each child to choose a letter to write on her barn. (She might choose the first letter of her name, the first letter of a family member's name, or just a letter that she likes to write.) Have each child glue her barn to her paper bag. Next, instruct each child to take her bag home and find two or more objects or pictures that begin with that letter's sound. Then have each child return her bag to school. During a group time, invite each child, in turn, to name the sound on her barn, then share the items inside. After each child's turn, sing the song below, substituting that child's name and her barn items in the appropriate places. E-I-E-I-Wow!

(adapted to the tune of "Old MacDonald")

Farmer [Heather] had a barn,
E-I-E-I-O.
And in that barn [she] had a [letter sound],
E-I-E-I-O.
With a [object name] here
And a [object name] there,
Sounds in the barn are everywhere!
Farmer [Heather] had a barn,
E-I-E-I-O.

Who's On The Farm-O?

Farm animals provide a familiar context for this activity that reinforces onsets and rimes. In advance, enlarge, photocopy, and cut apart the animal cards on pages 197–199. Then cut each animal card so that the onset and the rime are separated. Make stick puppets by taping a craft stick to the back of each of the pieces. Then, as you sing the song below, manipulate the appropriate puppets. When youngsters are familiar with the idea of the song, invite each child, in turn, to choose a puppet set. Then have him lead the class in a round of the song (substituting the appropriate words) as he manipulates the puppets.

Way Down On The Farm-O
(sung to the tune of "Bingo")

Down on the farm we'll find a /p/
And then we'll add an /ig/.
Now we have a pig.
Now we have a pig.
Now we have a pig.
Way down on the farm-o!

Books For "Everybody's Talking!"
(on page 189)

Barnyard Banter
By Denise Fleming
(Henry Holt And Company, Inc.)

Barnyard Lullaby
By Frank Asch
(Simon & Schuster Books For Young Readers)

Barnyard Tracks
By Dee Dee Duffy
(Bell Books)

Cock-a-doodle-doo: A Farmyard Counting Book
By Steve Lavis
(Lodestar Books)

Cock-a-doodle-moo!
By Bernard Most
(Red Wagon Books)

Cows In The Kitchen
By June Crebbin
(Candlewick Press)

Nothing At All
By Denys Cazet
(Orchard Books)

Quacky Duck
By Paul & Emma Rogers
(Little, Brown And Company)

More Barnyard Books

William Wegman's Farm Days
By William Wegman
(Hyperion)

Farmer Duck
By Martin Waddell
(Candlewick Press)

The Hullabaloo ABC
By Beverly Cleary
(Morrow Junior Books)

One Windy Wednesday
By Phyllis Root
(Candlewick Press)

The Thing That Bothered Farmer Brown
By Teri Sloat
(Orchard Books)

This And That
By Julie Sykes
(Farrar, Straus & Giroux, Inc.)

Order books on-line.
www.themailbox.com

Barn Patterns

Use with "What's In *Your* Barn?" on page 191.

en

Pig Pattern
Use with "Farmyard Families" on page 190.

ig

©The Education Center, Inc. • *THE MAILBOX®* • *Kindergarten* • April/May 1999

194

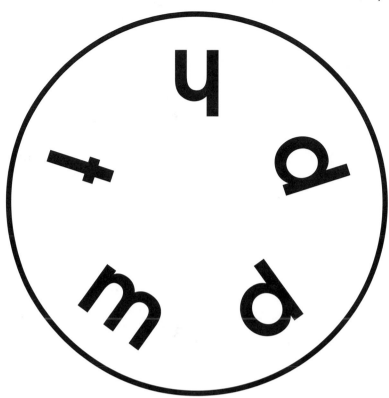

hen letter wheel

pig letter wheel

worm

bug

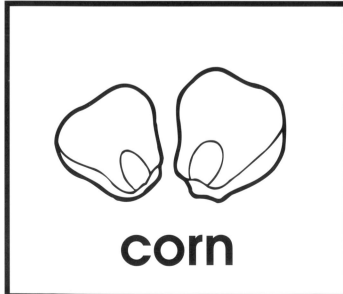

corn

scratch, scratch, scratch

hen

horse

dog

duck

Animal Cards
Use with "Who's On The Farm-O?" on page 191.

goat

cat

pig

cow

chick

goose

mouse

sheep

Calling All Cows!

With National Dairy Month in June, the "moo-oo-ood" is just right for contemplating cows! So use the herd of cross-curricular ideas in this unit to enhance your cow-related studies.

ideas contributed by Lucia Kemp Henry

What We Learned
- A cow is a female (that's a girl).
- A cow that makes milk is called a dairy cow.

What We Want To Know
- How big is a cow?
- What do cows eat?
- Can a cow jump?
- Are cows friendly?
- Do cows lie down?

What We Know
- Cows make milk.
- Cows say "moo."
- Cows live on a farm.

Setting The "Moo-oo-ood"

To introduce your study of cows, cut out three large construction-paper cows. (If desired, enlarge and trace the cow pattern on page 204.) Title the first cow "What We Know," the second, "What We Want To Know," and the third, "What We Learned." Display the cows where they can be easily seen by your students. Then ask children to share what they already know about cows. Record each response on the first cow cutout. Next ask students what they would *like* to know about cows and record these responses on the second cow. Then read aloud the delightfully written *Cow* by Jules Older (Charlesbridge Publishing, Inc.). After discussing the book—and throughout your cow studies—record new questions and discoveries on the corresponding cows.

* If *Cow* by Jules Older is not available, use suitable parts of *The Milk Makers* by Gail Gibbons (Scholastic Inc.) or substitute encyclopedia pictures as you paraphrase the text.

Colorful Cows

Isn't it cool that dairy cows come in a collection of colors? Use this idea to record this information and to reinforce specific color recognition, classification, and the scientific names of the different breeds of dairy cows. In advance, gather a supply of crayons in cow-color shades (light and dark brown, gold brown, orange brown, reddish brown, grayish brown, black, etc.). Then photocopy a class supply of the cow report form (page 204) on white construction paper. Ask each child to choose a breed of cow. Help him write the name of that type of cow on his page. Then have him study the appropriate pictures in the books noted in "Setting The 'Moo-oo-ood', " and color his cow to resemble that breed. After each child shares his page with the group, encourage students to graph their cows according to breed. This finished graph herds you right into math opportunities!

This is a _brown swiss_ cow. Jerome Name

This is a _holstein_ cow. Hannah Name

Just The Facts
A cow is a mature female of the cattle family.
A dairy cow is a cow that makes milk.

The Milk Makers

Use the song below to encourage children to creatively describe colors and shades of colors, and to reinforce the most distinguishing fact about dairy cows—they are the milk makers!

(sung to the tune of "Do You Know The Muffin Man?")

Some dairy cows are [black and white],
[Black and white, black and white].
Some dairy cows are [black and white].
And dairy cows make milk!

Some dairy cows are [reddish brown],
[Reddish brown, reddish brown].
Some dairy cows are [reddish brown].
And dairy cows make milk!

Repeat the song, encouraging children to substitute descriptive color words or phrases for the underlined parts.

— by Lucia Kemp Henry

Got Milk?

Once youngsters have studied those milk-making bovine buddies, invite children to explore the wide variety of foods that are made from milk. In advance, collect an assortment of empty, labeled food containers. Program one large paper bag with "Dairy Products" and a second bag with "Nondairy Products." Arrange the bags and the labeled containers in a center. To prepare youngsters for this activity, prompt children to brainstorm a list of dairy foods. Write their responses on chart paper. Afterward, have small groups of children visit the center and sort the food containers into the appropriate bags. Let's see…got milk?

And The Survey Says…

What is the most popular dairy food among your kindergarten families? Finding out will reinforce following directions, classification, math, and more! In advance, duplicate the dairy foods survey (page 205) for each child, plus one extra. Cut apart the pictures from the extra copy; then use them to program a class graph of the corresponding dairy foods. Next, instruct each child to take the survey home to discover what types of dairy fare reside in her refrigerator or pantry. When each child has returned with her survey, have her cut apart the circled pictures, then glue those pictures to the class graph. Afterward, discuss what the graph reveals. What is the most popular dairy food? The survey says it all!

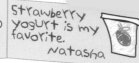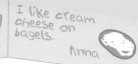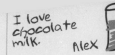
The Dairy Best

When each child reports on his favorite dairy food, the results will go a long way around your classroom—literally! In advance, duplicate the cow report form (page 204) on construction paper. Color and cut out the cow. Then cut the cow into two parts as shown above. Save these cow parts for later. Then give each child a 4 1/2" x 12" piece of construction paper. Ask each child to write about and illustrate her favorite type of dairy food (encourage children to provide as much detail as they can, such as a specific flavor of ice cream or type of cheese). Then tape all the pictures together, end-to-end. Glue the front end of the cow to the right side of the strip, and the back end to the left side. Display this delightful dairy report along a classroom wall for all to read and enjoy.

Cow Corral

What's going on down at the cow corral? Kindergarten cowboys and cowgirls are rounding up the cows! But only very special cows belong in this corral—those that are "branded" with a *c* word! To prepare for this activity, mount a construction-paper fence on a wall or board. Then photocopy a large supply of the cow cards on page 206. During your cow theme, encourage students to notice when they think of or see a word in print that begins with the hard *c* sound. Have each child write or glue each *c* word on a separate cow. Designate part of your group time for "Cow Corral." Ask each child who has "branded" a cow to share the word with the class, then mount her cow within the fence. How many cows can fill this corral?

Cows In The Kitchen!

Your little ones' imaginations will provide all the necessary inspiration to turn this countdown song into learning fun! After singing this song together, turn it into a class big book. Program a different large sheet of construction paper with each stanza of the song. (Split the last four lines of the song between two pages.) Then ask small groups of children to illustrate each page.

*You might like to partner this activity with *Counting Cows* by Woody Jackson (Harcourt Brace & Company).

(adapted to the verse of "Skip To My Lou")

Cows in the kitchen,
Oh, no, no!
Cows in the kitchen,
Oh, no, no!
Cows in the kitchen,
Oh, no, no!
Cows are in the kitchen!

Ten in the kitchen,
Shoo, cow, shoo!
Ten in the kitchen,
That won't do!
Ten in the kitchen,
Shoo, cow, shoo!
Nine cows in the kitchen.

Cows in the shower,
Oh, no, no!

(Repeat the second verse, substituting the appropriate number words each time. When you reach zero, speak the last four lines in unison.)

Ah, at last!
But what's that noise I hear in the shower?

Cows in the shower,
Oh, no, no!

I like milk and cookies. Seth

I like butter on my toast. Jerome

I like whipped cream on sundaes. Carla

How Now, Brown Cow?

With a theme like cows, you can hardly pass up the opportunity for a cow-related rhyming activity! To prepare, photocopy a supply of the cow cards (page 206) on brown construction paper. Cut apart the cards; then laminate them. Next encourage children to think of all the words they can that rhyme with *cow*. (See the list below and provide prompts, as needed.) As each rhyming word is mentioned, use a permanent marker to write it on a cow card. Also program one cow card with the word *cow* and each of several other cards with different words that do not rhyme with *cow*.

When you have a supply of cards, play How Now, Brown Cow? To begin, hold the card labeled *cow* in your right hand and another card of your choice in your left hand. Read (or have students read) the two cards aloud. If the words rhyme, have the class respond with a choral "How now, brown cow? Moo-oo!" If they do not rhyme, have the class say, "Not now, brown cow!" After the game, put the cards in a center and invite children to read and match the rhyming cow cards independently.

Words That Rhyme With *Cow*

bow	pow	chow
how	wow	plow
now	brow	meow

COW WOW COW green

'Til The Cows Come Home

This song can be used to get the wiggles out, strengthen fine-motor skills, practice following directions, and more. In fact, its uses just might go on 'til the cows come home! Before singing the song, explain to youngsters the meaning of the phrase " 'til the cows come home." Then sing the song below, inserting your own tailor-made actions as desired.

(adapted to the tune of "London Bridge")

I can hop on one foot,
One foot, one foot.
I can hop on one foot.
Hop 'til the cows come home.

I can snap my fingers,
Fingers, fingers.
I can snap my fingers.
Snap 'til the cows come home.

I can shake my neighbor's hand,
Neighbor's hand, neighbor's hand.
I can shake my neighbor's hand.
Shake 'til the cows come home.

Cow Books

Cows Can't Fly
By David Milgrim
(Viking)

Daddy Played Music For The Cows
By Maryann Weidt
Illustrated by Henri Sorensen
(Lothrop, Lee & Shepard Books)

George Washington's Cows
By David Small
(Farrar, Straus & Giroux, Inc.)

How Now, Brown Cow? (poetry)
By Alice Schertle
Illustrated by Amanda Schaffer
(Browndeer Press)

Luck With Potatoes
By Helen Ketteman
Illustrated by Brian Floca
(Orchard Books)

Metropolitan Cow
By Tim Egan
(Houghton Mifflin Company)

Moonstruck: The True Story Of The Cow Who Jumped Over The Moon
By Gennifer Choldenko
Illustrated by Paul Yalowitz
(Hyperion Books For Children)

No Milk!
By Jennifer A. Ericsson
Illustrated by Ora Eitan
(Mulberry Books)

No Moon, No Milk!
By Chris Babcock
Illustrated by Mark Teague
(Crown Publishers, Inc.)

The New Baby Calf
By Edith Newlin Chase
Illustrated by Barbara Reid
(Scholastic Inc.)

Two Cool Cows
By Toby Speed
Illustrated by Barry Root
(G. P. Putnam's Sons)

When Cows Come Home
By David L. Harrison
Illustrated by Chris L. Demarest
(Boyds Mills Press, Inc.)

Order books on-line.
www.themailbox.com

Cow Report Form

Use with "Setting The 'Moo-oo-ood'" and "Colorful Cows" on page 200 and "The Dairy Best" on page 202.

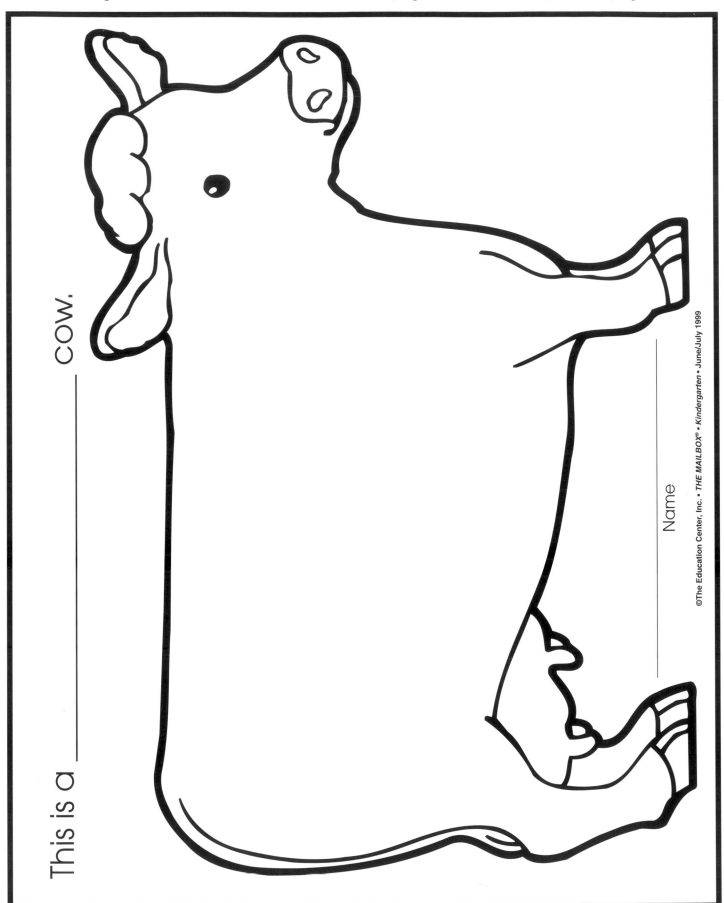

This is a _____ cow.

Name _____

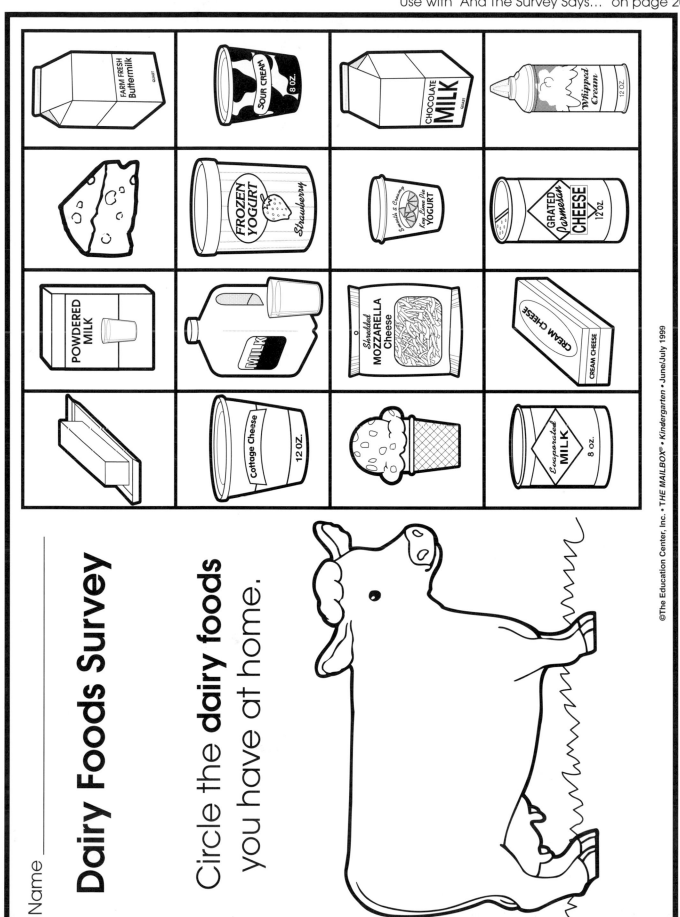

Name _____

Dairy Foods Survey

Circle the dairy foods you have at home.

©The Education Center, Inc. • THE MAILBOX® • Kindergarten • June/July 1999

Cow Card Patterns
Use with "Cow Corral" on page 202 and "How Now, Brown Cow?" on page 203.

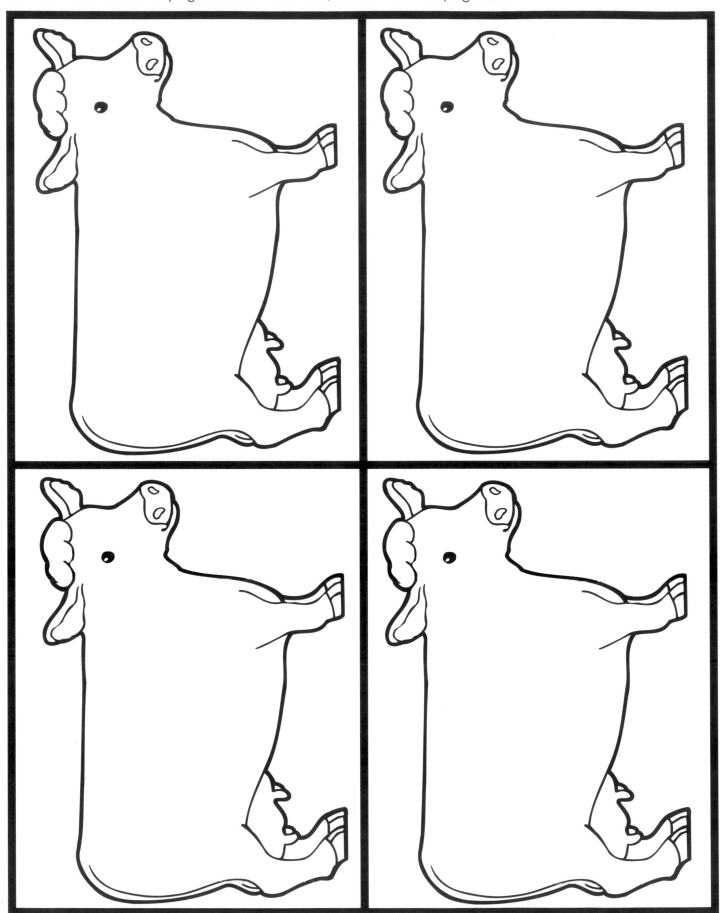

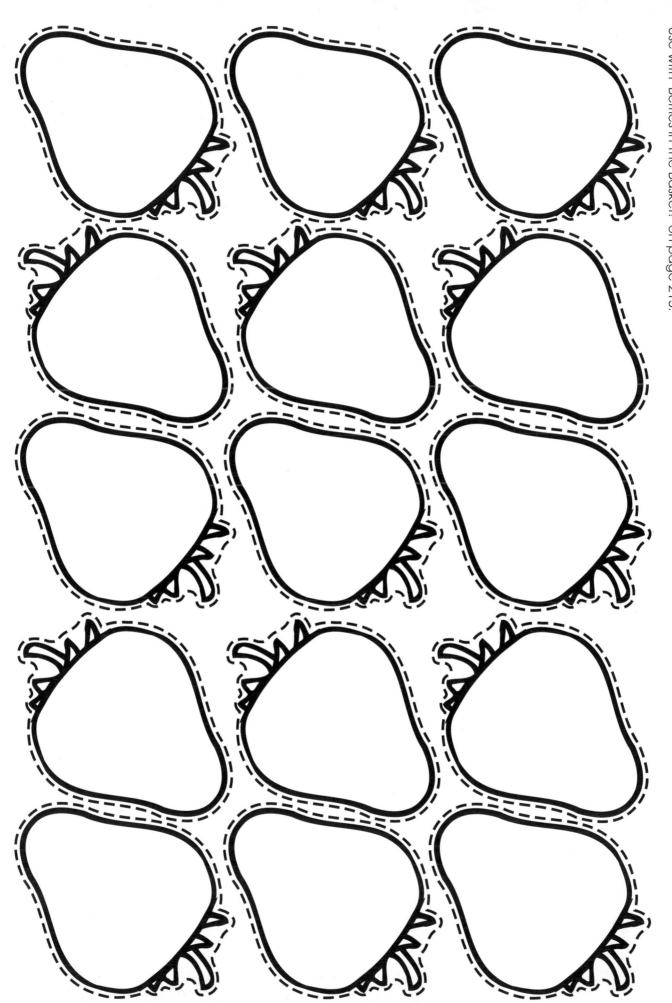

A Bounty of Berries

Blackberries, blueberries, raspberries, strawberries—summer's the season for these sweet, juicy treats! So pick from this patch of berry-related activities to serve your students a bushel of luscious learning.

ideas by Lucia Kemp Henry

A Juicy Little Secret

This delicious dilemma will pique your children's interest in your berry theme. In advance, hide a supply of berry-related items in a bag. (Appropriate items might include an empty berry basket, a jar of strawberry or blackberry jam, and a box of berry-flavored gelatin. Also include a basket of fresh berries.) Then pass out samples of blueberry, strawberry, and/or raspberry breakfast pastries. Tell students that these tasty morsels provide a clue to what your next theme is going to be. Then, one by one, show the clues that you have hidden in the bag—ranging from the more obscure to the most obvious. Once children have guessed the theme, invite each child to sample one of the fresh berries.

Rhyme Time

The time is ripe for rhyming! Cut out a large construction-paper berry (of any kind) and post it on a wall or glue it to a sheet of chart paper. Ask your youngsters to think of words that rhyme with berry. Write each mentioned rhyming word on the cutout. As your theme continues, encourage children to keep their ears out for more rhyming words. Add any new additions to the berry cutout. If your students fill up one berry, cut out another and another!

berry

cherry
dairy
fairy
hairy
Kerri
Mary
scary
very

Ripe For The Reading

In Bruce Degen's ever-popular *Jamberry* (HarperCollins Publishers), rhythm and rhyme pair together to create an exuberant celebration of berries. Before sharing this book, divide a sheet of chart paper into two columns. Label the chart as shown. Then read the book aloud just for the pure fun of it! Next share the book again, encouraging children to say, "Berry busters!" each time they hear the name of a berry. Each time they stop you, ask children to say the name of the berry that they just heard you read. Is it a real berry or a pretend berry? Write that berry name in the appropriate place on the chart and add a simple illustration if desired. Afterward, ask children if they know of any other real berries and record their responses on the chart. Display the finished chart and encourage children to incorporate this list of berry vocabulary in your read-the-room routine. Your youngsters will become berry buffs indeed!

Real	Pretend
blueberry	hatberry
strawberry	shoeberry
blackberry	canoeberry
raspberry	hayberry
cranberry	pawberry
huckleberry	quickberry
loganberry	quackberry
	trainberry
	trackberry
	clackberry

Berry busters!

The Berry Best

Taste testing is all in a day's work with this math idea! To prepare, photocopy a supply of the berry cards on page 212 on construction paper. Program a graph with a column for each different type of berry represented. Also provide a bowl each of fresh or frozen blackberries, blueberries, raspberries, and strawberries. (If desired, use the berry cards to label each of the bowls.) To begin, give each child a separate bowl and a spoon. Instruct her to take a sample of each different berry. When every child has all four berries, invite the class to taste each different one together. Then instruct each child to select the card for the berry that she likes best. Have her color the card, then tape it in the appropriate column of the graph. And the winning berry in your class is…?

Gobble The Greater Number!

Have you introduced your students to the symbols for *greater than* and *less than?* If so, here's an opportunity for practice! First photocopy each different berry on page 212 ten times. Then photocopy the *greater than* and *less than* characters on page 213. Laminate all the patterns. Also provide number cards from one to ten.

To do this activity, place one number card on the left side of a pocket chart and one number card on the right side. Ask children to manipulate sets of the berries to determine which number is greater. Then explain that the large part of the symbol (the mouth) likes to gobble up the biggest number. Invite a child to choose the correct symbol and place it in the pocket chart so that the mouth is facing the bigger number. When the correct placement is verified, have the child move the wider end of the symbol over the bigger number, while the whole class makes gobbling noises.

The Nose Knows

When youngsters visit this classification center, they can be as nosy as they like! In advance, collect several empty film canisters with lids. Pour different flavors of berry-flavored gelatin into several of the containers. Code the bottom of each of these containers with a berry sticker (or any available sticker). Then put different samples of non-berry-scented products in each of the remaining containers. (Examples include lemon and vanilla extract, mint toothpaste, floral perfume, cinnamon, cocoa, and bubble gum.) When a child visits this center, have her remove the lid of each container, in turn, and smell it—without looking! Then ask her to sort the scents into "Berry Scents" and "Non-Berry Scents." To check her work, she simply looks for the sticker on the bottom of the berry-scented containers.

The First Strawberries
A Cherokee Story
Retold by Joseph Bruchac
Illustrated by Anna Vojtech
Published by Dial Books For Young Readers

How do your youngsters think berries came into the world? This cherished Cherokee tale offers a sweet and meaningful explanation. After sharing this story with your class, you'll be ready for "Berries In The Basket!" on this page.

How My Berry Came To Be

Urge those creative-writing juices to overflow in this activity. To begin, ask each child to choose a berry that he'd like to write about. Then have him paint a picture of that specific berry. While the paint is drying, ask each child to write/dictate a real or pretend story about how his berry might have come into the world. When the painting is dry, instruct each child to cut out his berry picture, then tape it to his story. Display each child's work on a board titled "How My Berry Came To Be." In turn, give each child a pointer (a yardstick topped with a berry cutout would be nice!) and have him share his berry story with the class.

Blackberries rained when my gramma was six years old. —Jessie

God made the strawberries. —Josh

Blueberries came to the Earth from a blue planet. And for the bears. —Mable

Berries In The Basket!

Friendship, kindness, and respect make a child part of this batch of berries. In advance, duplicate the strawberries on page 207. Personalize one strawberry for each child; then store all of them in a produce basket. Next cut out and laminate a large tagboard basket. Mount the basket on a wall or board. After a class review of *The First Strawberries* (see above), ask children to recall what the strawberries came to mean to the Cherokee people. Then show youngsters the programmed strawberries and the basket on the wall. Explain that when a child receives friendship, kindness, and respect from a classmate, he may tape that classmate's strawberry to the basket. At the end of each day, honor the "berries in the basket" with special recognition. (If desired, use the awards on page 215.) Then empty the basket and begin the procedure again the following day. Can your class get *all* the berries in the basket?

Alison

Hugh

Anna

Joseph was a Berry In The Basket today!

My Berry Book

Berries abound in these child-illustrated books. For each child, duplicate pages 214 and 215 on construction paper. Also provide each child with five 9 1/2" x 7" white pages. After reading the text strips together, ask each child to cut her strips apart, then glue each strip to the bottom of a different page. Then have each child creatively illustrate her pages and the cover. (If desired, see the suggestions below for ideas.) When all the illustrations are done, have each child sequence her pages, then staple them together along the left side. During a group time, read the books together. Then encourage children to take their books home to share with their families.

Cover
Color the berries. Then glue on green yarn or green construction-paper strips to resemble a berry basket.

Page 1
Use a foam-ball half or a circle sponge and blue paint to make blueberry prints on the page. Use a dark blue marker to make a little starlike shape at the top of each blueberry.

Page 2
Use heart-shaped sponges and red paint to print strawberry shapes on the page. When the paint is dry, use a toothpick and yellow paint to add tiny seeds to the strawberries. Then use green glitter glue to add stems and leaves.

Page 3
Make thumbprint raspberry shapes on the page. When the paint is dry, add texture to each print by dabbing on little dots of pink- or red-colored glue.

Page 4
Use a cotton swab to cluster groups of purple paint dots. When the paint is dry, use a green marker to add stems.

Page 5
Use a paintbrush to paint one giant berry on the page. When the paint is dry, add details with crayons and markers.

Blueberries are delicious. 1

Page 1

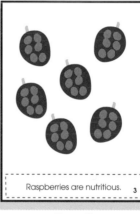

Strawberries are sweet. 2

Page 2

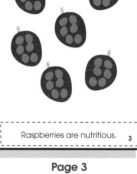

Raspberries are nutritious. 3

Page 3

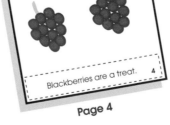

Blackberries are a treat. 4

Page 4

This ripe and juicy berry is my **favorite** one to eat! 5

Page 5

Books About Berries

Blueberries For Sal
By Robert McCloskey
(Viking)

The Grey Lady And
  The Strawberry Snatcher
By Molly Bang
(Aladdin Paperbacks)

The Little Mouse,
  The Red Ripe Strawberry,
  And The Big Hungry Bear
By Don & Audrey Wood
(Child's Play)

Greater Than Symbol

Use with "Gobble The Greater Number!" on page 209.

Less Than Symbol

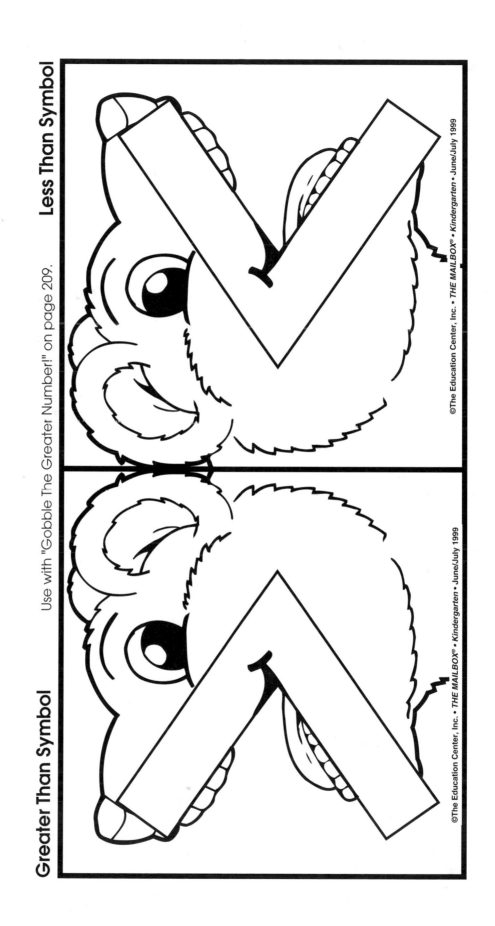

My Berry Book

Blueberries are delicious.

1

Strawberries are so sweet.

2

Raspberries are nutritious.

3

Blackberries are a treat.

4

This ripe and juicy berry
is my **favorite** one to eat!

5

awards
Use with "Berries In The Basket!" on page 210.

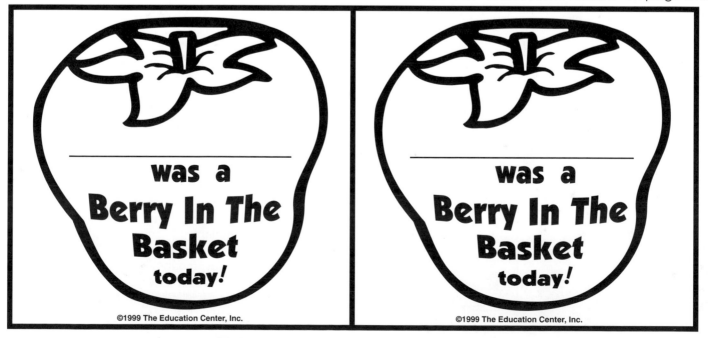

was a
Berry In The Basket
today!

©1999 The Education Center, Inc.

was a
Berry In The Basket
today!

©1999 The Education Center, Inc.

Hasn't This Been A Terrific Year?

The school year is drawing to a close…
and it's time to wrap things up. It's time to celebrate the
big moments and the little moments, the monumental milestones and the
tiny sparks of joy. Use the ideas in this unit to recognize and honor your students'
participation and progress throughout this school year.

—a collection of ideas contributed by kindergarten teachers

The Very Best Kindergartners

Reminisce over the year's accomplishments with this class-made book that follows the popular pattern in Eric Carle's *The Very Hungry Caterpillar*.

To prepare the book:

1. Caption the first page *"One morning the sun came up and—whoosh! —[insert a number] little children came to kindergarten at [school name]. They started to learn."*

2. Next, make a page for each month of the school year using this format: *"In September they [students suggest accomplishments/topics]. But there was still more to learn."*

3. For the months of summer vacation, write *"During [insert months], they played and played and played."*

4. Caption the last page *"Now it was [insert the first month of school] again—and the children were not little kindergartners anymore. They were ready for first grade! And there will be lots more to learn!"*

After each page is programmed, review *The Very Hungry Caterpillar* with your class. Afterward, share your original text. Then ask student volunteers (or small groups) to illustrate the pages. Bind all the pages together between construction-paper covers. After reading the finished book together, encourage your students to share this book with classroom visitors during the last days of school.

Barbara Goldman—Gr. K, Charlotte Sidway School, Grand Island, NY

One morning the sun came up and—whoosh!— little children came to kindergarten at ... entary. They started to learn.

In September they learned about shapes. But there was still more to learn.

During July and August, they played and ... ed and played.

Now it was September again—and the children were not little kindergarteners anymore. They were ready for first grade! And there will be lots more to learn!

MEMORY LANE

OCTOBER

Kimberly Richard

Memory Lane

For the last few weeks of school, invite children, parents, visitors, and other school personnel to stroll down your class's memory lane. To prepare, sort the photos that you've taken throughout the year according to month. Mount each month's pictures on a sheet of labeled poster board. Include child-dictated and teacher captions as desired. Then hang the posters in chronological order in the hall. Near the beginning of this display, mount a poster-board street sign labeled "Memory Lane." Everybody loves a trip down memory lane!

June E. Maddox—Gr. K
Calvary Baptist Day School, Savannah, GA

A "Sun-sational" Class

This cheerful puzzle display is perfect for reinforcing class spirit and teamwork! Begin by cutting a very large circle from yellow bulletin-board paper. With a black marker, draw a smaller circle in the center and write "Our 'Sun-sational' Class" inside it. On the outer circle, draw a sun ray for each child. (Be sure to vary the outer lines of each ray so that each piece will fit in only one place.) Cut apart the rays and give one to each child. Invite each child to decorate his ray with a variety of year-end art supplies. When all the rays are decorated and dry, display them on the floor with the sun center. Encourage small groups of children to take turns working on this giant floor puzzle. When each group has had an opportunity to assemble the puzzle, post it on your classroom door.

Barbara Spilman Lawson, Waynesboro, VA

Kindergarten March

Remember that old, familiar army marching song called "Sound Off"? Use the call-and-repeat pattern of that chant to inspire your kindergartners to march right into celebrating the kindergarten year.

We can say our ABCs
And we know our one, two, threes.
We are learning every day
And this is what we have to say:

Count off—1, 2
Count off—3, 4
Count off—1, 2—3, 4!

We know all our colors too
And we can write our names for you.
We are learning every day
And this is what we have to say:

Count off—1, 2
Count off—3, 4
Count off—1, 2—3, 4!

Kindergarten's almost passed
But kindergarten was a blast!
We're still learning every day
And this is what we have to say:

Count off—1, 2
Count off—3, 4
Count off—1, 2—3, 4!

adapted from an idea by Mary Anissa Chavers—Gr. K
Palm City Elementary, Palm City, FL

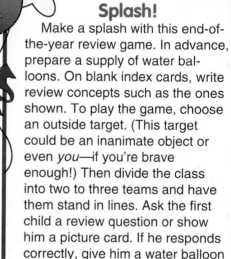

Splash!

Make a splash with this end-of-the-year review game. In advance, prepare a supply of water balloons. On blank index cards, write review concepts such as the ones shown. To play the game, choose an outside target. (This target could be an inanimate object or even *you*—if you're brave enough!) Then divide the class into two to three teams and have them stand in lines. Ask the first child a review question or show him a picture card. If he responds correctly, give him a water balloon to throw at the target. If he is incorrect, give the first person on each of the other teams a shot at it. Continue in this manner until all of the cards have been used—or you are dripping! Makes ordinary assessment seem kind of dry, doesn't it?

Jaimie K. Hudson—Gr. K
Can-Do Elementary Homeschool
Pace, FL

How Did Your "Kinder-garden" Grow?

Was there so much blooming going on in your kindergarten classroom this year, that it feels impossible to measure it all? This floral delight will help depict at least the physical growth of each of your little ones. To create this special garden, refer to each child's height at the beginning of the school year; then cut a corresponding construction-paper stem for each child. Next, measure the child's current height. Add a red length of paper to the stem to show the amount of growth. Have each child make a flower and leaves for her stem; then mount all the completed flowers along a wall with the title "Look How Much We've Grown!"

Barbara Spilman Lawson,
Waynesboro, VA

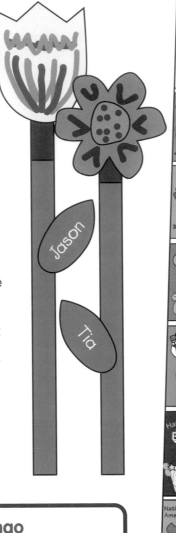

Beach Ball Bingo

Betty played Beach Ball Bingo by the breakers at the beach. Now your class can do the same! Well...maybe not by the breakers at the beach, but perhaps by the bookshelf beside the big box of blocks. To prepare, duplicate page 219. Program each beach ball with a skill that you'd like to reinforce, such as numerals or sight words. Then duplicate that programmed page for each child, plus one extra (to be cut apart for the Caller). Also duplicate the blank bingo card (page 220) for each child. Instruct each child to color her page of beach balls, then cut apart the boxes. Then have her glue all of the beach balls onto her bingo card however she chooses. When the glue is dry, each child has a tailor-made bingo card for end-of-the-year bingo bashes!

Barbara Spilman Lawson

Walking Through The Year

The end of the year is the perfect theme for this class-made walking book. In advance, collect 11 different-colored sheets of construction paper. Program each of ten of the sheets with a different month of the school year. Title the remaining sheet "Walking Through The Year." For each page, prompt students to recall activities and events that took place during each month, such as field trips, visitors, celebrations, birthdays, and themes. Write the events of each month on that page. Then invite different pairs of students to decorate each page with photos, stickers, and drawings. When the pages are complete, sequence them beginning with the cover, then the September page. Laminate the pages in order *and upside down,* leaving a small space between each page. (Be sure the pages are aligned and evenly spaced since this book will not be cut apart.) After laminating, trim the side margins and fold the book accordion-style for storage. To read this book, lay it flat and extended on the floor. Invite a child to walk beside each page as he (or the whole class) reads it aloud. You just walked through a whole year!

Barbara Spilman Lawson

Name _____

BEACH BALL BINGO

		FREE		

Author Units

The Remarkable Rosemary Wells

Author-illustrator Rosemary Wells believes that creating good writing is like looking into a kaleidoscope. "The design is yours to make," she says. "The exact image can never be repeated again." It's remarkable! With hard work, and lots of practice, Rosemary Wells has perfected the art of creating remarkably unique and engaging children's books. So collect these Rosemary Wells books; then invite your youngsters to peer into these kaleidoscopic designs. Ooooh, they're simply remarkable!

by Mackie Rhodes

All books are published by Dial Books For Young Readers

Characters: Charming And Challenging

Shy Charles

Are you feeling sheepish and shy, or boisterous and bold? Or perhaps somewhere in between? This rhyming story shows that even the shyest character can sometimes make the biggest statement. In advance, gather a half-pint milk carton and one craft stick for each child. Also duplicate a class supply of the boy and girl patterns (page 226) on construction paper. After sharing the story, have each child prepare a milk-carton prop and child puppet as shown. Then review the story. When students think Charles is feeling shy, have them pull their puppets down (and vice versa when they think he's feeling bold). Then describe situations that might elicit bashful or bold responses from your students. For example, you might say, "How would you feel if your mother asked you to sing for company?" Invite youngsters to manipulate their puppets to show their own reactions. Then discuss their responses.

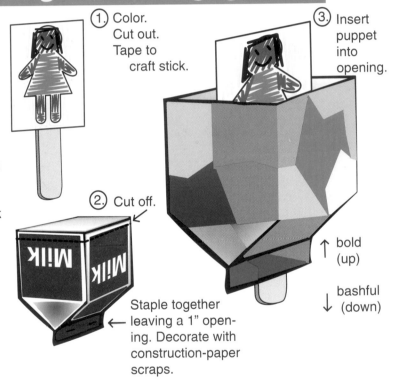

1. Color. Cut out. Tape to craft stick.

2. Cut off.

Staple together leaving a 1" opening. Decorate with construction-paper scraps.

3. Insert puppet into opening.

↑ bold (up)

↓ bashful (down)

Joe   Jake

A good friend plays with me.

Timothy Goes To School

After several miserable days at school, the unhappy Timothy finally finds a friend who helps turn his misery into bliss. To reinforce friendships, ask each child to illustrate himself and a buddy. Have the artist think about the characteristics that he thinks make a good friend. Record his dictation. Have each child share his picture during a group time; then prompt the whole class to brainstorm a list of good-friend characteristics. Write the ideas on a sheet of chart paper titled "What Is A Good Friend?" Post this chart to use in your read-the-room activities and to serve as a gentle reminder of good-friend qualities.

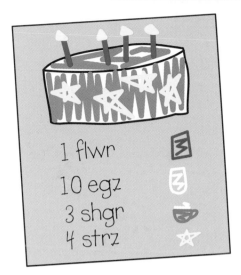

1 flwr

10 egz

3 shgr

4 strz

Bunny Cakes

Max and Ruby each have their own ideas about what kind of cake is best suited for Grandma's birthday. And they each have their own ideas about how to accomplish their goals. Encourage your youngsters to express their own cake-making ideas with this creative-writing assignment. Display cake ingredients, such as flour, sugar, eggs, milk, and butter. Invite each child to glue a cake cutout onto a large sheet of paper. Then instruct him to illustrate or write a cake recipe below the cutout. Just like Max in the story, each child will want to add his own special ingredients to his recipe. Then have each child use art supplies to decorate his cake. During group time ask each child to share his special cake recipe with the class. Then display all the pictures with the title "Kids' Cakes." And since you already have the ingredients on hand, you might as well get out your favorite cake recipe and whip up a real cake with your class!

Max's Dragon Shirt

Like most of us, Max and Ruby each have their own clothing preferences. After sharing this story, invite children to show off their clothing preferences *and* personalities with this design activity. To begin, help each child cut out a life-size clothing shape from butcher paper—a shirt, pants, a dress, or any other piece of clothing. Then ask her to embellish her cutout with craft items, such as sequins, buttons, feathers, and glitter confetti. Encourage her to add any original designs or effects she desires. Attach a paper-strip label with "A [Child's name] Original" to the decorated garment. Then display these special originals with the title "Designer Duds."

A Jamie Original

Bunny Money

Even in the storybook world of Max and Ruby, money seems to simply slip away. Help your youngsters begin to be accountable for spending money with their very own funny money. In advance, stock a classroom store with merchandise that children can buy, such as snack items, fancy pencils, and party favors. Label each item with a dollar amount. Next duplicate the funny-money pattern (page 226) for each child. Glue a copy of each child's school photo to his bill; then write his name in the box. Duplicate a set of bills for each child. After sharing the story, invite each student to purchase items from your classroom store. Afterward have the child report his spendings to you. Can he account for how his money was spent? Collect all the money; then redistribute it on other occasions for children to use to purchase tickets for special activities, privileges, and treats. Hold on to that funny money!

Andre Rhodes

$2.00

$3.00

Other Max And Ruby Books

Max's Chocolate Chicken
Max's Christmas
Max And Ruby's First Greek Myth: Pandora's Box
Max And Ruby's Midas: Another Greek Myth

Introducing...The Marvelous McDuff

McDuff Moves In

The irresistible aroma of vanilla rice pudding leads a little terrier to a tasty treat—and a new home! After sharing this heartwarming tale, invite youngsters to create a rice-pudding treat. As a class, follow the recipe shown. Then heat smoked sausage slices over low heat or in a microwave. Give each child a serving of pudding topped with sausage slices. Mmmm—no wonder McDuff wanted to stay!

Vanilla Rice Pudding
(makes 8 1/2-cup servings)

2 packages instant vanilla pudding-and-pie filling
4 cups milk
1 cup cooked rice
1 cup raisins
1 teaspoon nutmeg

Prepare the pudding as directed on the package. Add rice, raisins, and nutmeg.

McDuff Comes Home

Without a collar, the lost McDuff has no identification to help Mrs. Higgins return him to his home. But the clever terrier devises a way to steer his new friend in the right direction. After sharing this story, guide youngsters to realize the importance of knowing their first and last names, addresses, and phone numbers. Then invite them to create personal-identification collars. For each child, duplicate three bone patterns (page 226) on construction paper. After each child cuts out her patterns, have her write/dictate her name, address, and phone number on a separate cutout. Instruct her to punch a hole in each cutout, then thread them onto a length of ribbon. Tie the collar loosely around the child's neck. Throughout the day ask youngsters to imagine they are lost. Can they recite their personal information to you?

McDuff And The Baby

Since he can't talk, the sensitive McDuff expresses his feelings with facial expressions and actions. In each scene in the book, ask youngsters to imagine what McDuff might say if he could talk. Then have each youngster make a McDuff headband by gluing two triangle ears to a headband. Invite each student to don his headband. Then name a specific emotion, such as sad. Ask your student McDuffs to express that emotion without using words. Challenge youngsters to express as many emotions as they can in as many ways as possible.

Out Of This World!

Having a bad day? Sometimes just a little imagination can take you to a place that will get you looking on the bright side—and toward the day that should have been. Voyage with these cute characters of calamity who journey far beyond the moon and stars to just such a place.

Moss Pillows

Robert's visit with his relatives goes from bad to worse—and then even worse! It's no wonder Robert needs a visit to the gentle Bunny Planet. After sharing this book, invite children to talk about bad days they have experienced. Then invite students to make dreamy moss pillows. Have each child cover the front of a manila envelope with green felt or construction paper. Label the back of the envelope "Here's the day that should have been." Then invite each child to illustrate a perfect day for herself. Have her insert the picture into her moss pillow. During a quiet time, encourage the child to lay her head on her pillow for a few moments, imagining she is enjoying "the day that should have been." When you can, give each child a few private moments with you to express her feelings about her perfect day.

Here's the day that should have been.

The Island Light

Everyone is embarrassed now and then. And this book begins with Felix in one of those *very* embarrassing situations. Luckily, the Bunny Planet comes to the rescue just in time. Share this comforting story; then invite youngsters to close their eyes and imagine they are being swept away to the gentle Bunny Planet. While they're imagining, ask children to think about what kind of vehicle might take them to the Bunny Planet. Then encourage each child to use a variety of craft supplies to make a model of his imaginary vehicle. Write each child's dictation about his vehicle on a sheet of paper; then display the special transporters with the title "Bunny Planet Express."

First Tomato

Claire is having a miserable morning. She spills her cereal at breakfast, gets her shoes wet on the way to school, and by 11 A.M. she's already exhausted from too much math! From there, Claire's day only goes downhill. Can anything save Claire from such a terrible day? After sharing this book, point out that the story begins by telling *about* Claire and her day. But when Claire arrives on the Bunny Planet, *she* begins to tell about *her own* experiences using words like *I* and *my*. Invite each child to record an original Bunny-Planet story on a tape recorder. Ask him to tell about a pretend character's bad day. When he gets to the part where the character arrives on the Bunny Planet, have the storyteller imagine that he *is* that character. Guide him to tell about his visit using personal pronouns. After each child records a story, ask his permission to play it during group time. Would anyone like to illustrate his story during a free time?

On the Bunny Planet I walked into a huge room with one bazillion video games!

More By Rosemary Wells

Forest Of Dreams
Fritz And The Mess Fairy
Hazel's Amazing Mother
Night Sounds, Morning Colors
Noisy Nora
Stanley & Rhoda
The Language Of Doves

Patterns
puppet
Use with *Shy Charles* on page 222.

funny money
Use with *Bunny Money* on page 223.

bone
Use with *McDuff Comes Home* on page 224.

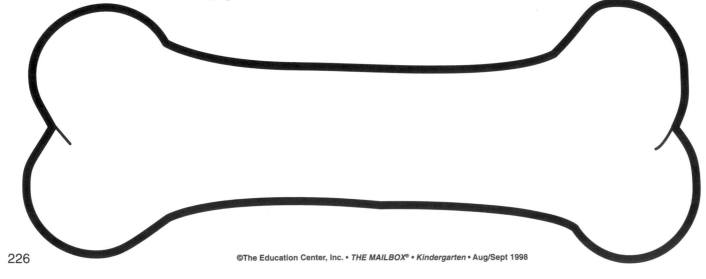

Forever Franklin

Paulette Bourgeois understands the trials and triumphs of childhood—and she conveys that perfectly in her tales of a lovable turtle named Franklin. In each story the author gently navigates Franklin through a common childhood dilemma, leading to the discovery of a satisfactory solution. Children are certain to identify with—and be inspired by—the many facets of Franklin. Thank you, Paulette Bourgeois, for this fabulous Franklin series!

by Mackie Rhodes

*All the books in this unit are illustrated by
Brenda Clark and published by Scholastic Inc.*

Franklin's Halloween

Just as Franklin eagerly anticipated the fun, fancy, and friendly fright of his town's Halloween costume party, youngsters will likewise anticipate their own costume-party activities. After sharing the book, invite each child to create an original costume using a variety of craft items, such as newspaper, fabric, paper bags, boxes, and paper plates. Then have youngsters line up for a special costume parade. Call out a costume category or feature—such as "animal" or "sharp teeth." Ask students whose costumes fit the named category to parade around the classroom, then return to the line. Continue naming different categories until each child has had a turn to show off his costume in parade fashion.

Franklin Has A Sleepover

Franklin is ready to host his first sleepover. But in spite of his careful planning, a few small problems arise. After reading this story, invite students to share their first sleepover experiences with the class. Then have each child personalize a manila envelope which has been prepared as shown. Have her glue construction-paper handles to the envelope to create a suitcase. Then ask her to illustrate and label a separate large notecard with each item she might pack for a sleepover. Instruct her to pack her suitcase with the illustrated items. During group time, invite each child to share the contents of her suitcase with the class, explaining why she chose to pack each item.

I can hop ten times in a row.

Franklin Fibs

In a round of friendly one-upmanship, Franklin learns that telling a little fib can cause big trouble. Here's a game that will keep youngsters grounded in *honesty*—and build self-esteem, too! After reading the story, discuss the importance of being honest about yourself to others. Then ask each student to think about the many different things she can do at school, such as hop on one foot, write her name, or tie her shoe. Invite each child, in turn, to name one thing she'd like to show the class. Lead the class in responding, "Show us!" Then have the child demonstrate her ability. Afterward lead students in a round of applause and praise for her special skill.

Franklin And The Tooth Fairy

Although losing a tooth marks a big event for each of his friends, Franklin learns that this is not the only way to feel grown-up. After reading this story, survey youngsters to find out how many have lost teeth. Then invite students to share their lost-tooth and tooth-fairy stories with the class. Afterward have each child color a copy of the tooth-fairy pattern (on page 231) and write his name on it. Instruct him to attach his cutout to a chart like the one shown to indicate the number of teeth he has lost. Throughout the year, update the chart as each child reports a lost tooth. Then celebrate each big event by having the class count and compare the number of lost teeth in each column. In this activity, each lost tooth equals a math gain for the class.

0 teeth	1 tooth	2 teeth	3 teeth	teeth
12	4	2	0	

Franklin Plays The Game

When Franklin's soccer team devises a plan that puts teamwork into practice, everyone's a winner. Discuss how each character in the story contributed to make the team plan work. Then guide youngsters to name some of the benefits of teamwork. Ask them to list some things at school that might be accomplished best by teamwork. Then divide the class into small teams. Assign each team a task, such as decorating a bulletin board, setting up a new center activity, or rearranging an area of the room. Encourage each group to devise a plan for its task before beginning the job. After teams complete their tasks, invite each team to say a little cheer for itself for a job well done. Go, team!

Franklin Is Lost

An innocent game of hide-and-seek turns into a frightening adventure when Franklin gets lost in the woods. Read this story up to the two-page spread picturing the owl. At this point, ask youngsters to author their own endings to the story. Have each child illustrate his ending on a treetop cutout; then record his dictation on a corresponding tree-trunk cutout. Display the trees in a woods setting around a decorated turtle-shell cutout. Title the display "Franklin Is Lost." Then read the remainder of the story to find out how Paulette Bourgeois chose to wrap up this story.

He falls asleep. The next day he remembers his way home.

A good fairy zaps Franklin back home.

The bear came to get him because bears can smell anything!

Franklin Wants A Pet

Franklin convinces his parents that he's ready to handle the responsibilities of caring for a pet. After sharing this story, discuss with your class the different kinds of pets and how to care for each one. Then ask youngsters to help set up a pet store stocked with pet supplies and stuffed animals. During dramatic play, have your pet-store browsers carefully survey the store's inventory. Invite each interested pet purchaser to dictate a list of supplies needed for his pet of choice. Then have him purchase the pet and items on his list. Encourage each pet owner to nurture and care for his new charge. Youngsters will reap the rewards along with the responsibilities of pet ownership.

Franklin And The Thunderstorm

The understanding and humor of good friends help Franklin overcome his fear of storms. Before reading the story, cut out a class quantity of paper circles the same size as a large, sturdy paper plate. Then decorate one paper plate to resemble the top of a turtle shell and another to resemble a turtle-shell bottom. After sharing the story, review that Franklin's fear made him want to hide in his shell. Ask youngsters to discuss any fears they have that make them want to "hide in their shells"—or under a bed, or in a closet! Then invite each child to illustrate the source of his fear on a paper circle. Bind all the illustrations between the turtle-shell covers; then title this class book "I Want To Hide In My Shell When…." During a group sharing time, use the class book as a springboard to talk about these childhood fears, and to affirm and reassure each child.

I Want To Hide In My Shell When...

I want to hide in my shell when I hear that monster at night.

Franklin's New Friend

Focusing on their differences makes Franklin hesitate to befriend his new classmate, Moose. Before reading this story, prepare a moose headband using construction-paper copies of the ear and antler patterns on page 232. After the story, guide students to predict how a new class member might feel in their class. Encourage them to brainstorm ways in which they might help a new student—regardless of their differences—become a welcome member of their group. Then challenge students to test their ideas. To do this, invite each student, in turn, to assume the role of a new class member. Ask the new student to wear the antler headband for identification. Instruct the veteran students to be a friend to the new student by following some of the class-generated suggestions. What a gentle reminder that it takes a friend a make a friend!

I can tie my own shoes.

I can write my last name too!

Tony Brown

Franklin Rides A Bike

After repeated episodes of "wibbly-wobbly, teetery-tottery" falls from his bike, Franklin's perseverance pays off as he proudly pedals to the park to join his friends. After sharing this story, invite students to share their experiences of perseverance and the resulting rewards, such as being able to tie their own shoes, or write their names, or pump themselves high on the swings. Then prepare an "I Can Do!" gallery to show off students' successes. In the gallery, display photos, work samples, student-dictation, and other items indicating student accomplishments. Add to the display throughout the year to reinforce youngsters' efforts as well as to encourage them to keep trying. Perseverance *does* pay!

More Franklin Turtle Tales

Franklin Is Bossy

Franklin Goes To School

Franklin's Bad Day

Franklin In The Dark

Franklin's School Play

Franklin's Blanket

Franklin Is Messy

Hurry Up, Franklin

Finders Keepers For Franklin

Patterns

Use with *Franklin's New Friend* on page 230.

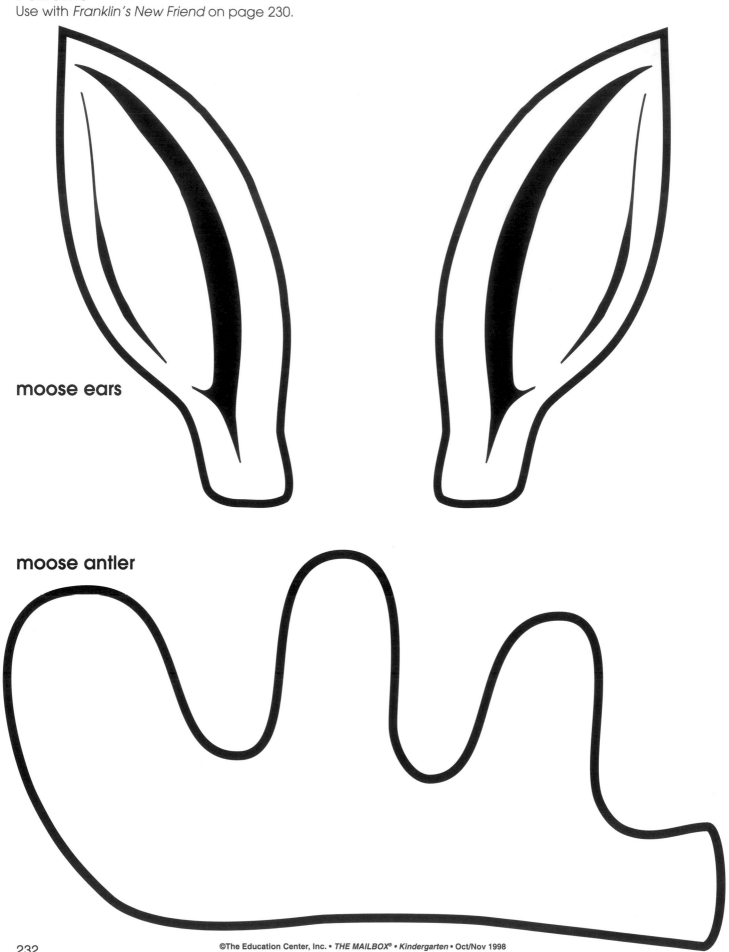

moose ears

moose antler

I would like to visit...

All In The Pinkney Family

When it comes to children's books, the Pinkney family has it all! Award-winning artist Jerry Pinkney has illustrated numerous books, including two that have been authored by his wife, Gloria Jean Pinkney. Following right along in their footsteps, their son, Brian, is also an accomplished children's-book author and illustrator. And—like father, like son—Brian has illustrated several books written by his talented wife, Andrea Davis Pinkney. This remarkable family brings to children's literature a unique richness that encompasses the heritage of Black Americans as well as other cultural groups. Their combined contributions have added new dimensions and insights in the world of children's books. To *all* the Pinkneys—*thank you* for the unique gifts you have offered to children's education!

by Mackie Rhodes

Note: All books are published by Dial Books For Young Readers (unless otherwise noted).

The Sunday Outing
By Gloria Jean Pinkney
Illustrated by Jerry Pinkney

On warm summer Sundays, Ernestine and her great-aunt Odessa take the trolley to the North Philadelphia train station, where they watch the trains rolling in and out. As they watch, Ernestine's utmost wish is to ride one of those trains to visit her relatives in North Carolina where she was born. But Mama and Daddy say they can't afford the fare right now. Before sharing this happy-ending story, duplicate the story starter on page 233 for each child. After reading the story, set the scene for creative writing by asking each child to imagine that *he* gets to go on a train trip. Then invite each child to make a special satchel, like Ernestine's. To make a satchel, give each child a large sheet of construction paper to fold in half. Have him glue just the side edges together. Then help him staple paper handles to the top. Invite each child to decorate his satchel as he likes. Then give each child a copy of page 233. Have each child write about and illustrate whom he would like to visit and why. Instruct each child to slide his completed paper into his satchel. Then have each child share about his dream trip during a group time. Hmmm…where would *you* like to go? Write about it!

Back Home
By Gloria Jean Pinkney
Illustrated by Jerry Pinkney

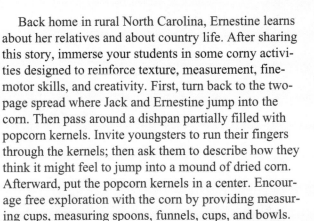

Back home in rural North Carolina, Ernestine learns about her relatives and about country life. After sharing this story, immerse your students in some corny activities designed to reinforce texture, measurement, fine-motor skills, and creativity. First, turn back to the two-page spread where Jack and Ernestine jump into the corn. Then pass around a dishpan partially filled with popcorn kernels. Invite youngsters to run their fingers through the kernels; then ask them to describe how they think it might feel to jump into a mound of dried corn. Afterward, put the popcorn kernels in a center. Encourage free exploration with the corn by providing measuring cups, measuring spoons, funnels, cups, and bowls. Later, suggest that each child create a piece of corn art. Provide markers, glue, construction paper, and the corn. Then invite students to use the supplies to create their own original corny masterpieces. When the glue is dry, display the artwork with the title "Corny Country Art."

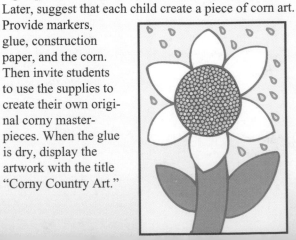

Sam And The Tigers
By Julius Lester
Illustrated by Jerry Pinkney

Dressed in colorful new duds, Sam from Sam-sam-sa-mara is forced to bargain his brand-new clothes away to five very threatening, very hungry tigers. But soon, a matter of pride turns the tigers into a buttery mess! Read this humorous tale aloud; then invite children to join the Sams in a batch of striped pancakes. For each small group of students, follow the package directions to mix up a batch of pancake batter. Then mix an additional half cup of batter in a separate container. Add chocolate syrup to the extra batter until it is medium brown. Using an electric frying pan, cook the plain pancakes on one side. Right before flipping each pancake, closely supervise a child in using a medicine-dropper filled with the brown mixture to create stripes on the pancake. Serve these "tiger-y" pancakes with butter and maple or chocolate syrup. Tasty!

Max Found Two Sticks
By Brian Pinkney
Published by Simon & Schuster Books For Young Readers

Launch the rhythm of your youngsters' imaginations with this delightful tale of a young boy and his rhythmic interpretation of the sights and sounds around him. Before reading the story, prepare a tape of simple rhythms. Tape each rhythm twice, leaving a five-second pause between each repetition. After reading the book, give each child a set of large craft sticks to use as rhythm sticks. Have children listen to the first rhythm, then repeat it several times. Then play the second taping of that rhythm. Did the class's rhythm match the tape? For an added challenge, invite a volunteer to listen to a rhythm through a set of headphones. Then have her tap out that rhythm with her sticks. Invite each child in the circle to repeat the rhythm in turn. After the last child plays her rhythm, play the second taped version for the whole class to hear. Did the last child's rhythm match the first one? Youngsters won't want to miss a beat of this fun game!

The Adventures Of Sparrowboy
By Brian Pinkney
Published by Simon & Schuster Books For Young Readers

In the tradition of Falconman, Henry's comic-book superhero, the young boy crosses paths with a small bird and finds himself zapped into the super-flying, evil-fighting *Sparrowboy!* Share this fanciful story with students; then invite each child to share his fantasy about possessing superhero qualities. What special powers and characteristics does he have? Do his abilities come from an animal, a machine, or some other source? After your sharing session, ask each child to draw himself as a superhero. Help him label his illustration with his superhero name and a few superhero qualities. Display all the drawings with the title "Our Class Superheroes!"

More Books Illustrated By Jerry Pinkney

The Hired Hand: An African-American Folktale
By Robert D. San Souci

The Patchwork Quilt
By Valerie Flournoy

Pretend You're A Cat
By Jean Marzollo

Rabbit Makes A Monkey Of Lion
By Verna Aardema

Tanya's Reunion (sequel to *The Patchwork Quilt*)
By Valerie Flournoy

The Timeless Tales Of MARGARET WISE BROWN

The uniquely talented Margaret Wise Brown (1910–1952) believed in a style of book-making that combines a child's interest in the here and now with his natural affinity for make-believe. And she was evidently on the right track—her books continue to be published again and again! Her picture-book classics have already captivated *three* generations of children, and they continue to delight first-time readers. So invite your class into a timeless tale created by Margaret Wise Brown. It will be time well spent!

by Mackie Rhodes

All books published by HarperCollins Children's Books unless otherwise indicated.

The Indoor Noisy Book

Illustrated by Leonard Weisgard

Poor little Muffin is confined to bed with a cold. But he discovers an interesting, new world when his finely tuned dog ears take him on an awesome auditory adventure! After sharing this story, ask students to sit very still with their eyes closed. Instruct them to listen for as many indoor noises as possible. Afterward, record on chart paper the noises your youngsters heard. Then invite each child to illustrate an indoor noise-making source with red, blue, and yellow markers—the colors used in the book. Assemble the pages into a class book; then read the book together. Close your eyes and perk up an ear. Oh, the wonderful things you'll hear!

The clock goes m m m m m m......

Four Fur Feet

Illustrated by Woodleigh Marx Hubbard
Published by Hyperion Books For Children

He walked in the woods on his four fur feet and he heard the birds go chirp-o.

This creature's four fur feet offer a veritable phonemic playground while adventuring around the world. As you read this story aloud, youngsters can't help but join in on the repetitive lines. Afterward, invite each child to create her own four-footed creature with an assortment of craft items including fur foot cutouts. Then have each child glue her creature to a construction-paper background. Guiding each child to follow the pattern of the book's text, record each student's dictation about her creature's adventure on that background. Then encourage each child to illustrate a background scene. Display the finished projects on a board titled "Four Fur Feet." Invite each child to read her page to the class. Then encourage the class to join in on a second reading of the same page. Neat-o!

Little Donkey Close Your Eyes

Illustrated by Ashley Wolff

Ease youngsters into rest time with the gentle, lulling rhythm of this sleepy-time book. After you share the story and children have settled in for rest time, take a photo of each resting child. Later, give each child a construction-paper cloud. Encourage him to illustrate/dictate a pleasant dream (or thought) he had during rest time. Attach each dream cloud to the corresponding child's photo. Then display all the photos on a starry background titled "Stars are quiet in the skies. Little child now close your eyes." So peaceful.

The Diggers

Illustrated by Daniel Kirk
Published by Hyperion Books For Children

Your kids will really dig this entertaining story about an assorted bunch of earth diggers. After reading and discussing the book, entice youngsters to dig into some counting practice. To prepare for this activity, gather a set of items; then secretly record the number of items in the set. (You might like to use a different set of items—such as play jewels, bones, rocks, or rubber worms—each time you do this activity.) Then bury the items in your sand table. Encourage each child, in turn, to use digging tools to dig up the buried items. When he thinks he has all the items, have him count and record how many he has found on a sticky note. Instruct the child to bury the items again for the next child. At the end of the day, have students share and compare their findings. Then reveal the exact number of hidden items. Is your number *more than, less than,* or *equal?*

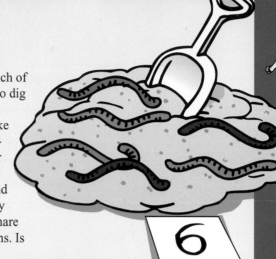

Wait Till The Moon Is Full

Illustrated by Garth Williams

Students will readily identify with this little raccoon who must wait and wait and wait until he can see the night. After reading the story aloud, ask students to share their personal experiences with being patient—such as waiting for a holiday, a birthday party, or a special trip. Then prepare this visual aid to help youngsters patiently gauge their waiting time for a special class activity. First, display an empty fishbowl to represent the moon. Place the moon, a container of clean sand, and a scoop in a prominent place in your classroom. Explain that the class must wait till the moon is full before the big event begins. Each day, invite a different child to add sand to the moon according to your directions. (Judge how many scoops of sand a child should put in according to the amount of time left before the activity.) When the moon is full, it's time to celebrate the long-awaited event. Finally!

The Days Before Now

An Autobiographical Note by Margaret Wise Brown

Adapted by Joan W. Blos
Illustrated by Thomas B. Allen
Published by Simon & Schuster Books for Young Readers

Would your students like to know a little bit more about Margaret Wise Brown? *The Days Before Now* offers just that! It has been newly edited and beautifully illustrated in storybook fashion. Youngsters will be delighted and intrigued to learn that, as a child, Margaret had 36 rabbits, 2 squirrels, a collie dog, 2 guinea hens, a Belgian hare, 7 fish, and a wild robin. As an adult, the talented author regretted having to sign her very long name!

More Timeless Tales

Animals In The Snow
Illustrated by Carol Schwartz
Published by Hyperion Books For Children

Big Red Barn
Illustrated by Felicia Bond

A Child's Good Morning Book
Illustrated by Jean Charlot

Goodnight Moon
Illustrated by Clement Hurd

On Christmas Eve
Illustrated by Nancy Edwards Calder

The Runaway Bunny
Illustrated by Clement Hurd

More JONATHAN

Since Jonathan London has no less than 30 children's books to his credit (and counting!), it's not surprising that children often ask how Mr. London comes up with ideas for all of his stories. His answer? A little bit of experience and a whole lot of imagination! In fact, according to Jonathan London, the experience he remembers is usually rather small, about the size of a dime. But his imagination is always rather large, about the size of a pizza—*extra large!* So use the ideas in this unit to get started on exploring the extra large imagination portrayed in Mr. London's literature. Odds are you'll go back for seconds…and thirds…and more!

by Allison Ward

oobie-doobie
scoobie-woobie
pip-pop-paddle-pam
skit, scat, skee
hi, hi, hiddle
giggle-y gee
me in the middle
skip, skip, ska-ree

Puddles
Illustrated by G. Brian Karas
Published by Viking

April showers bring May flowers, and they also bring *puddles!* On the morning after a storm, a little boy and girl expectantly explore their outside world. Among the young duo's many fascinating finds, perhaps the best find of all is puddles! This energetic story is sure to inspire some puddle-jumping urges in your classroom. So drip-drop into that teachable moment with this puddle-jumping measurement activity. To prepare, cut out and laminate various sizes of construction-paper puddles. Then tape all the puddles to your classroom floor. Provide standard and nonstandard measuring tools, crayons, and recording sheets nearby. (Use a permanent marker to label the puddles if appropriate for your students.) Invite each child to jump over a puddle, then measure and record the length of that puddle. Encourage children to make several jumps, measuring each of the corresponding puddles as they go. What was the longest puddle a child jumped? The shortest puddle? A puddle in the middle?

If I had a **dolfin**, I would… **rid on it to haye.** Allison

If I Had A Horse
Illustrated by Brooke Scudder
Published by Chronicle Books

Saddle up your imaginations—it's time for a magical horseback ride! Explore an array of sights and sounds as a young girl rides away on her dream horse. After sharing this story, invite students to think about their own dream pets. Then invite them to create a class sequel to Jonathan London's story. To begin, provide each child with a large piece of paper programmed with "If I had a _____, I would…" Assist each child in completing the story starter; then encourage him to illustrate the page. Bind all the pages between construction-paper covers and title the book. Keep the book in your reading center (along with London's book) for children to enjoy during reading times.

Hip Cat
Illustrated by Woodleigh Hubbard
Published by Chronicle Books

Shoobie do-wah bebop ditty! This book's about one hip cool kitty. Oobie-do John is a feline jazz musician looking for a place to play. But it seems all the good places are owned by the top dogs—who *don't* want cats! But when Oobie-do finally gets the chance to sing the blues, both the cats *and* the dogs go hog-wild! Use this unique book to introduce your little ones to *jazz.* Play selections from Miles Davis, John Coltrane, or Count Basie as you read the book aloud. Then transform your music center into a jazz center. First prompt youngsters to brainstorm a list of rhyming words or nonsense phrases similar to the sample scats in the book. Write their words on a sheet of chart paper. Post the list of words in a center along with some jazz selections. (For fun, add berets and child-safe sunglasses.) As youngsters listen to the jazz music, encourage them to use the words on the list to make up their own original scats. Wow—those kindergarten cats can wail!

Jake
1 = 24 worms
A

LONDON LITERATURE 6 Please!

Fireflies, Fireflies, Light My Way
Illustrated by Linda Messier
Published by Viking

A nocturnal walk through the summer woods has readers sliding with otters, sniffing with raccoons, and paddling with muskrats as fireflies light the way. Read the story aloud; then discuss each animal in the book. Next reinforce animal recognition and reading with these animal wheels. For each child, cut out a 2" x 2" window from a paper plate (as shown). Have each child paint the front of his plate black or dark blue. Then have each child cut out a construction-paper copy of the animal wheel on page 240. When the paint on the plate is dry, have each child add dabs of glow-in-the-dark fabric paint to resemble fireflies. When the fireflies are dry, help each child assemble his wheel by pushing a brass paper fastener through the center of both the paper plate and wheel. Invite each student to turn his wheel to the matching animal as you read the story again. Encourage each child to take his animal wheel home to keep in his own bedroom. Fireflies will light his way!

Like Butter On Pancakes
Illustrated by G. Brian Karas
Published by Puffin Books

Morning on the farm brings warm sunlight as a boy begins his daily routine that includes waking, eating breakfast, and doing the pajama dance. Soft, buttery illustrations accompany this gentle text. Extend this story by having your students each share a report on their own morning routines. To begin, give each child a sheet of white construction paper. Then ask her to illustrate a favorite part of her morning routine. Next have her paint a light yellow tempera wash over the drawing to represent sunlight. When the paint is dry, have each child share her report with the class. Then display the illustrations with the title "Sunlight Melts On Our Morning Like Butter On Pancakes."

I reed wit mi dad.

Karen

More Books By Jonathan London

At The Edge Of The Forest
Illustrated by Barbara Firth
(Candlewick Press)

The Candystore Man
Illustrated by Kevin O'Malley
(Lothrop, Lee & Shepard Books)

Jackrabbit
Illustrated by Deborah Kogan Ray
(Crown Publishers, Inc.)

Let's Go, Froggy!
Illustrated by Frank Remkiewicz
(Puffin Books)

Liplap's Wish
Illustrated by Sylvia Long
(Chronicle Books)

What Newt Could Do For Turtle
Illustrated by Louise Voce
(Candlewick Press)

Animal Wheel

Use with *Fireflies, Fireflies, Light My Way* on page 239.

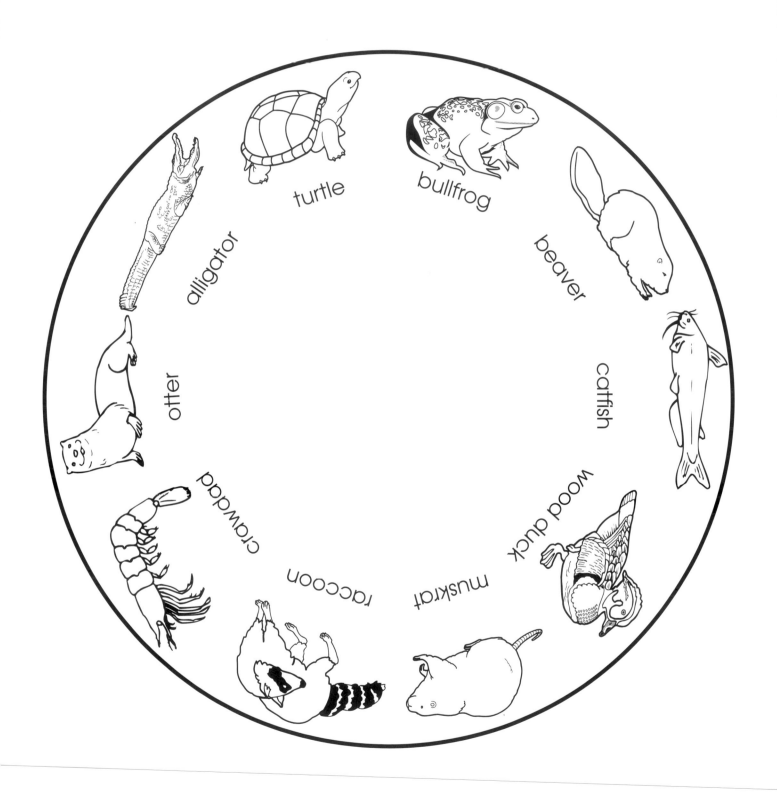

MR. AL
MUSIC AND MUCH, MUCH MORE!

Meet Al Rasso—lovingly known across the country as Mr. Al. This multitalented artist is "a musician turned educator turned entertainer-with-a-message." Mr. Al makes music out of education. Then, with contagious energy and enthusiasm, he uses his music to motivate both students and teachers alike. So add some Mr. Al to your music collection and get grooving with the fun curriculum-related ideas in this unit. You'll soon discover that Mr. Al is…well, music and much, much more!

by Mackie Rhodes

To order Mr. Al's recordings, call (800) 487-6725.

"The Train"
Mr. ALa carte
Cradle Rock Productions

Climb aboard for a rockin' ride on this imaginary train! After youngsters chug along with this action song, invite them to create a class train frieze. To prepare, program a large sheet of paper with "I will drive the train and ride it…." Then duplicate a class supply of this page on large construction-paper train cars. Ask each child to dictate/write a real or imaginary ending to the sentence and illustrate it. Next have each child cut out two construction-paper wheels and glue them to her train car. Then tape all the train cars together, end-to-end. Tape a simple train cutout to the front and a simple caboose cutout to the back. Mount this train along a classroom wall titled with a line from the chorus of the song, "C'mon Drive The Train And Ride It!" During group time, invite each child to read her page to the class. After each child reads a page, invite the class to recognize her good work with a hearty "toot-toot!"

"Creepy Crawlin' "
Mr. Al Sings And Moves
Melody House, Inc.

This fun song gets everyone in the act of following directions as they creep and crawl along. After youngsters get their fill of creepy-crawly movement, direct them to the art center to create their own creepy-crawly creatures. Stock the center with an assortment of craft items, such as cardboard tubes, small boxes, foam blocks, craft foam, pipe cleaners, craft sticks, and wiggle eyes. Then invite each center visitor to create an original creepy-crawly critter. Later, play the song again, this time having youngsters manipulate their critters according to the lyrics.

"Blowin' In The Breeze"
Mr. Al: Bop 'Til You Drop
Melody House, Inc.

Share this soothing song on a breezy, sunny day; then watch those imaginations fly up and away! On such a day, securely attach several lengths of bulletin-board paper to a fence or outdoor wall. (Or anchor the paper on the ground with rocks.) Then play the song and invite children to move to the music. Encourage them to talk about how the music makes them feel. Afterward, provide paint smocks, watercolor sets, a variety of paintbrushes, and containers of water. If you have a way of playing the song while you're outside, bring that with you! Then show students their giant outdoor "easel" and encourage them to paint their dreams, wishes, or whatever might breeze through their imaginations. Ahhh, creative expression at its best!

Here's More Mr. Al!
(Produced by Melody House, Inc.)

Sing Me Some Sanity

Mr. Al: Kids Wanna Rock

...And With His Friend, Stephen Fite

Back To School

Back To School Again

Just One World

Science Units

Wonders Never Cease
Simple Science For Young Children

A Bounty Of Bubbles

This introduction to "bubble-ology" (the scientific study of bubbles, of course!) will have your classroom bursting with discoveries all about the basics of bubbles.

ideas by Dr. Suzanne Moore

Objective: Students will learn that bubbles are made up of air that is surrounded by a thin liquid skin. They will also discover that bubbles can only be made through objects that have holes in them.

Bubble Brew

When you make the bubble recipe to the right, be sure to use bottled water. (Some tap water contains minerals that make bubble blowing more difficult.) Let this solution sit for about five days before you use it. The longer the bubble mixture ages, the better the bubbles! Why not mix up a big batch of Bubble Brew at the beginning of school to use throughout the year?

Basic Bubble Brew
Gently stir together:
1 gallon of water
2/3 cup Dawn® dishwashing liquid
1 tablespoon glycerin

Bubbling Over

This air-filled activity prompts youngsters to use their observing and predicting skills—but it might leave them just a little bit breathless!

You will need:
1 paper cup per child
1 plastic straw per child
water
Dawn® dishwashing liquid
paper towels for cleanup

After filling each cup halfway with water, give each child a cup and a straw. Invite children to use their straws to blow bubbles in the water. Ask youngsters why they think the bubbles were made. Then add two to three drops of Dawn® to each cup. Have each child gently mix the soap and water with her straw. Ask youngsters to predict what will happen when they blow into the soap-and-water solution. Then have them blow bubbles again. Were there more bubbles this time? Why?

Hint: Any place that bubbles land might become slippery. A vinegar-and-water solution can be used for easy cleanup.

Did You Know...

The outside of a bubble is a very thin film of liquid. Bubbles that are made of soap and water do not break as easily as plain-water bubbles. This is because soapy water sticks together better than plain water.

Blowing Bubbles

This activity gives each child a hands-on opportunity to explore the bubble-making process.

You will need:
- 1 small paper cup per child
- 1 plastic straw per child
- 1 foam bowl per small group
- Bubble Brew

In advance, use a sharp pencil to poke a hole about one inch from the bottom of each cup. (The hole should be slightly smaller than the circumference of the straw.) Then pour some Bubble Brew into each bowl. Next distribute a cup and a straw to each child. Help each child poke his straw through the hole in his cup. Instruct the child to turn his cup upside down, dip it in the Bubble Brew, and then turn it right-side up. What does he see? Have the child gently blow through the straw. What happens? Who knows why? Allow plenty of time for free exploration, encouraging children to try blowing hard, soft, and then not at all.

Did You Know...
Bubbles are filled with air or gas. When you blew into the straw, you filled the bubble with air.

A Rainbow Of Colors

Watch in delight as your youngsters discover a wonderful world of color in their bubbles.

You will need:
bubble pipes made in "Blowing Bubbles"

Following the same procedure used in "Blowing Bubbles," have each child blow a bubble with her back to the sunlight. Then have her move the bubble so that the sunlight passes through it. What does she see? Why? How many different colors can she identify?

Did You Know...
When the sunlight passes through the bubble, the colors of the rainbow can be seen on the outside of the bubble.

Bubble Catching

Your little scientists will be only too eager to get their hands on this bubbly activity.

You will need:
1 pipe cleaner per child
several small bowls of Bubble Brew
paper towels for easy cleanup

Begin by showing your students how to bend and twist a pipe cleaner to make a bubble wand. Then group children into pairs. Have one child in each pair blow bubbles, while his partner attempts to catch them. Then have the children switch roles and repeat the activity. Prompt children to discuss their discoveries. Then prompt youngsters by saying, "If a bubble breaks when it hits something *dry*, I wonder if it will still break when it hits something..." Then let your youngsters try out their thoughts. (Guide children to try catching bubbles on soapy fingers, straws, and bubble blowers. You can even have one child blow a bubble while another child sticks a soapy straw right into it!)

Did You Know...

A bubble's thin skin is made of liquid. When it lands on something dry, the liquid is absorbed by the dry object and the bubble pops. When a bubble comes in contact with a wet surface, the wet surface simply becomes part of the bubble.

Bubbles Or Bust

Exactly what kinds of things can be used to make bubbles? In this activity your students will be judges of that. Provide a supply of objects that children can immerse in bubble solution. (Be sure that you have a mixture of objects with and without holes, such as a pair of scissors, a plastic berry basket, a spoon, and a ruler.) Place the objects in a center, along with a large bowl of Bubble Brew and a copy of the recording sheet (page 247) for each child. When a child visits this center, have her choose one of the objects and write it (or draw it) on her recording sheet. Then have her indicate her prediction by drawing a happy face (for yes) if bubbles can be made or a sad face (for no) if bubbles can't be made. Next have her test it out and record the results. Extend this activity by asking children to bring in additional items to try out in this bubble-making center. Did you get bountiful bubbles, or was it a bust?

Some other bubble-making props:

mason jar lids	flyswatters	colanders
slotted spatulas	whisks	plastic bangle bracelets
cookie cutters	plastic six-pack rings	

Name _____

Can it make bubbles?

Object	Prediction	Result

Use with "Bubbles Or Bust" on page 246.

Wonders Never Cease

Simple Science For Young Children

The Magic Of Magnets!

These hands-on science activities will leave your youngsters highly attracted to magnets.

ideas by Dr. Suzanne Moore

Objective: Students will learn that magnets attract certain types of materials and that magnets may attract or repel other magnets.

Hocus Pocus! Abracadox! Fiddly, Faddly— Now, Out of the box!

Is It Magic?

Pique your youngsters' curiosity with the mystique of magnets. To prepare, cut out two construction-paper pumpkins (or any other thematic shape). Tape a large, metal paper clip to the back of the stem of one pumpkin. Then glue the two pumpkins together back-to-back. Tape a strong magnet to one end of a ruler; then cover the ruler with black and white construction paper to resemble a magic wand. Place the pumpkin in a box. Then announce that you are going to pull something out of the box with your magic wand. With dramatic flair, say some magic words as you touch the magnetic end of the wand to the pumpkin stem. When you "magically" lift the pumpkin out of the box, youngsters will be amazed—and the discovery process begins!

Magic Words	It still works without the magic words.
Pumpkin	We can only pick up the top of the pumpkin.
Magic Wand	Only one end of the wand is magic!

Exploring The Magic

After doing the activity in "Is It Magic?", ask youngsters to share their ideas about how the trick worked. Guide them to question and to test the different variables that might contribute to the success or failure of the trick. For example, are the magic words necessary? Will any part of the wand work just as well? How about any part of the pumpkin? Write students' comments on a sheet of chart paper. Then write their discoveries as you explore together. Finally, reveal the "magic" behind the trick.

The Magic Explained

A *magnet* is usually a piece of metal that pulls other metal objects toward it. The paper clip in the pumpkin is made of metal. When the magnet and paper clip were placed close together, the magnet's force pulled the paper clip until it stuck to the magnet.

Did You Know?

Magnets have an invisible force that can attract objects made of certain metals. This power to attract is called magnetism.

Discovery Center

Attract student attention and stick-to-itiveness with this center. To prepare, collect an assortment of magnets and a variety of metal and nonmetal items, such as those listed. Label one large foam meat tray with "Yes" and a smiley face; then label a separate tray with "No" and a sad face. Place the magnets, trays, and objects in a center. Invite student pairs to visit this center. Encourage the partners to predict whether or not each object will be attracted to a magnet, then try it out. Have them place each item on the corresponding tray. Ask children to determine which materials stick to the magnets. Is it metal? Plastic? Wood? Paper?

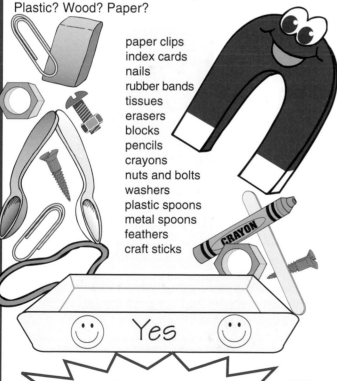

paper clips
index cards
nails
rubber bands
tissues
erasers
blocks
pencils
crayons
nuts and bolts
washers
plastic spoons
metal spoons
feathers
craft sticks

Did You Know?

Magnets attract objects made of the metals iron, steel, cobalt, *or* nickel.

Feature Attractions

by

Blake Harris

A magnet attracts a washer ,3

"Feature Attractions" Booklet

Once your students are familiar with the types of items that are attracted to magnets, the time is right to make these booklets. First, duplicate a class supply of pages 252 and 253. Also provide a class supply of four items that are magnetic and four that are non-magnetic. Have each child cut apart his booklet cover and pages, then sequence and staple them together. Have the child write his name on the cover. On each of pages 1 through 6, read the text together; then have the child tape or glue a corresponding item to the page. Next have him write/dictate to complete the text. For page 7, ask the child to write the name of an object with which he has not experimented, then attach that object to the last page. Finally, attach a length of magnetic tape to a tagboard strip; then attach the strip to the booklet with yarn. Invite each child to share his booklet with a classmate, demonstrating the attraction of each item to the attached magnet. Encourage each student pair to predict and then test out the magnetism of the object on the last page. Then encourage youngsters to share their booklets with family members and to display them as the feature attractions on their refrigerators.

Use The Force

Are all magnets created equal? Your students can be the judges of that. Collect several different sizes and shapes of magnets; then fill a bowl with metal paper clips. Program a copy of the chart on page 254 with the different types of magnets collected. Then duplicate the chart for each child. Have each child record her prediction of how many paper clips each magnet might attract. Then have each child test her predictions by placing each magnet, one at a time, into the bowl of paper clips. Help her count and record the actual number of clips attracted by each magnet. Then have the child compare that number to her prediction. Also, invite students to compare their data with each other. Which magnet has the greatest force?

Name __Ashley Dawson__

How Many Paper Clips?

Magnet	Prediction	Actual Number
⭕	15	34
▬	18	23
⋂	30	42
◼	20	

Chain Reaction

Now that your budding scientists have witnessed the force of different magnets, enlighten them with this experiment. Pick up one paper clip with a magnet. Then touch another paper clip to the end of the first clip. What happens? Youngsters will be amazed to see that it sticks to the first paper clip! Continue adding paper clips to the magnetic chain until the last clip keeps falling off. Then count the number of clips in the chain. Repeat the experiment with different magnets and compare the results. Why do the paper clips stick to each other to create a chain?

The Force Facts

The stronger the force of a magnet, the greater the number of magnetic items it will attract.

This Is Why

Some of the magnet's force moves into the first paper clip so that it, too, has some power to attract. Some magnetic force continues to move into each added paper clip. But this transferred force becomes weaker and weaker as the paper clips get farther away from the original magnet.

Attract Or Repel?

Use this activity to help youngsters discover that a magnet can both attract and *repel*. In small groups, have each child push the ends of two bar magnets toward each other. What happens? Now flip one of the magnets and push the ends together again. What happens then? Explain that each end of a magnet will either pull another magnet toward it or push the other magnet away. Then attach small bar magnets to a variety of toy vehicles. Place the vehicles and some magnets in a discovery center. Encourage youngsters to "drive" the vehicles using only the magnets' abilities to attract and repel.

More About Magnets

Mesmerized with magnets? If so, these books will attract your attention!

What Makes A Magnet?
By Franklyn M. Branley
Illustrated by True Kelley
Published by HarperCollins Publishers, Inc.

Science For Fun: Playing With Magnets
By Gary Gibson
Published by Copper Beech Books

The Science Book Of Magnets
By Neil Ardley
Published by Harcourt Brace Jovanovich, Publishers

Did You Know?

Every magnet has two places called poles. That's where the power is the strongest. The north pole *of one magnet attracts the* south pole *of another magnet. But when two north poles (or two south poles) are put together, the magnets push away from, or* repel, *each other.*

Use with " 'Feature Attractions' Booklet" on page 249.

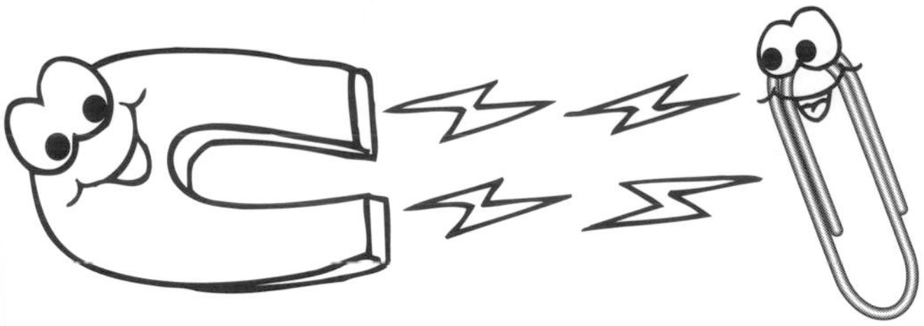

Feature Attractions

by

A magnet attracts a

_______________________, 1

but not a _______________. 2

A magnet attracts a

_______________________, 3

©The Education Center, Inc. • *THE MAILBOX®* • *Kindergarten* • Oct/Nov 1998

Use with " 'Feature Attractions' Booklet" on page 249.

but not a ___________.
4

A magnet attracts a
_____________________,
5

but not a ___________.
6

Would a magnet
attract a __________?
7

Name _____

 # How Many Paper Clips?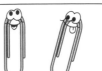

Magnet	Prediction	Actual Number

Note To The Teacher: Use this chart with "Use The Force" on page 250.

has a

MAGICAL

knowledge of

MAGNETS!

has a

MAGICAL

knowledge of

MAGNETS!

Investigating Eggs

Scramble up some scientific thinking with these egg explorations. (Also see "Egg 'em On!" on pages 182–188 for more cross-curricular egg-related ideas.)

ideas by Dr. Suzanne Moore

* Note: After handling eggs, be sure both children and adults wash their hands thoroughly.

What Do You Know?

Introduce your youngsters to egg investigations by posing the following riddle: What must be broken before it can be used? When someone guesses an egg—with your prompting, if necessary—pass around a few hard-boiled eggs. Ask youngsters to carefully examine the eggs and tell what they already know about them. Write children's responses on an egg-shaped cutout. Then ask what your youngsters would like to know about eggs. Write these queries on a different egg-shaped cutout. At the culmination of your egg studies, write a list of what your students learned on a third egg-shaped cutout. So that's what you know!

What We Know
• Eggs are white.
• Some are brown and blue too.
• Eggs crack.
• These eggs are cold and smooth.

What We Want To Know
• What happens to the baby chick?
• When the mom chicken sits on the eggs, why don't they crack?

Three In One

How many parts does an egg have? Crack open this mystery and see! Give each child in a small group a sheet of paper. Display a raw egg; then ask students how many parts they think the egg has. Then break open the egg (being careful not to break the yolk) and pour the insides onto a plate. Also position the eggshells on the plate. Pass the plate around, encouraging the children to visually examine the egg, then draw what they see. How many parts did they draw? Summarize your discussion by writing the actual names of each egg part: white, yolk, and shell. Have each child copy the words on the appropriate part of his illustration. Then encourage each child to take his illustration home and share this information with his family.

shell
white
yolk
Joey

Not Quite White

Clearly, there's some explaining to do about the egg white! For this activity, you'll need a raw egg and an electric skillet. After youngsters have examined the parts of an egg in "Three In One," draw their attention again to the egg white. Ask them what color it is. Did your students notice that the egg white isn't really quite white? Ask them why they suppose it is called the egg *white*. Then slide the raw egg into an oiled, heated skillet. Encourage children to observe the changes that take place. Any questions?

sizzle

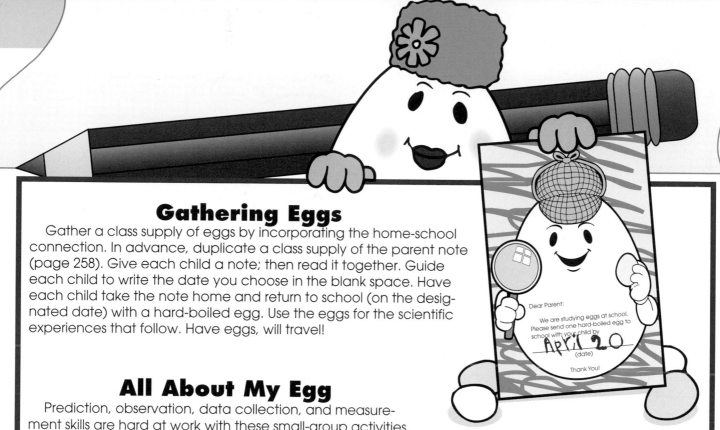

Gathering Eggs

Gather a class supply of eggs by incorporating the home-school connection. In advance, duplicate a class supply of the parent note (page 258). Give each child a note; then read it together. Guide each child to write the date you choose in the blank space. Have each child take the note home and return to school (on the designated date) with a hard-boiled egg. Use the eggs for the scientific experiences that follow. Have eggs, will travel!

Dear Parent:
We are studying eggs at school.
Please send one hard-boiled egg to school with your child by
April 20
(date)

Thank You!

All About My Egg

Prediction, observation, data collection, and measurement skills are hard at work with these small-group activities. In advance, mark a class supply of ten-ounce plastic cups at the halfway point. Also duplicate a class supply of the recording sheet on page 259. To do these activities, each child will need her egg, a marked cup, and a recording sheet. Each small group will need a pitcher of water and a balance scale to share. Let the egg investigations begin!

How Much Space?

Help each child fill her cup to the mark with water. Have her color in the bottom half of the cup on her recording sheet with a blue crayon. Then have each child gently place her egg in the water. What happens to the water? Invite children to share their observations and to brainstorm why the water level changed. After your discussion, explain that the egg and the water cannot take up the same space at the same time. So the egg pushed the water out of the way. Have children record the new water level with another color of crayon.

How Much Weight?

Have each child, in turn, position his egg on one side of a balance scale. Then have him add small blocks or counters to the other side until the scale is balanced. Encourage each child to fill in the blank under the scale.

How Many Squares?

Have each child look at the graphed square on his paper. Ask him to guess how many squares his egg will cover—whole and partial—and write that number in the space provided. Next have him place his egg on the graphed square and trace around it. Then have him remove his egg and count the number of squares within the egg shape. Instruct him to write that number on his recording sheet; then discuss the differences.

All About My Egg
by Jason

How Many Squares?

How Much Space?

My guess: 38 ☐ s.
It covered about 20 ☐ s.

My egg took up this much space.

How much weight?

My egg weighed 23 KUbz

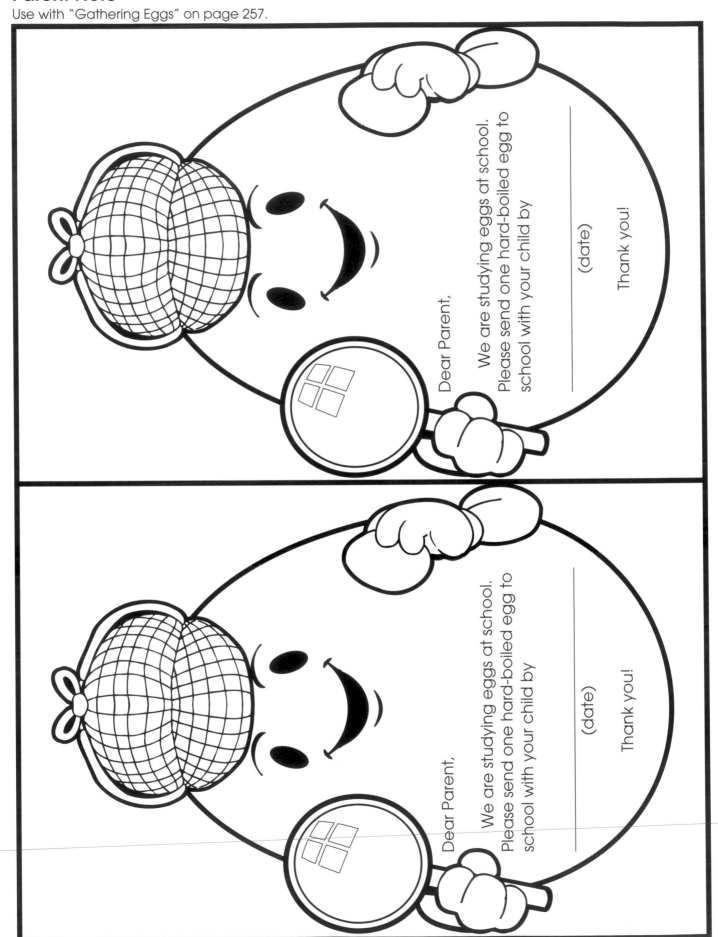

Dear Parent,

We are studying eggs at school. Please send one hard-boiled egg to school with your child by

_____
(date)

Thank you!

Dear Parent,

We are studying eggs at school. Please send one hard-boiled egg to school with your child by

_____
(date)

Thank you!

All About My Egg

by _____

How Many Squares?

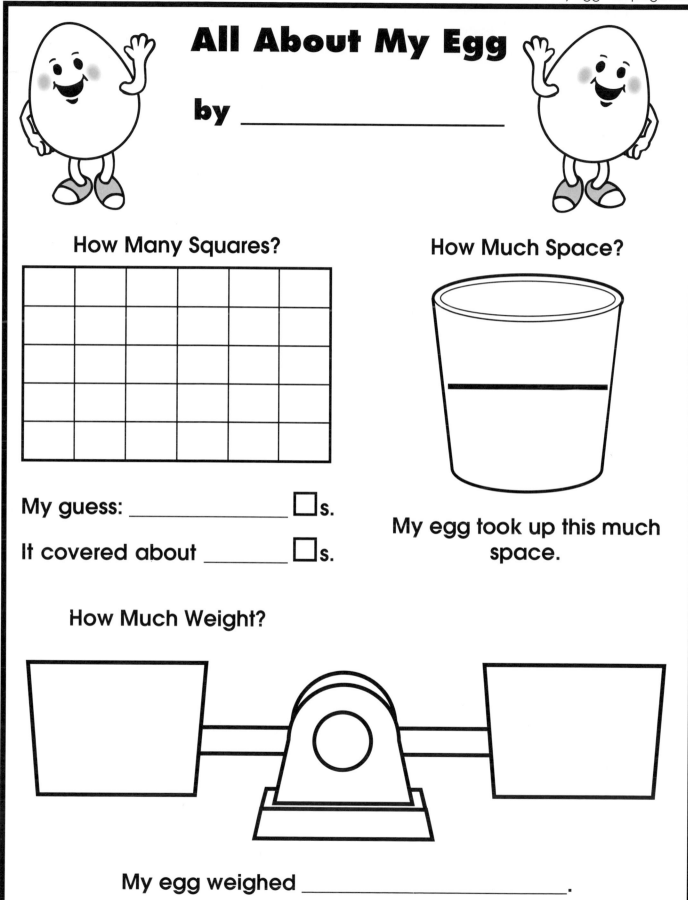

My guess: _____ ☐s.

It covered about _____ ☐s.

How Much Space?

My egg took up this much space.

How Much Weight?

My egg weighed _____.

Wonders Never Cease

Simple Science For Young Children

by Suzanne Moore

A Drop In The Bucket

Stir up lots of science fun with these learning experiences about water solubles.

Objective: Students will learn that some substances dissolve in water and that these substances are called *solubles.*

Getting Ready: To prepare for these studies, duplicate a class supply of the parent note on page 262. (If desired, indicate which supplies you'd like each parent to provide by checking the blank next to that item.) Several days before you begin this unit, send a note home with each child.

Pass The Sugar, Please!

Plunge into your study of solubles with this idea where the sense of taste does the testing.

For each child you will need
1 ten-ounce clear plastic cup
1 straw
1 plastic spoon

For each small group you will need
approximately 1/2 cup of sugar
1 pitcher of water

To begin, have each child in a group pour some water into her cup, then take a sip. What does it taste like? Then invite each child to watch the water carefully as she adds a spoonful of sugar to her cup. (Don't stir yet!) When the sugar settles on the bottom, have each child use her straw to experiment taking sips from the top, middle, and bottom of the cup. Finally, ask each child to gently stir the sugar into the water. What happened visually? Then invite them to take a sip. Where is the sugar? How can they tell?

The sugar dissolved in the water. It mixed in with the water so much that it can no longer be seen separately.

Prove It!

Just in case the taste testing wasn't completely convincing in "Pass The Sugar, Please!", the eyes have it in this activity—not to mention some great fine-motor practice!

For each child you will need
1 cup of sugar-water (from "Pass The Sugar, Please!")
1 foil tart pan

For each small group you will need
eyedroppers to share

Instruct each child to use his eyedropper to drop *just a few* drops of sugar-water into his foil pan. Arrange all the pans in a warm spot where they will not be disturbed during the day. Encourage children to predict what will happen. After 24 hours, have each child check his pan. What happened? Why? How does this prove that the sugar was really still in the water?

The water evaporated into the air so that only the sugar was left in the pan.

Did You Know?
When a substance dissolves in water, that substance is called a *soluble.*

It's A Race!

Observation and communication skills flow quite freely out of this small-group activity.

For each small group you will need
2 clear, plastic, lidded jars   1 teaspoon sugar granules
1 sugar cube   water

To begin, ask students which will dissolve faster in water—the sugar cube or sugar granules. Record students' predictions; then begin the process of finding out! Have two children in each group pour water in the two jars. Then invite another child to drop a sugar cube in one jar, while another child adds a spoonful of sugar granules to the second. Instruct students to tightly screw the lid on each jar. Then sing or chant the verses to the right as each child in the group takes a turn shaking the jars. Pause after each stanza to observe what is happening inside the jars. (Have children continue shaking the jars until you see that the sugar granules have dissolved.) Then ask children to communicate what they think happened and why.

(sung to the tune of "Row, Row, Row Your Boat")

Shake, shake, shake the jar.
Shake it up and down.
Shake it left and shake it right.
Then turn it upside down.

Granules or sugar cube,
Which will win the race?
Dissolving in the water first,
With nothing left to trace!

The sugar granules dissolved in the water quicker because they were broken into smaller pieces in the first place.

Whole "Lotta" Shakin' Going On!

Set up this free-exploration center to stimulate lots of discovery learning.

You will need
a duplicated supply of blank prediction charts
  (see the completed sample at right)
pencils
clear plastic cups and lidded jars
plastic spoons
paper towels
water
a sink or bucket for pouring out student-made solutions
a supply of solubles and insolubles, such as
  —bouillon cubes and granules   —cornstarch
  —powdered drink mixes   —flour
  —gelatin mixes   —dried beans
  —salt   —buttons
  —soap powder   —sand

When a child visits this center, invite her to choose an item to explore. Have her draw or write the name of that item on the chart, then predict whether or not she thinks it will dissolve in water. After each exploration, encourage the child to record the results. Then have her rinse and wipe out her cup or jar before beginning the process again with another item. Later, have each child bring her completed chart to a group time and discuss the results together.

If a substance does not dissolve in water, it is called insoluble.

Dear Parent,

We are studying about water solubles at school. During our studies, we will be discovering what substances mix with and dissolve in water. In order to stock our classroom for this project, we need a supply of the items listed below. If you are able to donate something from the list below, please send it to school by

_____.

Thank you for supporting your child's learning!

___10-ounce clear plastic cups
___plastic spoons
___sugar
___sugar cubes
___foil tart pans
___bouillon cubes
___bouillon granules
___dried beans

___soap powder
___flour
___salt
___cornstarch
___powdered drink mixes
___gelatin mixes
___buttons
___clean play sand

©The Education Center, Inc. • *THE MAILBOX® • Kindergarten •* June/July 1999

Dear Parent,

We are studying about water solubles at school. During our studies, we will be discovering what substances mix with and dissolve in water. In order to stock our classroom for this project, we need a supply of the items listed below. If you are able to donate something from the list below, please send it to school by

_____.

Thank you for supporting your child's learning!

___10-ounce clear plastic cups
___plastic spoons
___sugar
___sugar cubes
___foil tart pans
___bouillon cubes
___bouillon granules
___dried beans

___soap powder
___flour
___salt
___cornstarch
___powdered drink mixes
___gelatin mixes
___buttons
___clean play sand

©The Education Center, Inc. • *THE MAILBOX® • Kindergarten •* June/July 1999

KINDERGARTEN CAFÉ

Kindergarten Café

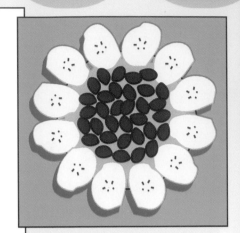

August
Sunflower Health Snacks

Ingredients For One:
1 large oatmeal cookie
smooth peanut butter
banana chips
raisins

Utensils And Supplies:
plastic knives for students
paper plates for students

Teacher Preparation:
- Arrange the ingredients for easy student access.

September
Caramel Apple-O's

Ingredients For One:
1 rice cake
caramel apple dip
chopped apples
cinnamon sugar

Utensils And Supplies:
plastic knives for students
paper plates for students
1 spoon

Teacher Preparation:
- Chop a supply of apples.
- If desired, toss the chopped apples in lemon juice to prevent browning.
- Arrange the ingredients for easy student access.

To prepare for each cooking activity, duplicate a classroom supply plus one extra of the recipe that you will be using (pages 265–266). Color one copy of the recipe; then cut these cards apart. Display the colored cards in sequence. Arrange the needed ingredients and utensils near the recipe cards. As a group of children visits the cooking center, ask each child to color a recipe, then cut the cards apart. Have each child sequence his cards; then staple them together, creating a small recipe booklet. Ask each child to explain the steps in the recipe. According to each child's abilities, have him read the directions (or circle familiar letters, numerals, or sight words). After each cooking event, encourage each child to take his recipe home and keep it in a box to make a collection of his very own cooking recipes.

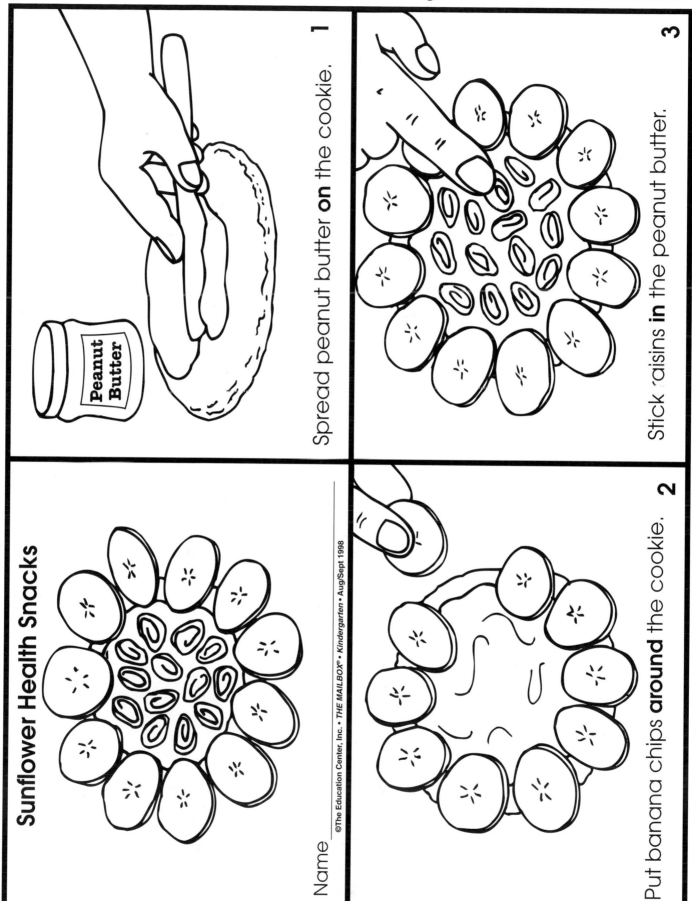

1

Spread peanut butter **on** the cookie.

3

Stick raisins **in** the peanut butter.

Sunflower Health Snacks

Name _____

©The Education Center, Inc. • THE MAILBOX® • Kindergarten • Aug/Sept 1998

2

Put banana chips **around** the cookie.

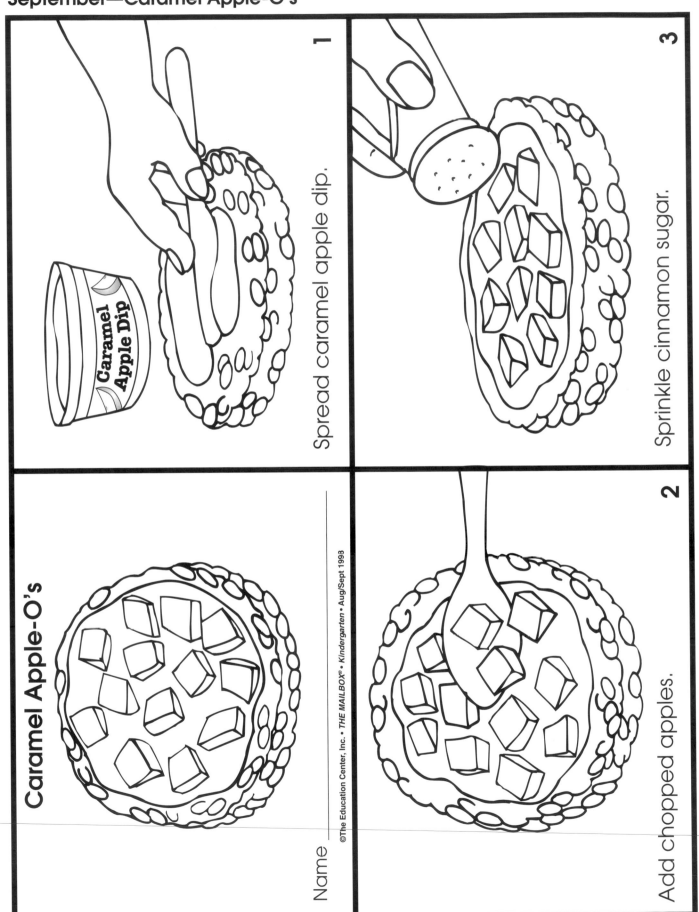

1

Spread caramel apple dip.

Caramel Apple Dip

3

Sprinkle cinnamon sugar.

Caramel Apple-O's

Name

2

Add chopped apples.

Kindergarten Café

October
Crunchy, Munchy Spiders

Ingredients For One:
1 large marshmallow
8 pretzel sticks
melted baking chocolate

Utensils And Supplies:
1 paper plate per child
plastic spoons

Teacher Preparation:
- Melt eight-ounces of semisweet baking chocolate according to package directions.
- Arrange the supplies and ingredients for easy student access.

Cathy Gust—Gr. K, Stiegel Elementary School, Manheim, PA

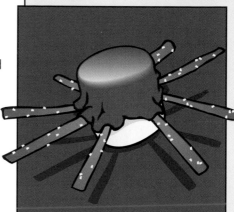

November
Helpful Squanto's Snack

Ingredients For One:
4 Oreos® cookies
3 candy corns
2 Gummy fish

Utensils And Supplies:
1 Ziploc® sandwich bag per child
rolling pin
1 clean plastic cup per child

Teacher Preparation:
- Introduce Squanto by reading *Thanksgiving Is...* by Louise Borden.
- Arrange the supplies and ingredients for easy student access.

Laura J. Robinson—Gr. K
Wheatley Elementary School
DuQuoin, IL

To prepare for each cooking activity, duplicate a classroom supply plus one extra of the recipe that you will be using (pages 268–269). Color one copy of the recipe; then cut the cards apart. Display the colored cards in sequence in your cooking center. Arrange the needed ingredients and utensils near the recipe cards. As a small group visits the center, ask each child in the group to color a recipe, then cut the cards apart. Have each child sequence his cards; then staple them together, creating a small recipe booklet. Ask each child to explain the steps in the recipe. According to each child's abilities, have him read the directions (or circle familiar letters, numerals, or sight words). After each cooking event, encourage each child to take his recipe home and keep it in a box to make a collection of his very own cooking recipes.

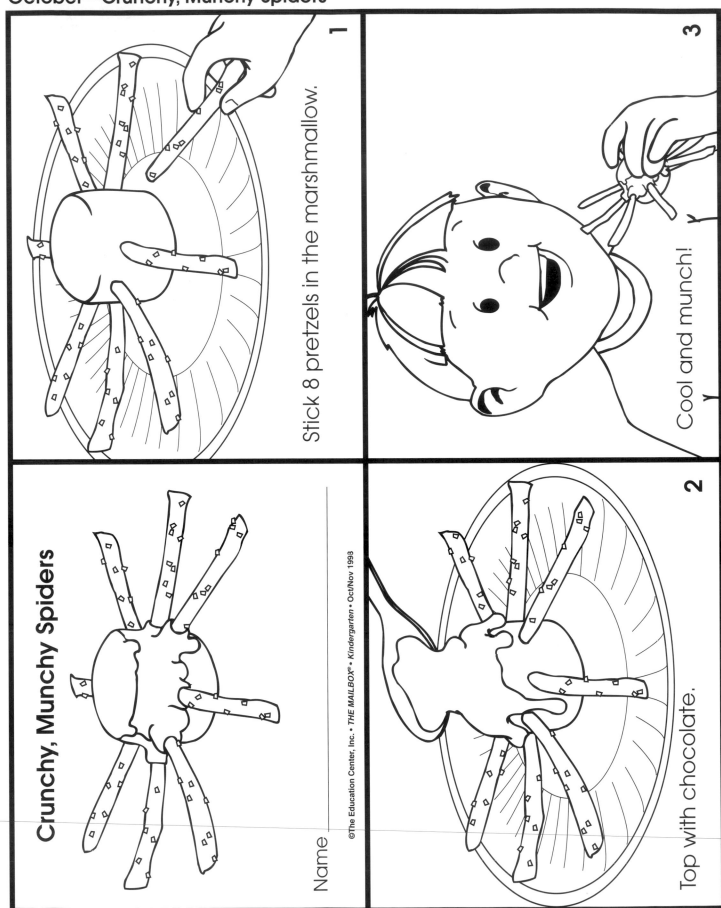

1

Stick 8 pretzels in the marshmallow.

3

Cool and munch!

Crunchy, Munchy Spiders

Name _____

2

Top with chocolate.

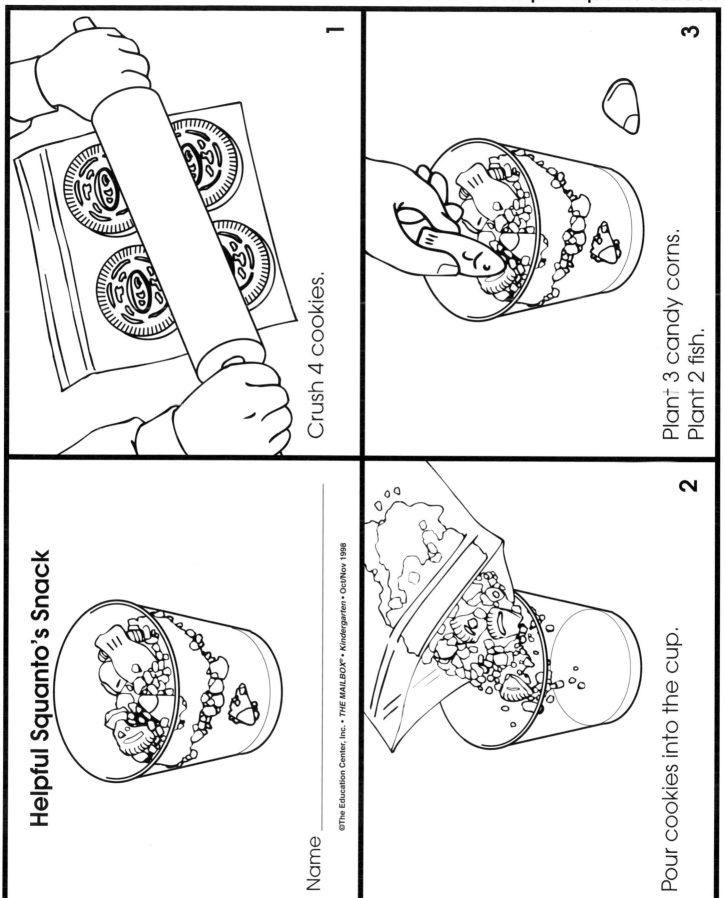

1

Crush 4 cookies.

3

Plant 3 candy corns.
Plant 2 fish.

Helpful Squanto's Snack

Name _____

2

Pour cookies into the cup.

Kindergarten Café

December-Reindeer Pops

Ingredients For One:

1 banana half   2 mini pretzels   melted chocolate
2 M&M's®   1 small red gumdrop   peanut butter

Utensils And Supplies:

waxed paper (one piece per child)
craft sticks (one per child)

Teacher Preparation:

- Cut bananas in half (as shown).
- Melt 16 ounces of semisweet baking chocolate according to package directions.
- Arrange the supplies and ingredients for easy student access.

January-Cheesy Treats

Ingredients For One:

1 large triangle-shaped   2 olive slices
   corn tortilla chip   1 strand of string cheese
2 pickle chips   pimento cheese spread
2 small pretzel sticks

Utensils And Supplies:

plastic knives   small paper plates

Teacher Preparation:

- Share one or more of the whiskery mice tales recommended on pages 60–65.
- Demonstrate how to cut off one edge of a pickle chip to make a mouse-ear shape.
- Arrange the supplies and ingredients for easy student access.

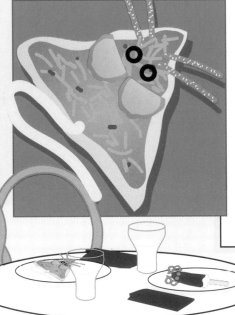

To prepare for each cooking activity, duplicate a classroom supply plus one extra of the recipe that you will be using (pages 271–272). Color one copy of the recipe; then cut the cards apart. Display the colored cards in sequence in your cooking center. Arrange the needed ingredients and utensils near the recipe cards. As a small group of children visits the cooking center, ask each child in the group to color a recipe, then cut the cards apart. Have each child sequence his cards; then staple them together, creating a small recipe booklet. Ask each child to explain the steps in the recipe. According to each child's abilities, have him read the directions (or circle familiar letters, numerals, or sight words). After each cooking event, encourage each child to take his recipe home and keep it in a box to make a collection of his very own cooking recipes.

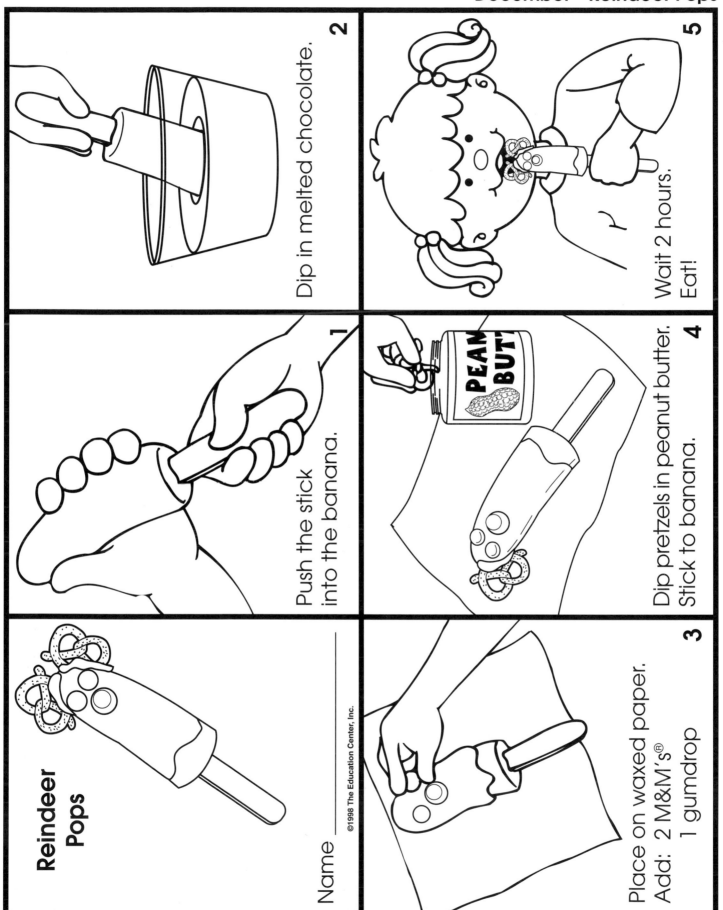

2 Dip in melted chocolate.

5 Wait 2 hours. Eat!

1 Push the stick into the banana.

4 Dip pretzels in peanut butter. Stick to banana.

Reindeer Pops

Name

©1998 The Education Center, Inc.

3 Place on waxed paper. Add: 2 M&M's® 1 gumdrop

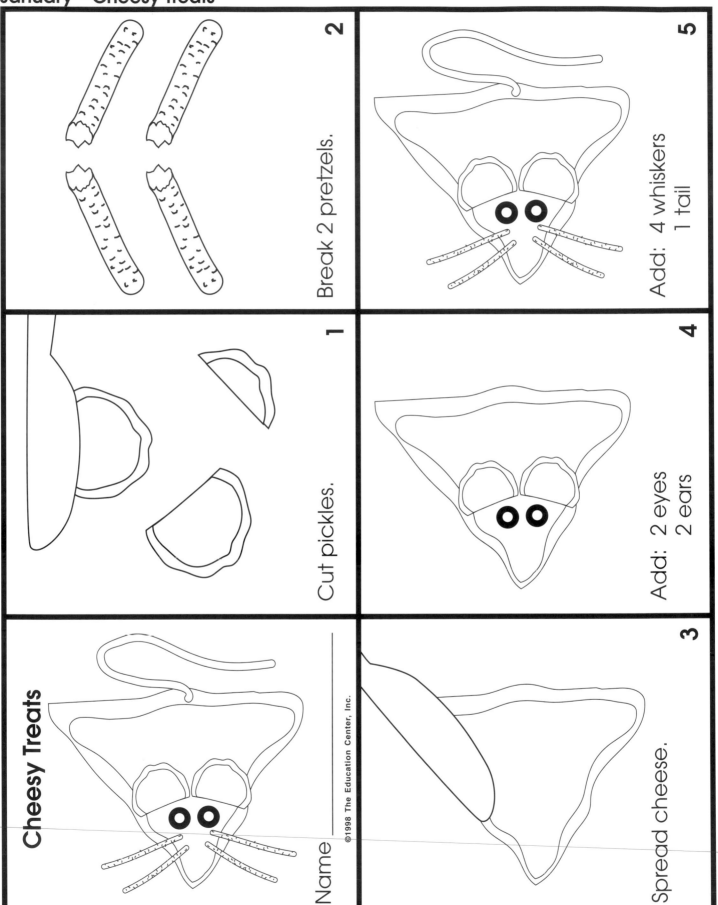

2 Break 2 pretzels.

5 Add: 4 whiskers
1 tail

1 Cut pickles.

4 Add: 2 eyes
2 ears

Cheesy Treats

Name _____

©1998 The Education Center, Inc.

3 Spread cheese.

Kindergarten Café

February—Raspberry Hearts

Ingredients For One:
1 slice of bread
raspberries *(fresh, or frozen
and defrosted)*
soft cream cheese
sugar

Utensils And Supplies:
heart-shaped cookie cutter(s)
1 paper plate per child
plastic knives

Teacher Preparation:
- Bring cream cheese to room temperature.
- Arrange the supplies and ingredients for easy student
  access.

Florence Paola, Briarfield Day School, Stratford, CT

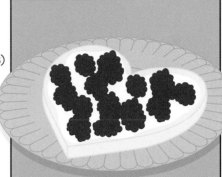

March—Green Eggs With Ham

Ingredients For One:
1 hard-boiled egg
green food coloring
1 slice of ham
water

Utensils And Supplies:
1 paper plate per child
1 paper cup per child
plastic spoons

Teacher Preparation:
- Hard-boil, cool, and peel a class supply of eggs.
- Read aloud *Green Eggs And Ham* by Dr. Seuss.
  Tell the children that Dr. Seuss was born in March
  (March 2, 1904). Then celebrate his birthday with
  a special treat!
- Arrange the ingredients for easy stu-
  dent access.

To prepare for each cooking activity, duplicate a class supply plus one extra of
the recipe that you will be using (pages 274–275). Color one copy of the recipe;
then cut the cards apart. Display the colored cards in sequence in your cooking
center. Arrange the needed ingredients and utensils near the recipe cards. As a
small group of children visits the cooking center, ask each child in the group to color
a recipe, then cut the cards apart. Have each child sequence his cards; then staple
them together, creating a small recipe booklet. According to each child's abilities,
have him read the directions (or do other appropriate phonemic activities). After
each cooking event, encourage each child to take his recipe home and keep it in
a box to make a collection of his very own cooking recipes.

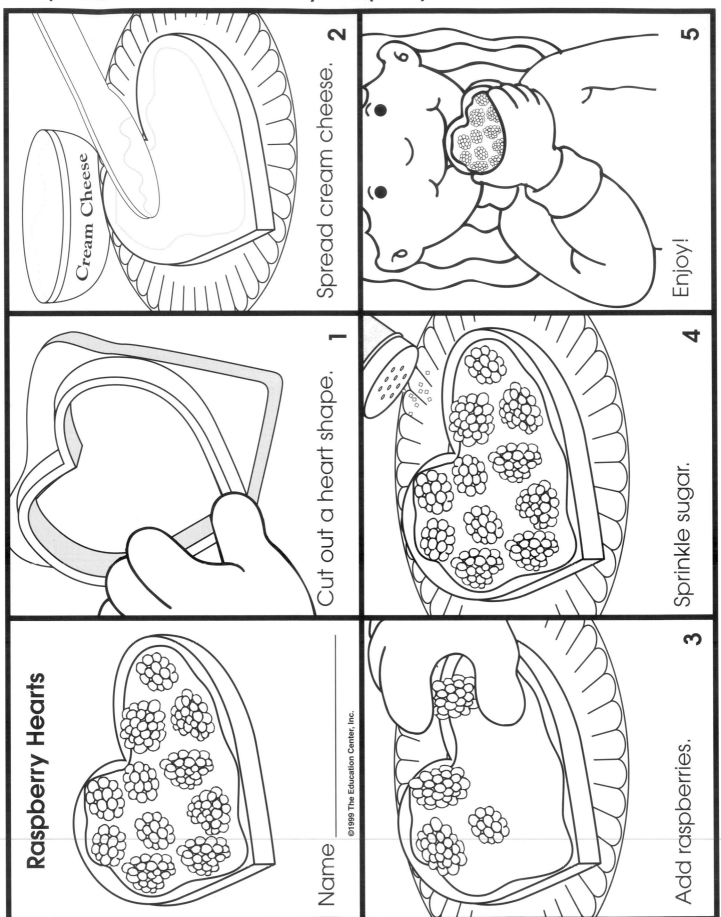

2 Spread cream cheese.

Cream Cheese

5 Enjoy!

1 Cut out a heart shape.

4 Sprinkle sugar.

Raspberry Hearts

Name _____

©1999 The Education Center, Inc.

3 Add raspberries.

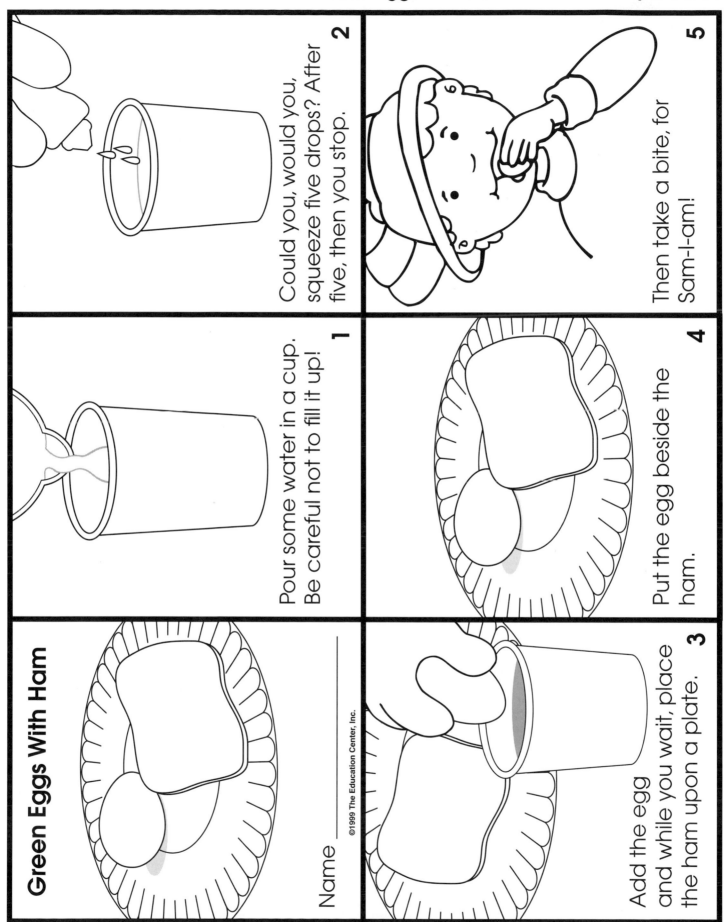

2

Could you, would you, squeeze five drops? After five, then you stop.

1

Pour some water in a cup. Be careful not to fill it up!

Green Eggs With Ham

Name _____

©1999 The Education Center, Inc.

5

Then take a bite, for Sam-I-am!

4

Put the egg beside the ham.

3

Add the egg and while you wait, place the ham upon a plate.

April
Bunny Patch Pound Cake

Ingredients For One:
1 slice pound cake
whipped topping
shredded coconut
3 BunnyMallows™

Utensils And Supplies:
1 napkin per child
green food coloring
1 large bowl
plastic knives

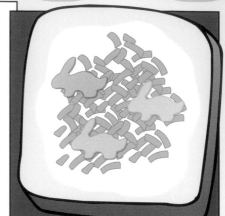

Teacher Preparation:
- Pour the coconut in the bowl and use green food coloring to tint it green.
- Slice the pound cake into half-inch-thick pieces.
- Arrange the ingredients for easy student access.

May
Arbor Day Tree Treats

Ingredients For One:
1 rice cake
4 raw broccoli florets
1 tablespoon soft cream cheese
1/4 teaspoon dry ranch dip mix

Utensils And Supplies:
1 napkin per child
1 small paper cup per child
1 tablespoon
1/4 teaspoon
1 plastic spoon per child

Teacher Preparation:
- Wash the broccoli.
- Arrange the ingredients and utensils for easy student access.

To prepare for each cooking activity, duplicate a classroom supply plus one extra of the recipe that you will be using (pages 277–278). Color one copy of the recipe; then cut the cards apart. Display the colored cards in sequence in your cooking center. Arrange the needed ingredients and utensils near the recipe cards. As a small group of children visits the cooking center, ask each child in the group to color a recipe, then cut the cards apart. Have each child sequence his cards; then staple them together, creating a small recipe booklet. After each cooking event, encourage each child to take his recipe home and keep it in a box to make a collection of his very own cooking recipes.

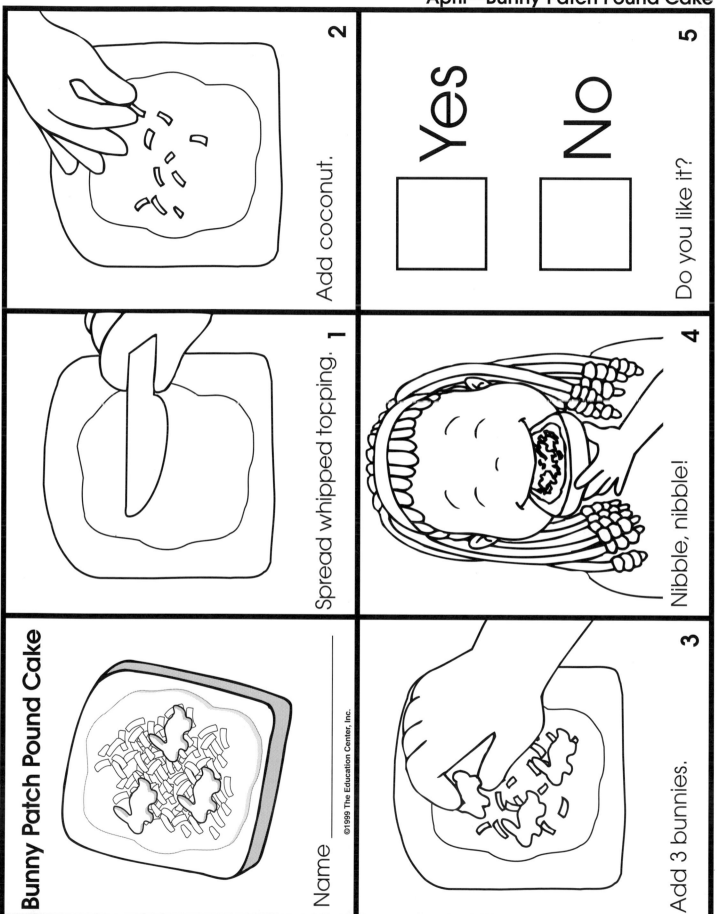

2 Add coconut.

5 Yes ☐ No ☐ Do you like it?

1 Spread whipped topping.

4 Nibble, nibble!

Bunny Patch Pound Cake

Name _____

3 Add 3 bunnies.

Recipe Cards
May—Arbor Day Tree Treats

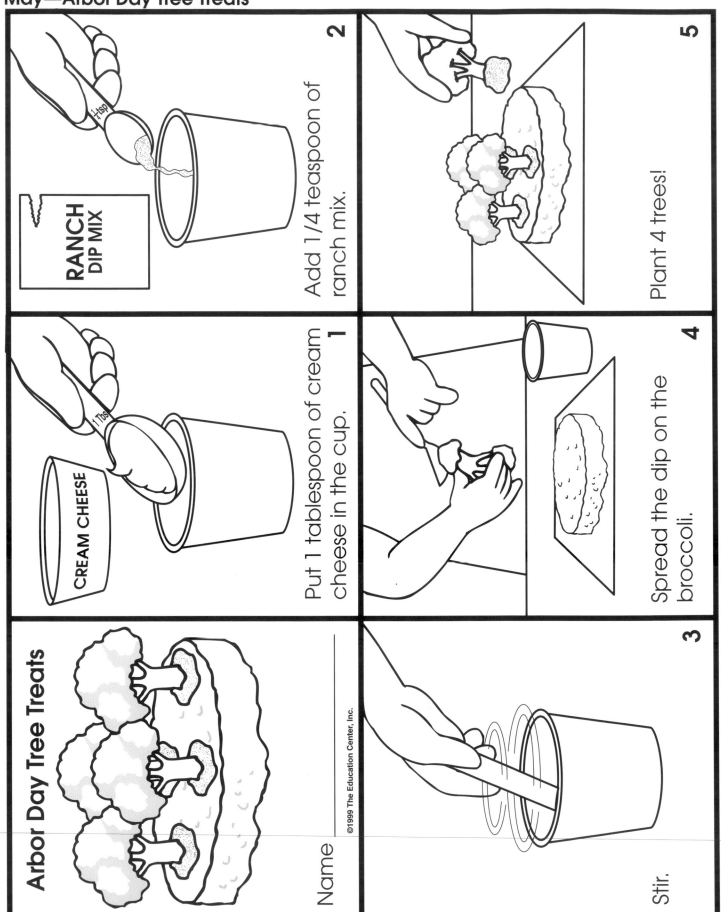

2 — Add 1/4 teaspoon of ranch mix.

RANCH DIP MIX

5 — Plant 4 trees!

1 — Put 1 tablespoon of cream cheese in the cup.

CREAM CHEESE

4 — Spread the dip on the broccoli.

Arbor Day Tree Treats

Name _____

©1999 The Education Center, Inc.

3 — Stir.

Fingerplays, Poems, Songs, & Rhymes

Season Song

The seasons and such will certainly sink into your students' minds with these activities. In advance make several copies of the season cards on page 281—you will need one season card for each child in your class. Then write the song on chart paper. Sing it a few times through until youngsters are familiar with it. Then have your students interact with the print on the paper. For example, you might ask different children to draw a blue box around the word *winter,* draw little pink flowers under the word *spring,* draw a green circle around the word *summer,* and underline the word *fall* with orange.

When children are comfortable with the lyrics of the song, divide your class into groups of four. Give each child in the group one season card. (If you have some children left over, you can give those children double roles, or you can play a part too.) Encourage each child to read the season on his card, then color the card to reflect that season. Back each season card with tagboard; then tape a large craft stick to it.

Have each group stand side by side in seasonal order, with each child holding his season card. Sing the song again, asking each child to hold his card high when the name of his season is sung. When your youngsters are ready, add the actions described below. This season song has just begun!

Pam Bishop—Gr. K, Stout Field Elementary, Indianapolis, IN

(sung to the tune of "Head, Shoulders, Knees, And Toes")

Winter, spring, summer, and fall—
We like them all!

Winter, spring, summer, and fall—
We like them all!

These are the seasons in a year.

Winter, spring, summer, and fall—
We like them all!

Winter, spring, summer, and fall—	*As your season is sung, hold your card high; then put it down.*
We like them all!	*Hold all cards high.*
Winter, spring, summer, and fall—	*(Repeat first two lines.)*
We like them all!	
These are the seasons in a year.	*Walk (in place) in a circle.*
Winter, spring, summer, and fall—	*(Repeat first two lines.)*
We like them all!	

Winter

©The Education Center, Inc. • *THE MAILBOX® • Kindergarten* • Oct/Nov 1998

Spring

©The Education Center, Inc. • *THE MAILBOX® • Kindergarten* • Oct/Nov 1998

Summer

©The Education Center, Inc. • *THE MAILBOX® • Kindergarten* • Oct/Nov 1998

Fall

©The Education Center, Inc. • *THE MAILBOX® • Kindergarten* • Oct/Nov 1998

Fingerplays, Poems, Songs, & Rhymes

Five Little Snowmen

Have youngsters recite this poem using their own five little fingers as snowmen.

Five little snowmen
Went out to play,
Over the hills
And far away.
When the sun came out,
It melted one away.
Four little snowmen came back that day.

Repeat the poem, replacing the boldfaced number words appropriately. When you get to zero, use the stanza below.

Zero little snowmen
Went out to play,
Over the hills
And far away.
But when winter came back,
It brought snow along the way.
Then **five** little snowmen came back that day!

Andrea Esposito—Pre-K And Gr. K
VA Child Care Center, Brooklyn, NY

Five Little Snowpeople

With a few simple props—such as a hat, a scarf, and a pair of mittens—your little ones will love acting out this poem. Choose five children at a time to be the featured snowpeople. And, of course, the best part of all is the drippy ending!

Five little snowpeople standing in a row.
The first one said, "We are made out of snow."
The second one said, "I have a hat and button eyes."
The third one said, "We look like funny guys."
The fourth one said, "Feel how the cold wind blows!"
The fifth one said, "It might freeze my carrot nose!"
Then drip, drip, went the snowpeople,
For it was a sunny day.
And the five little snowpeople drip, dripped right away.

Kathy Barlow—Gr. K
Southern Elementary
Somerset, KY

I'm A Little Snowman

(sung to the tune of "I'm A Little Teapot")

I'm a little snowman,
Short and fat.
Here is my nose
And here is my hat.
When the sun comes out,
I melt away.
But when it's cold,
I'm here to stay!

Markanne Gantt-Larberg, First Presbyterian Day School
Deland, FL

Ten Little Reindeer

This reindeer romp keeps all ten little fingers busy until they end up on top of each child's head as antlers!

One little reindeer, nose all aglow.
Two little reindeer, standing in the snow.
Three little reindeer, looking all around.
Four little reindeer, stomping on the ground.
Five little reindeer, all on Christmas Eve.
Six little reindeer, ready to take leave.
Seven little reindeer, hear the bells a-jingle.
Eight little reindeer, ready for Kris Kringle.
Nine little reindeer, hitched up to the sleigh.
Ten little reindeer bringing gifts on Christmas Day!

Joy Hollabaugh—Gr. K
Lake Trafford Elementary
Imokalee, FL

I'm A Little Penguin

If you're looking for a penguin tune, here's one that will hit the spot.

(sung to the tune of "I'm A Little Teapot")

I'm a little penguin.
Look at me,
Fishing and swimming
In the deep blue sea.
My wings are black
And my tail is white.
And I like sliding down the snow so bright!

Daphne L. Rivera—Gr. K
Bob Sikes Elementary School
Crestview, FL

The Crayons In The Box

Sing this colorful song to enhance students' color and color-word awareness. In advance, copy the song on sentence strips. Then label crayon cutouts with the color words from the song. Arrange all the word cards in a pocket chart. Sing the song several times together. Then, as you continue singing, invite students to take turns covering the color words on the pocket chart with the matching crayon cutouts.

(sung to the tune of "The Wheels On The Bus")

The crayons in the box are

Orange and blue,

Yellow and red,

Purple and green.

The crayons in the box are

Black and brown.

Colors all around!

Diane Parette—Gr. K
Durham Elementary
Durham, NY

Crunchy Apples

Here's a healthful snacktime poem that's sure to get your class in the mood for apples! For additional verses of the poem, replace the word *red* with other apple colors.

Oh, I wish I had a shiny [red] apple.
That is what I'd truly like to eat.
For if I had a shiny [red] apple,
I would have a crunchy, munchy treat!

Daphne L. Rivera—Gr. K
Bob Sikes Elementary School
Crestview, FL

M&M's® Candies Chant

This kid-pleasing chant does more than raise color awareness; it provides great motivation for hardworking students! To begin, give each child a handful of M&M's® candies on a small paper plate or napkin. Read the chant together. Then read the chant again, encouraging children to eat the corresponding candies as indicated in the chant. Mmmm, great-tasting language arts!

We've learned our colors and tried our best.
So now it's time for a colorful test!
Find some red ones if you would.
Munch them. Munch them. Aren't they good?
Choose some yellow ones from the bunch.
Taste them. Taste them. Crunch, crunch, crunch.
You know those blue ones taste good too.
Eat them. Eat them. Chew, chew, chew.
Now we're ready to eat the brown,
Chocolate candy—going down!
Are there green ones left for you?
I think *you* know what to do!
Orange ones are the very last.
Testing colors has been a blast!

adapted from an idea by Annette Hipp—Gr. K
Cleveland Elementary School
Cleveland, NC

Who's The Student Of The Week?

Honor each special Student of the Week with this lively song!

(sung to the tune of "Camptown Races")

Who's the Student of the Week?
[Patrick! Patrick!]
Who's the Student of the Week?
[Patrick] is the one!
He's/She's special, don't you know?
That's why we love him/her so! (*sign "I love you"*)
Who's the Student of the Week?
[Patrick] is the one!

Maureen Arbour—Gr. K
St. Dunstan School
Brighton, MI

Mr. Lobster And Mrs. Crab

Here's an ocean-related song with some fine-motor fun splashed in!

(adapted to the tune of "Old MacDonald Had A Farm")

Mr. Lobster and Mrs. Crab
Pinch and snap all day.
Mr. Lobster and Mrs. Crab
Pinch and snap all day.
With a pinch pinch here,
And a snap snap there.
Here a pinch,
There a snap,
Everywhere a pinch, snap.
Mr. Lobster and Mrs. Crab
Pinch and snap all day.

Betty Silkunas
Lansdale, PA

Do You See?

A wave of sea-related vocabulary washes in with this oceanic tune. As you sing, encourage your students to act out how each featured creature would look as it swims in the sea. After you sing the suggested verses, encourage children to brainstorm additional animals that might be seen in the sea. Then repeat the song, substituting a child-suggested creature each time. "Sea" ya!

(sung to the tune of "Do You Know The Muffin Man?")

Do you see [a jellyfish],
[A jellyfish, a jellyfish]?
Do you see [a jellyfish]
A-swimming in the sea?

Do you see a sea turtle…?
Do you see an octopus…?
Do you see a tiger shark…?
Do you see a sea urchin…?

Betty Silkunas

Getting Your Ducks In A Row—
Management Tips

GETTING YOUR DUCKS IN A ROW
Management Tips For The Classroom

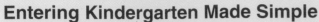

Entering Kindergarten Made Simple

Since kindergarten is sometimes the first school experience for children and parents (as parents!), use this idea to help organize the overwhelming odds and ends that can come with the start of school. For each child, label the outside of a two-pocket folder as shown. Add the child's name, your name, transportation information, and any other relevant information. Then gather your beginning-of-school paperwork, such as your welcome letter, a school handbook, and insurance forms. Indicate which of these papers must be returned to school by stamping them with a recognizable symbol, such as a star. (Be sure to write the code that you choose to use on the inside of the folder.) When you meet each parent, simply hand her a folder and encourage her to take it home and look over the information at her own pace. Then each child can use this folder to transport papers between home and school.

Beth Randall Davis—Gr. K, Lemira Elementary, Sumter, SC

Line-Up Chant

This little chant works wonders to help your children concentrate on forming and *staying in* a line. After practicing the art of lining up, introduce this chant to help with the task at hand.

Our line needs a leader
And it needs a caboose.
We'll make our line straight
And we'll keep our line loose.

No pushing, no shoving,
Our hands at our sides,
As we walk, walk, walk,
In our line.

Sandra Steele—Gr. K, Jefferson School, Princeton, IL

Pick A Pocket

Caught with just a spare minute or two? Here's the perfect spare-minute filler for review! Glue 10 to 20 library pockets on a sheet of poster board; then number each pocket. For each pocket, write a review activity on a blank index card (trimmed, if necessary, to fit the pocket). Slide a card into each pocket. When you have a spare minute to fill, ask a child to pick a pocket. Then have the class do the activity on that card. To add to the learning, turn the card over before replacing it in the pocket. Then have youngsters count how many cards have been chosen and how many are left, guiding them to make more and less statements. Change the activities on the cards as needed.

Debbie Reed—Gr. K, Satilla Elementary, Douglas, GA

Pick A Pocket
1 2 3 4

Say the alphabet.
Do ten jumping jacks.
Think of words that start with B.

Look Who Popped In!

Attendance taking has new appeal with this "pop-ular" display. To begin, mount the title and a large bowl cutout on a board. Have each child cut out a large piece of construction-paper popcorn, then write his name on it. Use pushpins to attach each popcorn piece to the board. As each child arrives, have him pin his popcorn piece above the bowl. With just a glance, you'll be able to tell who hasn't popped in for the day. (If desired, provide some microwave popcorn and invite each child to have a few pieces after he records his attendance. For a fun surprise, set out popcorn-flavored specialty jelly beans one day—and just sit back and watch the reactions and comments as children check in for the day!)

Lisa Cohen—Gr. K
Laurel Plains Elementary
New City, NY

Cleanup Party!

Do your classroom tables need a good cleaning? If so, throw a party! All you need is some shaving cream and about 20 pairs of little hands. First clear off your tables and invite each child to have a seat. Squirt out some shaving cream in front of each child; then encourage him to fingerpaint with the cream—swirling, twirling, and whirling it about. When the artistry subsides, have each child rinse his hands as you wipe off each table with a damp sponge. Your tables will be clean and your room will carry a clean, fresh scent!

Maddalena E. McKee—Gr. K, Trinity Regional School, Northport, NY

Stop Or Go?

Here's a simple tip to let your students know which centers are open for use and which are closed for the time being. For each center, cut out a black or yellow construction-paper rectangle (traffic light). Also cut out a green circle and an identically sized red circle for each center. Glue each green circle to a red circle. Then make a small slit in each traffic light as shown. Slide a paper clip through the slit. Post each traffic light near a center. If the center is open for use, slide the circle under the paper clip with the green side showing. If the center is closed, show the red side. So easy to know if it's stop or go!

Kimberly Armbruster—Gr. K
Grace Lane Kindergarten, Coram, NY

288

GETTING YOUR DUCKS IN A ROW
Management Tips For The Classroom

Field Trip Countdown

"How much longer?" Do your kindergartners get so excited about field trips and special events that they can hardly wait? Help them count down the days with this display. Begin by making numbered cutouts that match your trip theme or event (such as rockets for a trip to the planetarium or hearts for a Valentine's Day party). Decorate a wall or your door with the same number of cutouts as the days remaining until the trip. Remove one cutout each morning until the big day. When the display is bare, hit the road!

Eleanor L. Stout—Gr. K
Windsor Elementary
Elyria, OH

Hold Those Markers!

Try this idea to keep your dry-erase markers at your fingertips. Wrap a strip of Velcro® (hook side out) around each marker. Then stick a long loop-side strip of Velcro® to the wall beside your marker board. When the markers are not in use, attach them to the Velcro® strip. There you have it—markers everyone can find!

Cassie Hollatz—Gr. K
Lac du Flambeau Grade School
Lac du Flambeau, WI

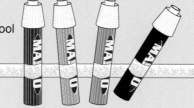

Box It Up

Use this tip to keep a week's worth of materials organized. Collect sturdy, flat boxes or tubs (such as plastic dishpans) and label each one with a different day of the week. As you plan for each day, place all the needed supplies into the appropriate boxes. With this storage system, you won't lose precious time searching for materials. These handy boxes are particularly useful for substitutes, since everything they need is in one place.

Jan Harding
Crescent Elementary
Sandy, UT

Literature-Extension Organizer

Do you spend valuable time searching through materials for literature-extension activities? Why not just keep them with the books they accompany? When you receive your latest copy of *The Mailbox®* magazine, cut out or photocopy the literature-extension activities. Then tape each activity inside the front or back cover of your copy of the book. When you want an activity to use with a certain book, it's right there!

Jennifer Travis—Gr. K
Bright Horizons
Randolph, MA

Carryall Jugs

Use this idea for easy-to-carry manipulative storage. Collect a supply of large, empty, and clean laundry-detergent jugs. Saw the top off each jug and file the rough edges with an emery board or cover them with masking tape. Cover the old label with white Con-Tact® paper. Then use colorful permanent markers to label each jug and illustrate its new contents. These jugs are perfect for kindergartners because they are easy to carry, materials are visible, and cleanup is a snap!

Elesa Miller—Gr. K
St. Catherine Laboure School
Wheaton, MD

Book And Tape Storage

Are you looking for a way to keep your read-along books and tapes together? Try this simple technique! Use clear mailing tape to attach a Ziploc® sandwich bag to the inside back cover of your book. Slide the accompanying cassette inside the bag and zip it closed. Store these book kits in a basket near your listening center. No more searching for a lost tape!

adapted from an idea
   by Linda Rasmussen
Sparks, NV

GETTING YOUR DUCKS IN A ROW
Management Tips For The Classroom

Sweet Storage

Do you need a place to store an abundance of small classroom supplies? If so, here's a lovely tip! Simply save a collection of heart-shaped boxes from Valentine's Day treats. Then use these boxes to store small supplies, such as beads, sequins, buttons, and stickers. What a sweet idea!

Mary E. Maurer
Caddo, OK

Curtain Calls

If you're about to do a messy project in your classroom, it's time for a curtain call! When you announce "curtain call," have students push tables together as you direct them. Then spread one or more shower curtains over the resulting surface. Students can work on top of the curtain while keeping the tables clean. Encore!

Colleen Thompson
Chosen Valley Elementary
Chatfield, MN

Special Delivery Envelopes

This special mail call provides a fun way to stay organized. After all, who doesn't love getting mail? To begin, give each child a business-size envelope and have him print his name on the front. Then encourage each child to decorate his envelope as desired. Store the completed envelopes in a mailbox. For special occasions, simply slide a note of praise or a seasonal treat in each child's envelope. To give a special assignment (such as a classroom job or center assignment), slip a note, picture, or photo depicting the desired event into the corresponding child's envelope. As an added bonus, these handy missives can also be used as place cards to assign seats during snacktimes and mealtimes. Your little ones will enjoy receiving their mail!

Beulah F. Cordell—Gr. K
An Academe For Children
Springdale, AR

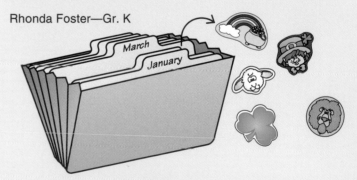

You are the pet feeder today!

Notes? No Problem!

Sending personalized notes home to parents is a snap with this idea! For each child's parent, program and sign a supply of decorative note sheets. Then file all the note sheets by name in a file box with A–Z dividers. When you observe a student doing something worth sharing, grab one of his personalized note sheets and jot down a quick message. The note is ready to go in just seconds! This system not only saves time, but you can also see which parents have not yet received positive news.

Rhonda Foster—Gr. K
West Central Elementary School
Francesville, IN

Dear Mrs. Cole,
Kelly was a great worker today!
Ms. Foster

S.O.S.
(Save Our Stickers)

Do you find yourself searching through drawers for just the right stickers at just the right time? You'll be stuck on this sticker-storage idea! Label the slots in a small accordion file with themes, seasons, etc. Then neatly file your stickers in the appropriate compartments. When you need a certain type of sticker, you'll know just where to look!

Rhonda Foster—Gr. K

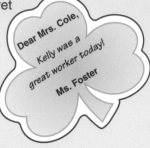

New-Student Welcome File

Make new-student arrival easy on yourself and the new child with this handy file! First label an accordion file "Welcome, New Students!" Then label each of the inner compartments with a different supply that is needed throughout the school year (such as nametags, cubby labels, permission slips, monthly calendars, book-order procedures, etc.). File each supply in its corresponding compartment. When a new student arrives, simply pull one item from each compartment. In no time at all, you and your new student will be up and running!

Karen Griffin—Gr. K
Rainwater Elementary
Carrollton, TX

GETTING YOUR DUCKS IN A ROW
Management Tips For The Classroom

Happy Hunting, One And All!

Take a crack at this teacher tip that helps egg hunts run smoothly, and also nestles in a little reading practice while you're at it. In advance, collect a supply of various colors of plastic eggs. Pack each egg with treats. Then, according to the number of students in your class and the colors in your egg collection, program a card (similar to the one shown) for each child in your class. (These cards serve to regulate the number of eggs each child may find.) For added fun, mix the egg colors! On the day of the hunt, give each child a card and send him hunting! In all the hunting excitement, you'll find your students becoming all for one and one for all!

Martha Alfrey
Southaven, MS

Anna
2 blue   1 blue & pink

Hey, I found blue. Who needs blue?

Rackin' Up Big Books

Looking for inexpensive, child-accessible storage for your big books? If you have a little-used laundry drying rack at home or see one at a yard sale, there's your answer! If desired, spray-paint the rack; then screw the legs onto a sheet of plywood. Hang your big books—front cover facing out—on the upper rungs of the rack. Hang earphones, bags of little books, and audio cassettes on the lower rungs. Big-book storage doesn't get any easier than this!

Catherine Turpin—Gr. K
Mohave Valley Elementary School
Bullhead City, AZ

A Bounty Of Borders?

Do you need a convenient way to protect and store a bounty of bulletin-board borders? Collect a clean, empty plastic frosting container for each border you wish to store. Cut off a sample of the border; then attach it to the front of a container with clear Con-Tact® covering. Next roll up the border and slip it inside the container. Snap on the lid and you're all set!

Mary C. Audsley—Gr. K, Attica Elementary, Attica, NY

Check Out These Books!

With just a little advance preparation on your part, classroom book checkout can run like a charm! Glue a library pocket inside the back cover of each take-home book. Label a different tagboard card with each book title; then slide each card in the corresponding book's pocket. Next photocopy a picture of each child in your class. Glue each child's picture to a different library pocket; then personalize the pocket. Arrange all these pockets on a planning chart near the take-home books. When a student is ready to check out a book, he removes the card from the inside back cover; then slides it into his chart pocket. With a simple glance at the chart, each child knows his own book status—and so do you!

Nancy Hopson—Gr. K
Hampton Elementary
Hampton, TN

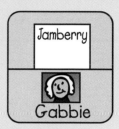

Jamberry

Gabbie

Cleanup Captains

Do you spend more time than you'd like transitioning from center time to the next activity? Here's a tip to ease your load and put the children in charge! After signaling students to begin cleaning up, select a hardworking child from each center to be the captain. Have her inspect the center and dismiss her group to the next activity when she thinks the center is neat and tidy. Remind students that if the captain excuses a group with a messy center, *the captain* must finish the work herself. Aye, aye, captain—these centers are shipshape!

Ginni Turoff—Gr. K, China Grove Elementary, Kannapolis, NC

"Bin" There, Read That!

Reading will be on the rise with this system for easy student selection and shelving. Program each of several large plastic bins with a different symbol; then fill it with books labeled to match. During reading time, set out several bins and assign a group of students to each one. Invite each child to choose books from her bin to read. When reading time is over, have her return her books to the bin with the matching symbol. Rotate bins and books frequently to provide each child with new reading choices. "Bin" there yet?

Kathleen Miller—Gr. K
Our Lady Of Mt. Carmel School
Tenafly, NJ

The Little Red Hen

Caps For Sale

291

GETTING YOUR DUCKS IN A ROW
Management Tips For The Classroom

Get The Point!

Are unsharpened pencils making your students' writing dull? Here's an easy way to stay organized and help your students get straight to the point. Cover a can with green construction paper and another can with red construction paper. Store sharpened pencils in the green can, and use the red can for collecting worn-down pencils. Then have children *stop* their dull pencils in the red can and go back to writing with a pencil from the green can! At a convenient time, choose a student helper to sharpen the worn-down pencils.

Karen Saner—Grs. K–1
Burns Elementary
Burns, KS

Bits & Pieces

If you find your classroom floor constantly peppered with stray pieces from puzzles, toys, and games, here's a simple way to keep track of those lost bits and pieces. Set aside a special tub for miscellaneous parts. When someone runs across a stray piece, simply toss it into the tub. Then, at a convenient time, choose a helper to find the corresponding places for the pieces in the tub. Finally, a way to make peace with the pieces!

Donna Leonard—Head Start
Monticello, IA

Homemade Sponge Shapes

You don't have to spend precious supply money on expensive sponge shapes! Instead, try making your own using household sponges, cookie cutters, stencils, and templates. Begin by wetting the sponge and squeezing out the excess water. Then allow the sponge to dry under a flat, heavy object. Next, place a shape on top of the dried sponge and trace around it. Then cut out the shape with a craft knife. Finally, wet the sponge again, wring out the water, and bring on the paints!

Peggy Anderson—Grs. K–1
Theodore Roosevelt Elementary
Pennsauken, NJ

Alphabet Partners

When your students choose partners, are they sometimes just a little bit too choosy? Use this tip to help eliminate hurt feelings and reinforce alphabet recognition. Prepare a set of lowercase alphabet cards and a set of uppercase alphabet cards. To determine partners, give half the class cards from the lowercase set and the other half cards from the uppercase set. (Be sure that each card given out has a mate.) Have students pair up by matching uppercase and lowercase letters. What a pleasant way to pick partners!

Laura Bentley—Gr. K, Captain John Palliser Elementary
Calgary, Alberta, Canada

Brag Tags

Here's an inexpensive way for you to "brag on your students" and build their self-esteem. Begin by collecting a file of cute clip-art pictures. When you have a good supply, cut out the pictures; then arrange and glue as many as possible on a sheet of paper. Write a positive comment on each picture; then duplicate a supply of the whole page. Color and cut out the pictures; then laminate them if desired. Store these brag tags in a handy place. When you'd like to recognize a student, simply reach for a brag tag, attach a loop of masking tape to the back, and pat it on!

Note: To keep your brag tags in stock and also reinforce the home-school connection, ask parent volunteers to help color the copies or cut out laminated pictures.

Norma Stotts—Gr. K
Jonesboro Kindergarten Center
Jonesboro, AR

Simple Drying Racks

When it comes to drying art projects, is there any classroom that has enough space? This drying rack takes up very little room and is easy to make. Simply turn a plastic file organizer on its side. Then cut a piece of cardboard to fit inside each divider. Cover each piece of cardboard with Con-Tact® paper. Then slide the covered cardboard pieces onto the dividers to make shelves. These racks are ready to go!

Jackie Wright—Grs. K–2
Summerhill Children's House
Enid, OK

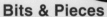

PHONICS FUN

PHONICS FUN

Giant Letter Creations

These impressive letter displays reinforce phonics and can be made in a center or as small-group projects. For each letter that you introduce, cut out a large tagboard shape of that letter. Then provide (or ask children to provide) a large supply of an object or craft that begins with that particular letter (see the list at right for suggestions). Have children glue the objects or apply the crafts to the giant letter shape. When the glue is dry, display the letter on your classroom wall. Eventually the entire alphabet—with phonetic clues—will be displayed around your classroom!

Gina Sciscioli
Bright Beginnings Preschool
Chandler, AZ

a- apple prints	m-macaroni
b- buttons	n- nuts
c- cotton	o- orange prints
d- dog biscuits	p- popcorn
e- eggshells	q- quilt squares
f- feathers	r- rice
g- gold nuggets	s- suns
(spray-painted	t- turkeys
gravel or beans)	u- umbrellas
h- handprints	v- valentines
i- insects (drawings)	w-wood pieces
j- jack-o'-lanterns	x- x-rays
k- kites	y- yarn
l- leaves	z- ziti

ABC Apron

This readiness activity will produce miles of smiles and go a long way to help reinforce each letter and its sound. To prepare, you'll need an apron with four (or more) pockets. For each letter that you introduce, each of the pockets will have a function. In the first pocket, hide objects that begin with that particular letter. Hide a letter card in the second pocket. In the third pocket, "hide" the sign-language sign for that letter (your hand, of course!). And in the fourth pocket, hide a puppet or other mascot to represent that letter.

To introduce each letter, sing the song at the left; then show children the objects from the first pocket, asking them to say the name of each object. When they guess the letter (or sound), remove and display the letter card from the second pocket. Then "pull out" the sign for that letter and encourage each child to make that sign with you. Lastly bring out your puppet or mascot to interact with your students.

Susan Showalter Hayden—Gr. K, Lorane Elementary School, Reading, PA

---

*(sung to the tune of the song,
"I Have Something In My Pocket")*

I have something in my pocket;
It's our letter of the week.
I keep it very close to me
So I can take a peek.
And I bet that you can guess it
If you think about my clues.
So I'll take them out and show you now—
What letter do you choose?

PHONICS FUN

Buried Treasure

Ahoy, mateys! There's valuable letter-sound association buried in this activity. To begin, arrange objects that begin with letters you have studied around your sand table. Then bury corresponding alphabet tiles in the sand. Have each child choose an object, identify the initial letter, and then find the matching letter tile in the sand. Vary this activity for more advanced children by having them spell the object's entire name with the letter tiles. Shiver me timbers—your spelling is better than gold!

Chrissy Casey—Gr. K, Bring 'Em Young Day Care Center, Frazer, PA

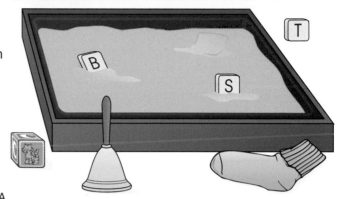

Ahhhh...Olives

Here's a unique way to reinforce the short o sound—with a graphing twist! Prepare a large graph with three columns. Label the first column "black," the second column "green," and the third column "no, thank you." Then cut out a supply of large black, green, and red construction-paper olives. Tell students that you're going to be talking about olives; then prompt them to chorally say, "Ahhhh, olives!" Next invite each child to taste a black and a green olive. If she likes the taste, she responds by saying, "Ahhhh, olives!" Then have each child indicate her olive preference by choosing an appropriately colored olive cutout. Ask each child to write her name on the olive, then tape it in the corresponding graph column. Interpret the graph with your students; then display it on a classroom wall. Ahhhh—do you like olives?

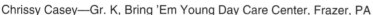

My Favorite Olive

black — Halley, Albert, Bill

green — Ashlee, Will, Ryan

no, thank you — Lauren, Scott

Donna Livingston—Gr. K, Embry Hills Methodist Church Kindergarten Atlanta, GA

Letter Golfing

Fore! Your little ones will enjoy this center that combines letter-sound association with golf. First, obtain a child's plastic golf set (or use a golf club, plastic golf balls or Ping-Pong® balls, and large plastic cups). Next, program each golf ball with a different letter that you have studied. Then set up several putting holes in a center area. (If you're using plastic cups for the holes, be sure to tape them securely to the floor.) Also arrange an assortment of objects that begin with the letters you have programmed on the golf balls. To do this activity, have a child try to putt a golf ball into a hole. When she sinks one, have her retrieve the ball and read the letter on it. Then have her match that ball to one of the objects. Have the child continue in this manner until each object is matched with a ball. It's a phonemic hole in one!

Kim Hohlbein—Gr. K
Our Lady Of Lourdes School
Toledo, OH

PHONICS FUN

Hop To It!

Your students' reading skills will improve by leaps and bounds when they play this version of hopscotch. In advance, draw a hopscotch pattern on a large vinyl tablecloth. Then use a permanent marker to write a letter or simple word in each box. Next, to prevent the tablecloth from slipping, use duct tape to tape the edges to the floor. The game begins with the first player tossing a beanbag into the first hopscotch box. She then hops over the first box into the next box and the next, etc., until she reaches the end. Then she hops back in reverse order, picking up the beanbag and saying the sound of the letter or reading the word in the box. The game continues until all players have tossed their beanbags into each box. When students have mastered the skills on this hopscotch board, use hairspray to wipe off the old programming; then write in a whole new board!

adapted from an idea by Melissa Miller—Gr. K, Kleven Boston Elementary, Woodstock, GA

Password Day

Top off your letter-of-the-week activities with this fun password game. The day before the last day of the week, tell your students that in order to get into the classroom the next morning, they must tell you a secret password. This password can be any word that begins with your current letter of study. (Encourage originality!) The following morning, stand outside your classroom door with a rubber stamp and ink pad. If a child says an appropriate word, stamp his hand and invite him to enter the classroom. If he has difficulty, give him clues until he responds correctly. What a smart way to start the day!

Kelly Larson—Gr. K, St. Joseph Elementary, Shawnee, KS

Slinky® Spelling

Your little visual and kinesthetic learners will love this Slinky® activity designed to help them hear and "see" parts of words. Begin the lesson with a simple two-syllable word, such as *turtle*. Hold the Slinky® in front of you; then stretch it as you say the first syllable, *tur*. Pause, then continue stretching the Slinky® as you say the second syllable, *tle*. Next, have the students say the entire word, *turtle,* as you bring the Slinky® back together. Practice with many words. If your children are ready, use the same process to "stretch" the individual letter sounds in simple words such as *hop*. When your students are familiar with this activity, place a few Slinky® toys in your writing center for independent student use.

Diane Brownlee—Gr. K, Westview Elementary, Canton, IL

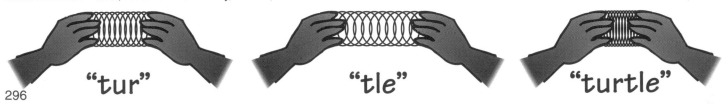

"tur"   "tle"   "turtle"

OUR READERS WRITE

Our Readers Write

First-Day Photos (For Holiday Fun)

If you take a minute to snap a first-day photo of each child, you'll have the makings for treasured holiday keepsakes. Save each child's first-day photo. Then cut out a theme-related shape from a double thickness of construction paper. Cut a photo-sized hole in one of the shapes; then tape the child's photo behind it. Back the first cutout with the second one. Write the information as shown, adapted to your needs; then laminate the cutout. When the holidays roll around have each child punch a hole in the top of his cutout, then tie on a length of ribbon to make a hanger. Each parent will be thrilled to receive this holiday ornament and reminisce with his child about the first day of kindergarten.

Diane Parette—Gr. K, Durham Elementary
Durham, NY

My first day at Kindergarten August 18, 1998

Set The Mood With Music

Tune in to a new way of stimulating (or "de-stimulating") your students with music! The use of a handy CD player and a variety of music might be just what your students need. You can use this music during creative-writing times, quiet times, work times—however it works best for you and your students. For a separate activity, introduce a particular music piece; then have children listen to it and verbalize what they hear, think of, and feel. Have children express their ideas through writing and/or drawing. Follow up this activity with an artist/author sharing time. You'll be surprised how music can set the mood and the pace of your classroom! (A nice selection of instrumental music is available from Gary Lamb. To order, call 1-800-772-7701).

Lisa Hughes—Gr. K, Winston Park Elementary
Coconut Creek, FL

Take-Home Kit

After a new and exciting (and sometimes exhausting!) first day in kindergarten, send each child home with a decorated bag containing the following items and messages:

Adapted from an idea by
Lauren Giles—Gr. K
Oakview Elementary
Simpsonville, SC

You're a star in my class!
Starburst®

You're going to learn so much in school this year!
Smarties®

We all need hugs now and then. If you need one, let me know!
Hershey's® Hugs®

Remember, it's OK to make mistakes. That's how we learn!
Eraser

I'm nuts about you!
Peanut

Busy! Busy! Busy!

Do you have an Open House near the beginning of the year? Try this project to give parents and family members a glimpse into just how busy their little ones are. Start by having each child use art supplies to decorate a paper plate to resemble himself. Tape a large craft stick to the back of each plate. Then tape each craft stick to the back of a chair. Drape each child's paint shirt (or shirt that he brought in) over his chair so that it appears as if the child is sitting at his desk. On each desk (or table space), display something that a child might do during the day. For example, you might put pattern blocks in one child's space, math counters in another, and color-word cards in another. There's just no end to how busy we can be!

Colleen Thompson
Chosen Valley Elementary
Chatfield, MN

Supply Slips

To save time and help children remember to bring necessary supplies to school, try these handy supply slips. In advance, type (or write) a list of simple sentences. Duplicate the page as needed; then cut apart the sentences. Store these supply slips in an envelope. When a child needs a certain supply, simply hand him the appropriate slip, have him write his name in the blank, and take it on home.

Lori Hamernik—Gr. K
Prairie Farm Elementary
Prairie Farm, WI

_____ needs a new glue stick.

Birthday Show-And-Tell

Highlight each birthday child with this special activity. At the beginning of the year, write a letter asking each parent to send in a photo of her child at each of the following ages: birth, age 1, age 2, age 3, age 4, age 5, and age 6 (if appropriate). Shortly before each child's birthday, send a copy of the letter home with the birthday child. On her birthday, invite that child to share the pictures with the class. If parents agree that it's OK for children to touch the photos, place the photos in a special center and invite one child at a time to visit the center and sequence the photos. My, how you've grown!

Betty Silkunas, Lansdale, PA

Portfolios: A Method Of Management

Use this method of making portfolios to help each parent, child, and yourself make a permanent record of that child's school year. At the beginning of the year, make a folder for each child. During the course of each month, save a few pieces of each child's work. Be sure to save a variety of work, and ensure that each piece has a name and date! Store the work in the folders. At the end of each month, mount each child's work on large sheets of construction paper. Embellish the pages with die-cut characters, stickers, or pages from teacher notepads. If you do just one page per child each month, by June you'll have an impressive portfolio that is ready to be hole-punched and tied together with ribbon. If you'd like to use these portfolios for midyear conferences, simply bind them together with a removable binding such as a metal ring or ribbon.

Elizabeth B. Ozol—Gr. K
Accompsett Elementary School
Smithtown, NY

Cutting Control

Could your little ones use some scissor practice? Here's an idea to help accomplish just that. Cut a large supply of strips of adding-machine paper or construction paper a little bit longer than headband size. Place the strips at a center along with children's scissors. After demonstrating how to fringe-cut the paper, have each child fringe-cut his own paper. If he makes a mistake and goes all the way through, no big deal! Have him simply get another strip of paper and try again. When he makes it successfully to the end of his strip, instruct the child to bring it to you so you can tape it together to make a crown. You did it!

Annette Hamill—Gr. K
Collins Elementary
Collins, MS

Learning Mats

The beginning of the year is the perfect time to introduce these learning mats. Then, when each child is ready for a particular skill, he'll know just where he can find it. To make a learning mat, glue the skills of your choice on a sheet of construction paper. For example, you might include a number line, a color-word chart, an alphabet strip, and a 100 grid. Glue all the skills to a large sheet of construction paper; then laminate it. Keep these learning mats in a child-accessible place so youngsters can get their hands on them anytime they'd like.

Sue Christopher—Gr. K
Dawson Boyd Elementary
Dawson, MN

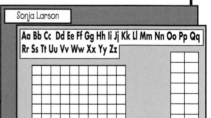

Yearlong Display

This yearlong display will bring back fond memories and remind each child how much she has accomplished. Each month, section off a small area of a wall with butcher paper and bulletin-board border. Label the section with that month. Display photos, artwork, writing samples, and captions from that month on the wall. Then look around and see what's been going on at school!

Amy Pierce
Pierce Private
 Day School
Irving, TX

We studied bubbles.

Jacob had
a birthday!

Special Recognition

These unique medallions will make your students feel like a million bucks! In advance, start saving yogurt lids. To make one medal, wash and dry a lid; then cover both sides with an adhesive covering. Use a permanent marker to write a special message on the lid. Then glue on colorful cutouts, stickers, or stars. Next poke or punch two small holes at the top of the rim. Thread a length of cord or ribbon through the holes; then tie the ends together. Have these medallions ready to provide special recognition at a moment's notice.

Maureen Tiedemann—Gr. K
Holy Child School
Hicksville, NY

Alphabet Illustrations

There's nothing better than kindergarten artwork in a kindergarten classroom. And here's a way to get some for your permanent displays. Throughout the year, be on the lookout for child-created pictures that are just the right size and subject to go along with your alphabet chart. When you find one, ask the artist's permission to laminate it and display it with your alphabet chart. Before long you're bound to have an alphabet entirely illustrated by your class. Some particularly generous children might even insist that you keep their illustrations for next year. If they do, don't be surprised if you see their little first-grade eyes peeking into your room to see if their artwork is still there!

Judith Wrenick—Gr. K
Fraser Valley Elementary School
Fraser, CO

I-Can-Read-It-Myself Books

Use these books to help build self-esteem and independent reading skills. At the beginning of the year, ask each child to bring in a composition notebook. Each time you learn a poem or song as a class, type it in large print on a separate sheet of paper. Then photocopy a class supply. Have each child glue her page to a page in her composition notebook. Invite each child to add illustrations to the pages as desired. Before long each child will have an entire book that she can read all by herself!

M. Lynne Sypher—Gr. K
Brook Avenue School
Bay Shore, NY

Sequencing With A Smile

A touch of humor can be just the ticket to motivate youngsters to practice sequencing. As you read the comics in the newspaper, keep an eye out for comics that have an obvious sequence to them and good kid appeal. Cut out the comic strip; then laminate it. After cutting apart each frame of the comic, store it in an envelope. When you have collected a few good comics, put them in a center for your children to use for sequencing practice.

Michelle Myers
Tutor Time Learning Center
Bradenton, FL

Bloom Where You're Planted

These fabulous flowers will affirm that each child is indeed blooming where he is planted. For each child glue a flower center, stem, and leaf to a sheet of paper. Cut out and glue a copy of the child's photo to the center of the flower. Then cut out a large supply of construction-paper petals. Each time a child achieves a goal, write it on a petal; then have him glue that petal to his flower. When his flower is complete, watch him carry that blooming flower home with pride!

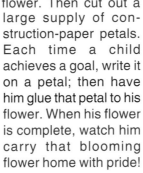

Patti Sutphen—Gr. K
College Park Elementary
LaPorte, TX

Puffy Practice Cards

Add a little dimension and interest to your skill cards with puffy fabric paint. When you make your skill cards, use puffy paint to write the skills on them. The colors appeal to children and the raised texture gives an added tactile cue.

Connie Powell—Gr. K Special Education
Cloud Elementary
Wichita, KS

Phone-Number Practice

Here's a neat idea that enables children to practice their phone numbers and get visual feedback. Write each child's name and phone number on a separate sentence strip. Place the strips in a center along with a calculator. Encourage children to practice "dialing" their phone numbers on the calculator. When a child has memorized his phone number, reward him by letting him call home on a real phone to announce the good news!

Betsy Ruggiano—Gr. K, Laurence Harbor, NJ

Sing A Song

Sing a simple song to practice color recognition and to help youngsters learn one another's names. Begin by singing the song "Mary Wore Her Red Dress." When your children are familiar with the song, sing a question in the form of this song. For example, you might sing:

Who is wearing green pants, green pants, green pants?
Who is wearing green pants, all day long?

Encourage your group to sing their response to you using the appropriate child's (children's) name(s).

Lara Renfroe—Gr. K
Heber Springs Elementary School, Heber Springs, AR

Our Readers Write

Daily Review

Summarize each day's activities with a special class meeting. Announce a memorable moment or activity into a toy microphone. Then invite each child, in turn, to do the same. Acknowledge each child's shared experience with a positive response. What a great way to wrap up the day!

Carol Chess—Gr. K, North Lauderdale Elementary
North Lauderdale, FL

It was neat when we learned about fire safety.

Nature Patterns

Promote patterning skills with this neat idea. Collect an assortment of fall nature items such as leaves, pinecones, and acorns. Have each child create a pattern with several different items on a poster-board strip. Then have her glue the items onto the strip. Use the pattern strips in a display or as bulletin-board borders. How beautiful—naturally!

Jackie Jones—Gr. K, Blairsville Elementary, Blairsville, PA

It Isn't Just *Circle* Time Anymore!

Reinforce shape recognition and keep your youngsters on their toes when they get ready to sit down. Once your children have become accustomed to the seating arrangement of circle time—surprise them! Use masking tape to outline other shapes on the floor. Then have your children come to *square time, rectangle time,* or even *triangle time!* Later, for an added challenge, have children come to a named shape time without the tape markings to guide them!

Pam Bishop—Gr. K, Stout Field Elementary, Indianapolis, IN

Leaf Shadows

Those wonderful, freshly fallen leaves are the subject of this "shadow-y" craft. First use a piece of rolled tape to attach a leaf to dark construction paper. Then place the paper in direct sunlight for several hours. Later, remove the leaf to examine the "shadow" created on the paper. Invite each child to use a marker to outline each leaf on his page, then use art supplies to decorate his page as he likes.

Daphne
  Orenshein—Gr. K
Yavneh Hebrew
  Academy
Los Angeles, CA

Every Vote Counts

During the election season, demonstrate the democratic process by conducting a class vote on special issues. Prepare a cardboard-box voting booth. Program a ballot with two simple illustrations for each class issue, such as students' favorite book, song, snack, or activity. Send each child to the booth to mark her vote on a copy of the ballot. As a class, tally and record the results on a graph. Post the official results; then refer to the results as each issue is addressed during the day.

Barbara Surgeon—Gr. K
Jupiter Elementary
Palm Bay, FL

My Favorite:

Bat Jamboree

Itsy Bitsy Spider

Quick-And-Easy Cleanup

For fast table cleanups, keep a package of wet wipes handy. When a table needs to be cleaned, simply pull out a wipe, clean the table, and then toss the wipe into the trash. It's as easy as one, two, three! (Bonus tip: The empty containers are great for storing small items and manipulatives.)

Megan Schubert—Gr. K, Farmington Elementary
Germantown, TN

301

Happy Birthday Cassette

Here's a unique birthday gift sure to make your birthday students smile! Using a cassette recorder, tape the birthday student stating his name, age, and favorite things. Next record the class singing "Happy Birthday" to him. Then give each child a chance to record any individual birthday greetings that they'd like. The recipient will enjoy sharing this special gift with friends and family.

Traveling Books

Send your class-created books home with youngsters in this durable package. Design a parent letter explaining that a class book will be sent home with each child to share with her family. Include a reminder to return the book to school the next day. Attach the letter to a large manila envelope; then laminate the envelope. Place a book in the envelope. Each day send the book home with a different child. These well-traveled books will quickly become well-loved favorites!

Stacy L. Fritz—Gr. K, Gilbertsville Elementary, Gilbertsville, PA

Seedy Socks

Have you ever seen socks growing? Well, you will now! Have each child bring a large, old sock to school. Have him put his sock on over one shoe. Then go for a nature walk through the woods, a field, or any other area that is likely to have seeds on the ground. When you return, place each sock in a different Ziploc® bag; then dampen it with water. Seal the bags; then hang them in the sunlight. Periodically check the bags for any signs of growing socks!

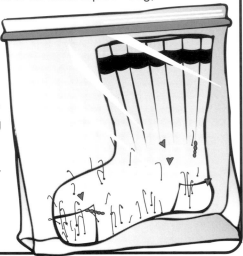

Jennifer Reimann—
  Gr. K
Walnut Creek
  Dayschool
Columbia, MO

Bean-Bag Creature Count

Count those popular bean-bag creatures as valuable teaching tools! Gather a collection of bean-bag creatures to represent the characters in counting songs (or rhymes), such as "Five Little Ducks" or "Five Little Monkeys." Line up the set of characters; then appoint students to manipulate the creatures as the class sings the song.

Sue Lewis Lein—Four-Year-Old K, St. Pius X School
Wauwatosa, WI

Take-Home Kits

Promote your home-school connection with these handy kits designed to help parents reinforce skills at home. Place a note and the items used for each skill in a labeled, resealable plastic bag. For example, label a bag "Patterns"; then include a set of plastic shapes and a note explaining how to create patterns with them. Send the kit home with any student who needs practice with that particular skill. Parents will be thrilled to have appropriate materials to use with their children without the expense.

Emile Blake—Gr. K
Sherrills Ford Elementary
Sherrills Ford, NC

Squish Art

Create beautiful, colorful masterpieces with this sensory activity. Place a few blobs of a child's choice of fingerpaint colors onto a piece of cardboard. Wrap the cardboard with plastic wrap. Invite the child to squish the paint around with her palms, fingers, and fists. Afterward remove the plastic wrap to allow the paint to dry. Display the masterpieces for all to enjoy. Squish!

Bonnie McKenzie—Pre-K & Gr. K
Cheshire Country Day School, Cheshire, CT

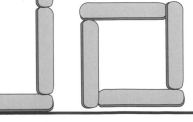

Stick Shapes

Give each child ten craft sticks; then challenge her to create a given shape using a specified number of sticks. For example, ask, "Can you make a triangle with three sticks?" or "Who can make a rectangle using all ten sticks?" This is a great way to shape up youngsters' stick-to-itiveness!

Rhonda Chiles—Gr. K, South Park Elementary
Shawnee Mission, KS

Scented Ink Pads

If you have a few drops of scented oil to spare, here's a great tip that makes "scents." Simply apply a few drops of an oil fragrance onto a colored ink pad. Then invite youngsters to make their own ink-stamp creations. What a wonderful blend of designs and scents!

Sue Lewis Lein—Four-Year-Old K, St. Pius X School
Wauwatosa, WI

Precious Pasta Jewelry

Try this new twist for coloring pasta to use for stringing activities. Use gold and silver spray paint to color an assortment of pasta shapes. After the paint dries, invite students to string the pasta onto gold or silver string to create beautiful pieces of jewelry. Gorgeous!

Peggy Carr—Gr. K
Lancaster West School
Glasford, IL

Grin And Share It

My class often listens to CDs. One day, I was unable to find the song I was looking for on a CD, so I brought in an old record album from home. As I removed the record from its jacket, one little girl remarked in awe, "Wow—that's the biggest CD I've ever seen!"

Laura Bentley—Gr. K
Captain John Palliser Elementary School
Calgary, Alberta, Canada

Silver And Gold

Give this special going-away gift to students who move during the school year. Purchase two pencils—one silver and one gold. Tie the pencils together with ribbon. Then attach a copy of this precious, old-time rhyme as an encouraging memento for the child.

Make new friends,
But keep the old.
One is silver
And the other gold.

Peggy Carr—Gr. K

Make new friends,
But keep the old.
One is silver
And the other gold.

Group Names

Use this idea to help reinforce concepts throughout the day. For each student group, select a name related to a concept that you are currently studying. For example, each group might be named for a different shape, planet, or zoo animal. Change the group names periodically to correspond to current topics of study. The repeated use of these names will help youngsters learn concepts with little effort!

Jean Goins—Gr. K, Miamitown Elementary, Miamitown, OH

Counting With Erasers

Count on this math-center game to be a hit with youngsters. Draw a large grid with ten sections on a sheet of poster board. (Or increase the number of sections to suit your youngsters' abilities.) Label each section with a different numeral from 1 to 10. Place the grid in your math center along with a collection of small, theme-related erasers. (These little erasers are often available in large quantities at paper-goods stores.) To do this activity, a child creates an eraser set in each space on the grid to equal the labeled numeral.
Cool counting!

Mary Tamporello—Gr. K
Wyandotte Elementary
Morgan City, LA

Tasty Numerals

Creating and recognizing numerals has never been so delicious! Give each child a length of Twizzlers® Pull-n-Peel™ candy and a paper plate. Have her gently separate the twisted candy laces. Then challenge her to form specific numerals with the laces. Afterward invite each child to enjoy her tasty math manipulatives. Yummy!

Kimberly Faraci
The Roberto Clemente School, Brooklyn, NY

Coin-Protector Ornament

Looking for a way to make easy and inexpensive Christmas ornaments? Head to your local discount store and purchase a class supply of coin protectors. To make an ornament, simply center a child's photo in the round window of a protector; then trim the photo and fold the protector around it. Secure the photo with double-sided tape. Use tiny stickers and colorful markers to decorate the frame around the photo; then add a loop of ribbon for hanging. Or add a length of magnetic tape to the back to create a very merry magnet!

Melanie M. Thompson
Loxley Elementary
Fairhope, AL

How Are They Alike?

If your holiday studies include explorations of various celebrations—such as Hanukkah, Christmas, and Kwanzaa—ask youngsters to think about how these holidays are alike. Have them make a list of things these holidays have in common, such as the use of candles, the giving of gifts, or feelings of joy. Your diverse group of youngsters may have more in common than they think!

Carmen Carpenter, Highland Preschool, Raleigh, NC

Listen And Respond

Get more out of your listening center with independent response sheets. Program a sheet of copy paper similar to the one shown; then duplicate a large supply. Keep these response sheets in a folder in your listening center. Then your students can not only listen to, but also think, write, and draw about the stories they hear!

Carmen Rufa—Gr. K
Bethlehem Children's School
Slingerlands, NY

Listening Center

Name _____ Date _____

I listened to _____

This story was 🙂 😐 🙁
(circle one)   good   OK   not good

This is a picture of my favorite part

I liked this story because _____

Project Linus

Do you involve your students in making a quilt when you study the letter *Q?* If so, here's a great way to extend your letter study into a community service project. Donate your finished quilt to Project Linus, a volunteer organization that provides blankets and quilts to seriously ill or traumatized children across the country. To find out more about Project Linus, call (303) 840-1116 or visit www.projectlinus.org.

Patty Schmitt—Gr. K, St. Patrick's School, Portland, MI

Let It Shine!

This holiday bulletin board will add some sparkle to dreary December days. Begin by cutting a large Christmas-tree shape from green felt. Cut small holes in the felt tree; then insert the bulbs from a string of Christmas-tree lights. Use duct tape to attach the light string to the back. Mount the tree on a bulletin board and plug in the lights at the nearest outlet. Finish the tree with a treetop bow and any other lightweight ornaments you wish to add. Complete this display by wrapping pieces of poster board with holiday gift wrap and adding bows to make pretty packages.

Melissa Jenkins
Arkansas School For The Deaf
Little Rock, AR

Ho, Ho, Ho!

Here's a fun holiday twist on a word wall. How about a word chimney—complete with Santa peeking over the top? To make this display, use a thick black marker to draw bricks on a length of red bulletin-board paper. Mount the paper on a wall or bulletin board. Add a white paper chimney top; then mount a favorite Santa Claus decoration above it. Onto each brick, attach a length of a sentence strip on which you've printed a sight word or a vocabulary word your children can identify. Add a picture clue to each strip, if desired. Finish this display with the title "Ho, Ho, Ho! Look At The Words We Know!"

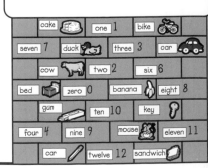

Sheila Jeffries—Gr. K
Theodore Jones Elementary
Conway, AR

Shimmering Icicles

Create a wintry look in your classroom with this idea. Squeeze a thick line of glue onto a length of blue construction paper. Then hold the paper up so that parts of the glue line run down to resemble icicles. Sprinkle silver glitter on the glue and allow it to dry. Shake off the excess. Make several strips of these icicles; then tape them along the tops of doors, bulletin boards, or bookcases to put a chill in the air. Brrrr!

Melissa Stanek—Substitute Teacher
Delaware Academy Central School
Delhi, NY

A Nifty Gift Exchange

Here's a neat way to randomly distribute gifts during your annual classroom gift exchange. Gather a supply of discarded Christmas cards and trim off the back half of each card. Cut each of the card fronts to make a two-piece puzzle. Form two groups of puzzle halves—one group for gifts and one group for students—with the halves of each puzzle being in opposite groups. As each child enters the classroom on the day of the exchange, attach a card half from the gift group to his gift; then give him a different card half from the student group (to make sure he doesn't receive the gift he brought). When it's time to open the gifts, have each child find his gift by completing his Christmas-card puzzle.

Helen Bintz—Gr. K, Danz School, Green Bay, WI

Christmas-Tree Bags

Going home for the holidays is easier with these festive bags. Collect a class supply of brown paper grocery bags. Use dimensional fabric paint to draw a Christmas tree on one side of each bag. Give a bag to each child. Invite him to use more of the paint to decorate his tree with colored dots to resemble lights. If time (and paint) allow(s), encourage him to add a few presents under his tree as well. Save the bags for the last day of school before winter break. Then have each child load up his sack and "Ho, ho, ho!" all the way home.

Karen Franz
Apple Valley, MN

Soup-Can Snowman

Express your thanks to classroom volunteers during the holidays with these snowman goodies. In advance collect a supply of cleaned soup cans. To make a snowman, spray-paint the outside of a can white. After the paint is dry, add facial features with markers or paint pens. Cut out a hat shape from tagboard and glue on a strip of ribbon to resemble a hatband. Hot-glue the hat near the top of the can to complete this frosty character. Then line the can with a piece of tissue paper, and fill it with candy or a packet of hot cocoa. Mmm, mmm, good!

Tina Townsend—Gr. K
Gorin R-3
Gorin, MO

Cups To Hang Up

Trimming the tree with cups? It's a cool thing to do with this hot idea! Purchase a supply of 16-ounce plastic party cups (red and green ones look especially festive for Christmas). Prior to introducing this activity to your class, place one cup per child upside down on a foil-lined cookie sheet. Put the cookie sheet in a preheated oven at the broil setting. Leave the cups in the oven for a minute or two until they melt into round or oval shapes. Allow the shapes to cool completely. Then hot-glue a loop of ribbon to the back of each ornament. Have each youngster decorate her ornament with glitter and glue. These melted keepsakes are sure to warm hearts year after year!

Michelle Myers—Pre-K
Tutor Time Learning Center
Bradenton, FL

Personally Yours

Help each of your youngsters make a batch of stationery to give to someone special. If desired, show them several examples of packaged stationery. Then give each child a piece of 8 1/2" x 11" paper labeled "From The Desk [or House] Of" at the top. Have her write the receiver's name under the heading. Duplicate this page onto a few sheets of colored paper. Provide an assortment of envelopes (ask your local printer for donations) and watercolors for each child to make several designer envelopes. When the paint is dry, put the colored papers, envelopes, and a pen in a plastic resealable bag. Write on!

From The Desk Of
Dad

Daphne M. Orenshein—Gr. K
Yavneh Hebrew Academy
Los Angeles, CA

Gift Tags To Go

Add a festive touch to Mom and Dad's holiday present with this easy gift tag idea. To make a tag, cut a 2" x 6" rectangle from a discarded gift box. Fold it in half so it measures 2" x 3". Use pinking shears to cut a 2" x 3" rectangle from holiday fabric. Glue the fabric rectangle to the front of the folded tag. Invite each child to sign her name on the inside of her gift tag. Then punch a hole in the upper left corner and use ribbon to attach the tag to her gift.

Debra Nehlsen—Gr. K
Wait Primary School
Streetsboro, OH

Easy-To-Cut Snowflakes

If your youngsters have trouble cutting snowflake designs from construction paper, try using coffee filters instead. The filters are thinner than construction paper, making folded designs easier for little hands to cut. Yet they're still durable enough to make beautiful snowflakes, whether you choose to leave them white or color them before cutting.

Jean Harrison—Pre-K, Peace Lutheran Preschool, Palm Bay, FL

Snowfall Gauge

Turn the excitement of a fresh snowfall into a science lesson with this simple project. Explain that meteorologists use various tools to help them learn about the weather. Then invite youngsters to help you make a simplified snowfall gauge. To make one, cut off the bottom of a gallon milk jug. Starting at the bottom, measure and mark off one-inch increments. Then take the gauge outdoors and push the cutaway end into the snow. Have youngsters look at where the snow line hits. How many inches of snow are on the ground? Do they get the same reading at different places? Hey, snow is fun *and* scientific!

Sue Lewis Lein—Four-Year-Olds
St. Pius X
Wauwatosa, WI

Calling All Students!

Here's a fun way to give students special attention, encourage good behavior, *and* help students memorize their phone numbers! Cut a large telephone shape, and mount it on a wall or bulletin board. Add sponge numeral keys. Post a list of students' telephone numbers nearby. Then cut a class supply of telephone receivers from construction paper. Label each receiver with a child's name and phone number; then laminate for durability. Invite each child to keep her receiver at her table. (If you have metal desks, a strip of magnetic tape on the back will keep the receiver handy.) Periodically, walk over to the display telephone and read a child's phone number aloud as you punch the numerals. Students will quickly catch on to answer your call. Ask how the day is going, give a little praise, and say good-bye. Your kindergartners are bound to love this telephone talk!

Karen Saner—Grs. K–1
Burns Elementary School
Burns, KS

Recycled "Snow"

Got a leaky beanbag chair? Don't toss it! The tiny beads of Styrofoam® inside make beautiful snow for all kinds of wintry art projects. Invite students to cut out construction-paper snowmen and paint them with glue. Then unzip the chair and have youngsters dip their cutouts into the filling for a glistening 3-D effect. Use the beanbag snow to embellish icebergs, mountains, and snowy bulletin-board backgrounds, too.

Gwen Broder
Bedford Mothers Club School
Bedford, NH

Fortune Cookie

Add these cute cookies to a bulletin board for a Chinese New Year display. To make a cookie, a child paints the back of a paper plate beige. She then folds the plate in half and staples all around the open edges. She bends the plate in half to resemble a fortune cookie, then attaches a dictated fortune on a strip of paper.

Randi Rote—Gr. K
Wesley Learning Center
Sandy Hook, CT

Chinese Dragon Puppets

Celebrate the Chinese New Year with these fiery dragon puppets. To make a puppet, fold down the bottom of a flattened paper lunch bag; then cut out a mouth. Paint the bag or decorate it with colored tissue-paper scraps. Glue on wiggle eyes and staple colorful streamers to the open end of the bag. For added excitement, tape lengths of orange and red crepe-paper streamers to a toilet-tissue tube. Invite a child to hold a tube, then slip the puppet over his arm, inserting the tube into the open end of the puppet. When those fiery streamers emerge from the puppet's mouth—voilà! A festive, fire-breathing dragon!

Kathy Curnow—Gr. K
Woolridge Elementary School
Midlothian, VA

A Sign Of Love

Have students use a favorite sign—the one for "I love you"—to make a special card for a friend or parent. For each child, provide two sheets of construction paper, one red and one skin-toned. Help her fold the sheet of red construction paper in half, trace a half-heart shape on the fold, and cut along the line to make a heart. Then trace the child's hand on the skin-toned construction paper. (If appropriate, have partners trace each other's hands.) Have each student cut out her own hand shape. Instruct her to fold and glue the middle and ring fingers of her hand cutout to the palm to make the sign for "I love you," then glue the completed hand sign to her red paper heart. Invite her to copy the words "I love you" onto the heart. Lovely!

Amy Pierce—Pre-K
Pierce Private Day School
Irving, TX

I Predict...

Groundhog Day is a perfect time for predicting. After discussing the meaning of a groundhog seeing or not seeing his shadow, have each youngster make his own prediction. On a small square of paper, have the child illustrate a groundhog with or without a shadow. Graph the predictions to see what the class thinks. Then wait for the news on Groundhog Day to reveal the actual outcome. What a forecast for fun!

Sue Lewis Lein—Four-Year-Old K
St. Pius Grade School
Wauwatosa, WI

A Dental-Health Ditty

This song will bring lots of toothy grins during your dental-health studies.

(sung to the tune of "Row, Row, Row Your Boat")

Brush, brush, brush your teeth,
Morning, noon, and night.
Brush in circles all around
To make your teeth look bright!

Stacy Richardson-Bond—Preschool And Gr. K
Cabell County Public Library
Huntington, WV

Music From The Heart

Liven up your rhythm band with these heart-shaped shakers. To make one, simply put beans, rice, bells, or buttons inside a small, empty heart-shaped box. Then securely glue or tape the box shut. Next, hot-glue a large craft stick to the back of the box. If desired, cover the box panels with decorative self-adhesive paper. Now, shake it!

Mary E. Maurer
Caddo, OK

Bye-Bye Baby Teeth!

Celebrate lost teeth with this fun display. Make a pair of lips from red bulletin-board paper. Then cut out and label a white construction-paper tooth for each month in the school year. Attach the teeth inside the lips. When a student loses a tooth, write his name on the corresponding tooth in the display. (If desired, "pull" each month's tooth and post it near your calendar activities.) At the end of the school year, tally and compare the monthly tooth counts. Then add them together for a grand total!

Melanie Fried—Gr. K, J.G. Johnson Elementary, Pahrump, NV

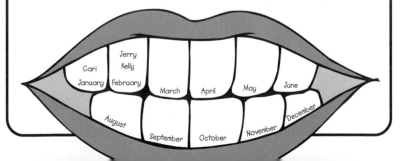

Stuck On You

These attractive valentine gifts are sure to find their way onto refrigerators everywhere! In advance, collect a class supply of metal lids from frozen-juice cans. To make one magnet, attach a piece of magnetic tape to the back of each lid. Then write (or have a child write) "Stuck on you!" on a construction-paper heart. Glue the heart to the lid. Next, have a child accordion-fold four construction-paper strips, then attach them to the back of the lid to resemble arms and legs. Finish the magnet by gluing the student's photo to the top of the lid as shown.

Amy Regan—Gr. K
Amy Martin—Gr. K
Woodfern Elementary
Neshanic Station, NJ

Hearts Full Of Love

Creative writing fills the heart in this lovely display! To prepare, have each child trace his hand on red construction paper, then cut it out. (Depending on the number of children in your class, you might need to have each child make several hand cutouts.) Mount all the hand cutouts to form a large, open heart. Label the display as shown. Then stock your writing center with a supply of writing paper. Encourage each child to write "I love" on her paper, then complete the sentence. Mount each child's paper on black construction paper; then display it within the large heart. Just lovely!

Laura Cozzi—Gr. K
Truman School
Parlin, NJ

HEARTS FULL OF LOVE

I love my mom and dad.

Cereal-Box Furniture

With an assortment of empty cereal boxes and a little creative ingenuity, you'll have more furniture for your play areas! In advance, ask children to bring in empty cereal boxes. (They'll pile up fast!) When you have a wide variety of boxes, arrange the boxes and tape them together with packing tape to create the desired furniture. The illustrations below show several configurations that work well. But your youngsters might like to explore some new designs of their own! If desired, cover the finished furniture with an adhesive covering.

Linda K. Lilienthal—Gr. K, Hayes Center Elementary
Hayes Center, NE

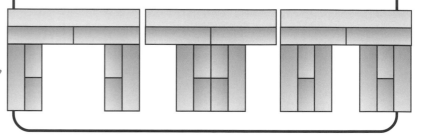

Wishing Just For Fun

When you've got a spare minute or two during the month of March, recite the poem below to your class. Then ask each child, in turn, to share a wish with the class. Use this poem again and again for transition times and you'll be sure to gain lots of insight into each of your little wishing ones.

If you found a four-leaf clover,
That makes wishes all come true,
And you thought your wishes over,
What would you wish for you?

adapted from an idea by Angelena Pritchard—Gr. K
Fountain Inn Elementary, Fountain Inn, SC

Valentine Line

Here's a simple way to make pretty valentine displays. After children have received their valentines, give each child a long length of ribbon. Instruct each child to staple his valentines on the ribbon as shown. If there is extra space at the end of the ribbon, have that child create a special valentine decoration to staple to the bottom of the ribbon. These valentine lines can be hung for display at home or school.

Tracey J. Quezada—Gr. K
Presentation Of Mary Academy
Hudson, NH

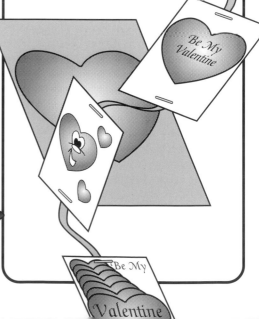

It's Abraham Lincoln!

This special Abe has multiple uses during February! If you're studying coins or collecting pennies, use it as a class bank. If you're celebrating Presidents' Day, it's the perfect collecting spot for children's creative writings. Or have each child make his own Abe Lincoln, and use them for valentine mailboxes. To make one, cut out a slit in the top of an oatmeal container. Then cover the sides of the container with black construction paper. Draw a face, hat brim, and beard (as shown) on construction paper; then cut them out. Slide the hat brim halfway down the container; then glue the tabs to the container. Fringe-cut the beard; then glue the face and the beard under the hat. If appropriate for your use, decorate the hat with heart cutouts.

Trevor Cottle—Gr. K
Washington School
Beardstown, IL

I "A-Door" You!

Youngsters will be proud to make these doorknob hangers for the special people in their lives. For each child, cut out a doorknob hanger from oaktag as shown. (These can also be purchased at craft supply stores.) Then have children use rubber stamps and colorful stamp pads to decorate their cutouts. When each hanger is fully decorated, have its designer write a message on the back; then laminate it. Trim off the excess laminating film; then encourage children to deliver these handmade hangers to people they adore.

Diane Parette—Gr. K, Durham Elementary
Durham, NY

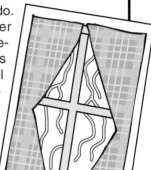

That's A Good Sign!

If you're converting one of your centers into a store of some kind, give it a truly authentic touch with real signs. Purchase one or more inexpensive signs from a local office supply store. Encourage children to use the signs in the center. For example, encourage students to use signs such as "Open," "Closed," and "We'll return at…" What pride your little merchants will have!

Sue Lewis Lein—Gr. K, St. Pius X Grade School
Wauwatosa, WI

Mother's Day Matinee

Are your little ones hosting a Mother's Day tea this year? If so, this entertainment idea will be a heartwarming hit. In advance, ask children to think of why their moms (or any female family members or caretakers) are special to them. Then encourage students to illustrate their thoughts on a large sheet of paper. Videotape each child sharing his picture and his thoughts. After each child has shared, group your class together to sing a song for all the moms to enjoy.

My mom is special because we always have story time no matter what.

Cindi Zsittnik
Surrey School
Hagerstown, MD

Bright Umbrellas For Dreary Days

Brighten up a damp and dreary day with these umbrella projects. To make an umbrella, trace a child's handprint (fingers pressed together) onto white construction paper. Draw lines from the heel of the handprint as shown. Color the sections and cut out the handprint. Tape a pipe-cleaner handle to the back of the umbrella. Glue one or more umbrellas onto a blue or gray sheet of construction paper. Then use a Q-tips® swab and paint to scatter blue raindrops on the page. Tut. Tut. Looks like rain!

Maureen F. Guerin, Lowell, MA

Raindrops Trickle

Have the spring rains set in? Call attention to trickling raindrops on your classroom windowpanes. Then show your students how to make trickle artwork. Place a small amount of thin blue watercolor or tempera paint on the top of a sheet of construction paper. Gently blow through a drinking straw, causing the paint to trickle downward like real raindrops do. Use construction paper and fabric scraps to resemble the windowpanes and curtains. Children will love the unusual art technique and the equally unusual results!

Maureen F. Guerin

Have You Ever Tasted A Raindrop?

These sweet raindrops are sure to turn dreary-weather frowns upside down! To make a class supply of raindrops, give each child a slice of refrigerated sugar-cookie dough. Invite each child to form his dough into a raindrop shape. Shower blue sprinkles on the raindrops; then bake them according to the package directions. Mmmm, what a sweet rain!

Maureen F. Guerin

Look Who GREW In Our Kindergarten!

These colorful keepsakes make lasting mementos for years to come. In advance, program a large sheet of construction paper (lengthwise) as shown; then duplicate a class supply. Provide bowls of red, yellow, and blue colored water; paintbrushes; and coffee filters. Instruct each child to use the colored water to paint a coffee filter. When the filters are dry, have each child fold his filter to resemble a flower; then help him staple it to a programmed page. Next, have each child color a stem and leaves under his flower. Add the finishing touch by gluing each child's photo to the center of his flower. My, how you've grown!

Barbara Cohen—Gr. K, Horace Mann School
Cherry Hill, NJ

Alphabet Fish

Cast your nets for language practice! To prepare this center, brainstorm a list of ocean-related vocabulary words with students. Write the list on a chart; then place it in a center with a supply of fish-shaped crackers and long tagboard sheets. When a child visits this center, invite him to choose one of the vocabulary words and illustrate it on a sheet of tagboard. Then use a marker to write the word he chooses in large letters on the tagboard sheet. Finally, have the child glue fish crackers to the letters. When the glue is dry, invite him to take his word-scene home to share. There's an ocean of possibilities for language growth in this center.

adapted from an idea by Betty Silkunas, Lansdale, PA

Mystery Writing

Students will be drawn to this kinesthetic guessing game that includes writing practice and visual imagery. To begin, pair students. Assign one child to be the writer, and the other to be the reader. Instruct the writer to "write" a letter with her finger on the reader's back. Encourage the reader to call out what is "written" on his back. If he guesses correctly, have the two children switch roles and continue in the same manner. If he guesses incorrectly, encourage the writer to "write" the letter again. If needed, have the writer supply clues such as, "This letter is at the beginning of *dog*."

Nicole Cook—Gr. K, St. Rosalie School
Harvey, LA

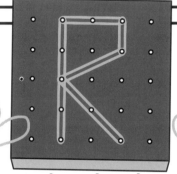

Geoboard Genius

For a new twist on an old favorite, use Geoboards to practice letter formation! Simply have students stretch rubber bands on the boards to form different letters of the alphabet. It's great for fine-motor skills as well as letter formation and problem solving.

Tara Kicklighter
Bunnell Elementary School, Bunnell, FL

Portfolio Possibilities

If you have an abundance of class-made books at the end of the year, use them to add to your students' portfolios. To do this, simply take apart a few of your class-made books (if the pages are not dated, you might like to date them first). Then insert each child's pages into his portfolio. By looking through these entries, the parent, the child, and you can see the student's growth and development throughout the year!

Ann-Marie Blake—Gr. K
Spring Glen Elementary School
Hamden, CT

Submarine Center

Submerge your dramatic-play area in submarine fun! First paint a large appliance box and let it dry. Then attach a periscope made from a painted wrapping paper tube. Cut out small, round windows in the sides; then cover them with laminating film scraps. Cut along only three sides of a door area so it will open and close. Invite children to draw controls and radar screens inside the submarine, then finish the outside with painted shells, fish, and seaweed. Prepare to submerge!

Cynthia Sayman—Gr. K, Harpursville, NY

Father's Day Frame

These frames make fabulous Father's Day gifts! To begin, make a batch of your favorite salt dough recipe. Use that dough to form the letters in *DAD*. Bake the letters according to your recipe; then paint them as desired. Also paint four craft sticks. When the paint is dry, glue the sticks together to form a frame. Hot-glue the letters to the front of the frame. Glue a child's picture to the back of the frame; then add a construction-paper backing. Make a hanger by hot-gluing a soda can flip-top to the top of the back of the frame. Happy day, Dad!

Carol Corcoran, Bayonne Recreation Preschool, Bayonne, NJ

Rubber Cement Solution

Apply rubber cement neatly and quickly with this handy tip. Clean an empty laundry spot-treatment bottle that has a plastic brush top. Fill the bottle with rubber cement and replace the top. The brush attachment makes for easy application over large surfaces. No more messy brushes!

Linda Gilchrest—Pre-K and Gr. K
DeLeon Elementary School
DeLeon, TX

Junk Jars

One person's trash can be a teacher's treasure! And that holds true for these math manipulative collections. First, gather a supply of clean, empty plastic jars (with lids). As you peruse yard sales and flea markets, collect small items to be used as math manipulatives, such as old keys, shells, dice, game pieces, barrettes, or erasers. Store each different type of manipulative in a separate jar. (You'd probably have lots of child volunteers willing to help you sort out your collection!) For a center activity or a five-minute filler, encourage children to sort, count, seriate, stack, or measure items in the junk jars.

Connie Powell
Early Childhood
    Special Education
Wichita, KS

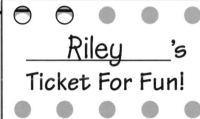

_____Riley_____'s
Ticket For Fun!

Just The Ticket!

Here's your ticket to positive behavior management! First, draw a page of tickets with approximately ten dots along the border of each ticket. Duplicate the tickets as needed; then cut them apart. When you observe positive behavior, punch out one of the spots on that child's ticket. When all the spots have been punched, invite that child to choose an appropriate reward.

Allissa M. Pendleton—Gr. K
Stanford Elementary School
Stanford, KY

Watch The Clock!

Time flies when you use this transition activity! Have children watch the second hand on your classroom clock and perform a simple movement when the hand reaches a given numeral. For example, have children sit down when the second hand points to the four, or pat their heads when the second hand points to the nine. As abilities permit, use more advanced concepts, such as instructing students to clap when the second hand is on the sum of two plus three. Watch that clock!

Nancy Kleinke—Gr. K
Trinity Evangelical
    Lutheran School
Bay City, MI

Bare Those Crayons

When you need a bunch of bare crayons, is it difficult for your students to remove the paper wrappings from them? Try soaking them in water overnight. Or even add them to the water table for a center time. After soaking, the soft paper slides right off!

Lisa Kuecker—Gr. K
Adams Elementary School
Arkansas City, KS

Graphing Made Easy

This space-saving attraction can be used over and over again. First, use electrical tape to make a graphing grid on the side of a cabinet. Then create a name magnet for each student. To do this, write a child's name on a small paper circle; then glue it inside a plastic milk cap. Attach a piece of magnetic tape to the other side of the cap. To use this graph, write a title on a sentence strip and label each heading with a programmed sticky note. Then have each child place her magnet in the appropriate column. To change the topic, simply program a new sentence strip and sticky notes. Graphing doesn't get any easier than this!

Sandy Dufrin—Gr. K, New Covenant Christian School
Lansing, MI

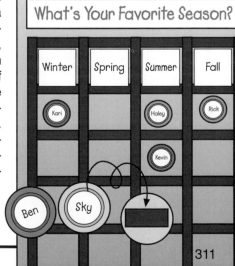

What's Your Favorite Season?

| Winter | Spring | Summer | Fall |

Personal Thanks

Picture personal thank-you notes for class volunteers and guests. To prepare, take a group photo of your class in which the front row of children are holding a large thank-you banner. Then duplicate a supply of color copies of the photo. When you need a thank-you note, simply enclose a copy of the group photo with a handwritten note. What a picture-perfect way to say thanks!

Kathy Pitcher—Gr. K
Grove Elementary School
Montrose, IL

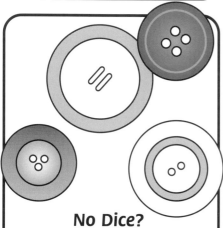

No Dice?

You don't need dice to play games if you have buttons! Just put a quantity of buttons into an opaque bag. Have a child draw a button from the bag, then count the holes to determine the number of spaces to move. It's your move!

Karen Smith—Grs. K–1
Pine Lane Elementary Homeschool
Pace, FL

Beautiful Briny Sea

When you make ocean bulletin boards, add this special sea appeal. When the scene is complete, cover the entire board with blue plastic wrap. Staple the wrap only at the top and bottom of the board. Enjoy this view of the shimmery shiny sea!

Tammy Melissa Griffith—Gr. K
Ridge Baptist Preschool
Summerville, SC

Our line leaders show good manners

You behaved very nicely on our field trip to the zoo!

You were so polite to our guests!

Our class line was so quiet and straight!

You have done so well practicing safety on the playground.

Computer Cover-Ups

If you have a table of computer equipment in or near your classroom, here's an attractive way to keep that valuable equipment dust-free. Use vinyl tablecloths—available in seasonal patterns and a variety of lengths—to drape the entire table. If desired, change the tablecloths to match the seasons. There you have it—attractive, easy-care dustcovers.

Patsi Hendricks—Gr. K
Galveston Elementary School
Galveston, IN

A Great Bunch

Reinforce social graces with this unique, reusable system. Cut out and laminate several construction-paper balloons. Display the bunch of balloons on a board or wall. When you observe your class showing positive behavior, use a permanent marker to write a relevant compliment on one of the balloons. Also record compliments that your class receives from other school personnel. When all the balloons display a compliment, reward the class with a treat such as a popcorn-video party or extra recess time. To start again, use some hairspray to wipe the balloons clean.

Kay Chabot—Gr. K
Long Beach Elementary
Long Beach, WA

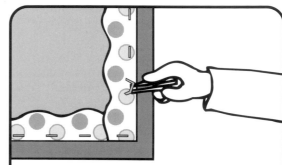

"Staple-Ease"

Do you find that traditional staple removers sometimes tear your bulletin-board background or wallboard? If so, use an ordinary pair of tweezers to remove the staples. You can even reinforce fine-motor skills by asking a child helper to remove staples using this method.

Karen Griffin—Gr. K
American Heritage Academy, Carrollton, TX

Patriotic Pops

Uncle Sam would approve of these patriotic pops! To make one, scoop blue-tinted whipped topping into a clear plastic cup. Insert a craft stick; then let it freeze. Layer softened vanilla ice cream on top of the blue layer; then freeze it again. Finally, add the last layer by pouring red Kool-Aid® into the cup. Freeze the pop until it has set. To loosen the frozen pop, run tap water over the cup. Oh say, can you see these popular pops disappear!

Michelle Myers—Pre-K and Gr. K
Tutor Time Learning Center, Bradenton, FL

Index